Pain, Play and Music

Also Available from Bloomsbury:

Decolonizing Contemporary Gospel Music Through Praxis, Robert Beckford

The Bloomsbury Handbook of Religion and Popular Music,
Edited by Christopher Partridge and Marcus Moberg

Exploring the Spiritual in Popular Music, Mike Dines and Georgina Gregory

Pain, Play and Music

Death and Healing Rites among the Wana

Giorgio Scalici

BLOOMSBURY ACADEMIC

LONDON • NEW YORK • OXFORD • NEW DELHI • SYDNEY

BLOOMSBURY ACADEMIC
Bloomsbury Publishing Plc, 50 Bedford Square, London, WC1B 3DP, UK
Bloomsbury Publishing Inc, 1359 Broadway, New York, NY 10018, USA
Bloomsbury Publishing Ireland, 29 Earlsfort Terrace, Dublin 2, D02 AY28, Ireland

BLOOMSBURY, BLOOMSBURY ACADEMIC and the Diana logo
are trademarks of Bloomsbury Publishing Plc

First published in Great Britain 2024
Paperback edition published 2026

A catalogue record for this book is available from the British Library.

Library of Congress Cataloging-in-Publication Data
Names: Scalici, Giorgio, author.
Title: Pain, play and music : death and healing rites among the Wana / Giorgio Scalici.
Description: London ; New York : Bloomsbury Academic, 2024. |
Includes bibliographical references and index.
Identifiers: LCCN 2023041050 (print) | LCCN 2023041051 (ebook) |
ISBN 9781350236257 (HB) | ISBN 9781350236295 (paperback) |
ISBN 9781350236264 (ePDF) | ISBN 9781350236271 (eBook)
Subjects: LCSH: Ritual–Indonesia–Morowali (Indonesia). | Music–Religious
aspects–Indonesia–Morowali (Indonesia). | Wana (Indonesian
people)–Religious life. | Wana (Indonesian people)–Rites and
ceremonies. | Death–Indonesia–Morowali (Indonesia). |
Death–Religious aspects–Shamanism.
Classification: LCC BL605 .S33 2024 (print) | LCC BL605 (ebook) |
DDC 299/.9222–dc23/eng/20231115
LC record available at https://lccn.loc.gov/2023041050
LC ebook record available at https://lccn.loc.gov/2023041051

ISBN: HB: 978-1-3502-3625-7
         PB: 978-1-3502-3629-5
         ePDF: 978-1-3502-3626-4
         eBook: 978-1-3502-3627-1

Typeset by Integra Software Services Pvt. Ltd.

For product safety related questions contact productsafety@bloomsbury.com.

To find out more about our authors and books visit www.bloomsbury.com
and sign up for our newsletters.

This book is dedicated to the memory of
Nanju (d. 2013)
Indo n'Tibe (d. 2014)
Indo n'Pino (d. 2016)
Indo Jaka (d. 2016)

Contents

Figures

Tables

Foreword

Through cumulative exposure to a series of vibrant cultural events Georgio Scalici has achieved his intentional goal of inducting us into an experience of the Wana of Indonesia. Mirroring his own anthropological insights and gradual immersion in Wana culture, step by step, he invites us to share in his own developing sense of community events as description and interpretation complement each other in framing and extending our grasp of the long-standing topic of Shamanism. Sickness, death and a group's sense of being marginally inferior to others all pivot around behaviours that express the triumph of life and, above all, the emotional dynamics grounded in the key sense of community or *kasintuwu*. His frequent use of such local terms ever reminds us of our distance from the Wana yet his humane description ever prompts our empathy and recognition of the trials of life that we all face.

In this, theoretical concepts drive Scalici's Wana narrative, whether in the idiom of centre versus periphery or 'densification' and rites of densification that intensify cultural behaviours seeking to foster life. Phrases set the scene – 'stay, drink, and joke', or 'pain, play, and music'. Here we encounter playfulness associated with ritual, indeed, this ludic dimension pervades much of this study, not least when related to laughter and especially to music as a prime driver of Georgio Scalici's work as an ethnomusicologist. But no single description or vogue fashion restricts this book, in fact it is notable for its easy acceptance of and critical objection to scholarly ideas from the nineteenth through to the twenty-first century. What is especially pleasing to me is to see ethnographic work and the European tradition of the history of religions in concert. Much the same could be said for its relevance to the modern development of medical humanities.

I warmly commend this study for its realistic recognition of the problems of fieldwork, something many postgraduates will appreciate. So too, for the excitement offered to undergraduates and readers at large, for this comes from a scholar for whom teaching is a joy, something I saw first-hand when Giorgio worked with me here at Durham University. This, indeed, is the very point at which his recognition of 'the polluting sense of meaninglessness' engages with the meaningful life of the research-grounded teacher who invites others to join the venture of informed living.

Douglas Davies FBA
Durham University

Acknowledgements

My deepest gratitude goes to:

My masters Mariella, Gigi, Giovanni, Alessandro, Douglas and Simon who guided me with great kindness, patience and understanding.

All of the Wana people I encountered in Morowali, especially the families of Apa Rau, Apa Ingus, Apa Dheri and Tandau, and my loyal guide Ajeran.

The owners of the *Penginapan Sederhana,* who treated me like a son.

The market stall owner who gave me free doughnuts.

Sam for his friendship.

My dad for his trust.

My wife for her patience.

Special thanks to Kevin.

Last but not least, thanks to my own stupidity without which I would never end up doing this research.

These are just some of the people who really deserve thanks. I am afraid, however, that there would not be enough pages in this whole thesis to thank all the people who played a role in bringing me to where I am today.

I thank you all.

Note on the text

The audio and video material, including first-hand interviews, referred to in this academic work was accompanied by permission from each of the Wana with whom I worked and lived. Due to the low level of literacy in the Indonesian community where I worked, I recorded their oral permit in Wana language. Moreover, to work with the Wana inside the Morowali natural reserve I had to obtain a research permit from the Indonesian government, to carry research in Indonesia, and from the Ministry of Forestry, to live inside a natural reserve.

Throughout my fieldwork in Indonesia, all ethical considerations of my work have been supervised by Durham University. The university's ethical committee granted me its ethical authorization.

In addition, all the material shown in this work is available on my personal website, giorgioscalici.eu, and I am the only author of everything present there, thus I take all responsibility for any misuse of all video and audio material.

Glossary

Adat (BI)	Tradition and system of traditional laws
Agama (BI)	Religion
Bahasa Indonesia (BI)	Indonesian language
Bahasa Taa	Wana language
Banua	House
Banua mate	Grave
Baraka	Mythical power
Belanda	The Netherlands
Chaptikus	Palm wine
Diodio	Small rattle tied to the machete of a warrior to attract women
Do'a	Spell
Dumbaru	Ritual hut of the *kayori*
Eo	Sun
Ganda	Drum
Geso	Spike fiddle
Gunung (BI)	Mountain or hill
Joe n' tana	The edge of the world where the Tau Baraka live
Kasintuwu	Sense of community
Katuntu	Mythological tales
Kayori	Funerary ritual
Kayu	Wood
Kayu paramba	Money tree
Kepala suku (BI)	Village chief
Kios	Shop, stall
Koro	Soul
Jampu	Invisibility
Langu	Ritual tray
Lengke	Shadow
Linga-linga	Song
Mandeke	The ritualized expression of pain and sorrow
Mankoni	To eat
Malae	To go to the *momago*
Mata	Rattan thread with sixteen or eighteen knots tied in it. It is used to keep track of the days of the *kayori*
Mate	Death, dead or to die
Mea	Shyness

Measa	Demon
Miskin (BI)	Poor
Moapu	To cook
Molawo	Esoteric shamanic ritual
Momago	Main shamanic ritual
Motaro	Male shamanic dance
Patoe	Shamanic chant
Pitu	Seven
Poloisong	Wana mythical hero and trickster
Pompolonzu	Ritual cloth used during the *momago*
Pongas	Rice wine
Popondo	Chest resonator
Pue	Wana god
Rando	Decoration
Salia	The biggest shamanic ritual, usually held during the harvest festival. Also known as *masalia* and *padunku*
Salonde	Female shamanic dance
Setan	Demon
Siu	Comb
Soga	A torch used during the *kayori* to let the spirit of the deceased seeing the human world
Soo	Sound, musical note
Sopu	Blowpipe
Suruga	Heaven
Tana	Land, territory
Tana Taa	Wana land
Tanuana	Dream agent
Tau	Person
Tau Baraka	People of the mythical era
Tau Rumbi	Giant
Tau Walia	Shaman
Tempo	Time
Togo	Three
Tulali	Flute
Tunda'n tana	Navel of the world and mythical mountain
Uba	Wana bag, but also the funeral bag that during the funeral represents the deceased
Urat	Hand nerves that indicate the spiritual and moral inclinations of a person
Vaiansivangu	The sacred vine that connected the earth to the sky
Walia	Spirit
Wuri	Night
Yoku	Funerary bracelet

Map

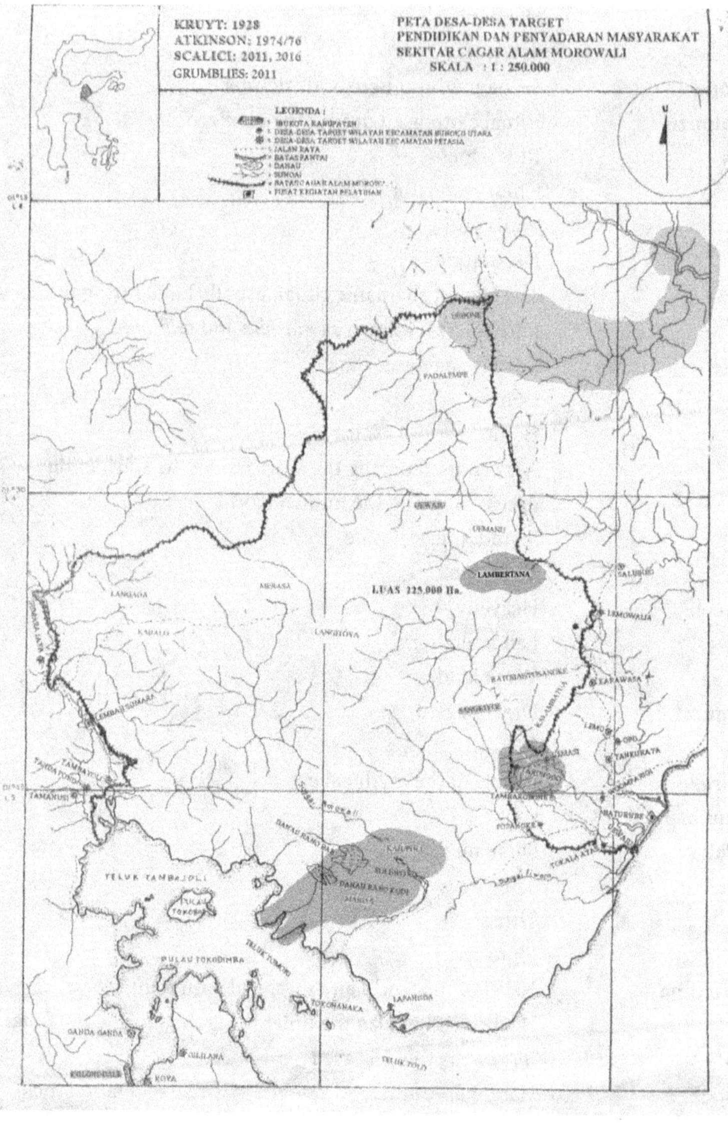

Map 1 Natural reserve of Morowali with the fieldwork localities explored by other key researchers of Wana culture highlighted. The Indonesian Ministry of Forestry kindly contributed this map for the purposes of this fieldwork. Source unknown. Rearranged by Scalici.

1

Introduction

This book is the product of a research started in 2011 when I was an Ethnomusicology MA student in Rome, Italy. It aims to explore, discuss and analyse the rituals of the Wana people of Morowali, the values that these rituals carry and how they use music, emotion and religion to not only heal the single member but the entire community. It will examine how a small community reinforces social relationships among its members through the one-night-long shamanic healing ritual, *momago*, and the almost-three-weeks-long funeral, *kayori*. Fortifying these relationships contributes to the physical and emotional survival of an endangered community that historically has constantly been under the attack of the colonial empires (Indian, Muslim and Dutch), the Indonesian government and Christianity.

The wretched of the earth

While approaching and discovering Wana culture, I tried to cope with the culture shock arising from the contact with this new world and to look for reasons, meanings and aims behind the rituals I was observing. Of course, the intricate intertwinement of rituality, mythology and mundane life made it necessary to employ a holistic approach that took into consideration various elements of Wana life. It meant focusing part of my efforts on seeing connections between many different situations, from watching B movies in the jungle to the organization of a funeral. The keyword was: *kasintuwu*, the sense of community that fuelled all Wana actions.

My aim is to uncover the key values of Wana life through the analysis of the two most important rituals of this culture. At the same time, it is to see how Wana people use these rituals, and the values reinforced by them, to maintain what I call the 'density'[1] of their community, and to cope with the pain and the wretchedness they believe are a central part of their existence since the end of the mythical space-time. The Wana describe themselves as *miskin* (poor) people, but the word refers to far more than economic status: it refers to a state of existence. In an attempt to summarize all the different meanings Wana people invoke with the word *miskin*, the term 'wretched' will be used in this work. There are several reasons behind this decision. First, it literally means 'low quality'. According to the Wana I met, both their life and status are inferior in quality to those of other people (especially Christians[2]). As Atkinson pointed out: 'Wana are fully aware that they are at the bottom of an ethnic ladder, dominated and despised by their neighbours – Bugis, Mori, Pamona, Gorontalo, and others – who subscribe to one or another world religion. Wana represent themselves as poor and degraded' (Atkinson 1988: 55). They have also been treated as lower quality human beings since the arrival of the Indians who sold them as slaves. Another reason behind the choice of the term 'wretched' is its etymology; the term derives from the old English *wrecca*, meaning 'exile', 'to drive out' or 'to punish' (Online Etymology Dictionary). This etymology reflects the situation of the Wana people, in that they see themselves as 'exiled' from the golden era, albeit as a result of mythical space-time leaving them rather than the other way around. They are doomed to live a wretched life while deprived of the power of the golden era. Finally, the term seems appropriate in connecting the Wana situation to key works in postcolonial studies, particularly *Les Damnés de la Terre* by Franz Fanon (1961), translated into English with the title *The Wretched of the Earth*. The original term used by Fanon was '*damnés*' and this word comes from the opening lyrics of *L'Internationale*: *Debout, les damnés de la terre* (Stand up, damned of the Earth) (Pottier 1871). The term *damnés* derives from the Latin *damnum* (loss), and this can be related to the Wana people's loss of primordial power along with dissolution of mythical density, and it is also linked with the status of being cursed. Indeed, Wana people are damned to be poor and to exist at the bottom of the social ladder until the return of the *Tau Baraka* (the people of the myth) and the restoration of the golden era.

Ultimately, the purpose of this book is to describe and analyse how Wana people view the world they live in, and to uncover the coping methods put into action during the rituals. These methods are not only about dealing with a life considered full of pain, but they are also about transforming the negative energies resulting from the illness or death of a member of the community into a powerful and playful positive energy that heals both individuals and the community as a whole.

Reasons behind this research

In 2011, when I was a student, my plan was to 'simply' study the ritual music of Wana main shamanic ritual, the *momago*. I was very inexperienced and naïve researcher, and my only source about the Wana people was the only other existing book on them: *The Art and Politics of Wana Shamanship* (1989) by Jane Monnig Atkinson. Once on the field, everything changed very quickly, there I started to see interconnections between many elements of Wana life and I observed their never-documented-before funeral.[3] My interest moved towards the coping mechanisms of Wana people, and their ability to transform negative events into playful opportunities that reinforce *kasintuwu* (the sense of community) and heal the entire community. Alongside these personal interests, there is the urge to document and study this endangered community that will soon drastically change and that is, in fact, already transforming some of its defining cultural characteristics. Considering that already in 2011 collecting and recording Wana traditional music required a great effort and that I could not find many musical instruments or people able to play them, it would not be a surprise if this musical tradition were to disappear altogether, or at least to become deeply impoverished or unrecognizable, within the next twenty years. Sadly, anthropology is, in some way, similar to astronomy, in fact as Atkinson's publishing her book in 1989 based on a fieldwork done in the 1970s and I am publishing this book in 2024 based on facts observed in 2011 and 2016, we describe things that are not there anymore when the readers learn about them. We analyse a time that is already in the past, like a star far from us many light years, we can see only its past.

The Wana people have never received a great deal of attention from academic researchers, especially in comparison with other communities in Indonesia or even in the same island of Sulawesi. The Toraja people, for instance, are a cultural group known to both academics and others, and are one of the most important tourist destinations in Indonesia.[4] Curiously, they live less than 400 kilometres from *Tana Taa* (Wana land), and there are many studies with a range of interests, from ethnomusicology (Rappoport 2004) to textiles (Christou 1997) to emotions (Waterson 2018), that have produced dozens if not hundreds of books, articles and recordings. It is not clear, on the other hand, why the Wana people have never attracted so much attention. Published works about them will be discussed in Chapter 2 but they hardly exceed a dozen in number. Furthermore, half of this work is produced by only one person: the US anthropologist Jane Monnig Atkinson.

Therefore, one of the factors behind my research is the desire to bring knowledge of this culture to a wider audience, not because the Wana people need in any way to become famous, and there are countless examples of traditional communities being damaged by superficial images of them being presented by outsiders. It is a culture that I truly consider fascinating and that could potentially reveal much about how people can effectively manage emotions and foster coherent communities – perhaps providing insights regarding how other societies (such as our own) may effectively address this issue. I trust the role of anthropological research in preserving the memory and recording testimonies of a culture. I do not, however, desire to put Wana people 'under a glass dome'. Instead, I note a quotation attributed to the composer Gustav Mahler:[5] '*Tradition ist nicht die Anbetung der Asche, sondern die Weitergabe des Feuers.*'[6] I strongly believe that one of the main duties of anthropology is to serve as a respectful archive and museum for information about different cultures. I intend for my work to offer a source of information and a record of the state of Wana rituality between 2011 and 2016, especially for the benefit of Wana people themselves. The photos, descriptions, video and audio files will preserve a testimony of a religion, culture and musical art that are deeply changing. For this reason, I've created, and I am constantly working on, a website, *giorgioscalici.eu/fieldwork*, where everybody can have access to the data collected during my fieldwork. This is an even more important considering that the Wana people in Taronggo are planning to build a *rumah adat* (house of traditions) that will preserve and display their artefacts and culture, and the data and material collected could help them in preserving their culture. My great interest in visual anthropology means that photos will have an important role in this book. They are not used exclusively as a visual aid and as an opportunity to show the Wana world, but they will also be integrated into the analysis and analysed themselves. Moreover, the interaction between the many ritual participants, the importance of the visible and the non-visible in Wana culture, and difficulties in giving a clear and complete description of the complexity of Wana rituality has forced me to 'rethink certain categories of anthropological knowledge in the light of understandings that may be accessible only by non-verbal means' (Sweetman 2009: 491). As stated by Cox and Wright 'visual media are appropriate for the production and dissemination of anthropological knowledge because they can convey distinct forms of knowledge that writing cannot and they provide a means to experience and understand ethnographic complexity, richness and depth' (2012: 21). The written media has its limits and words alone are not sufficient to describe a culture (Prosser and Loxley 2008), especially a geographically and culturally distant reality such as the Wana one. Thus, the *giorgioscalici.eu/fieldwork* website will have a pivotal role in this work, giving me the freedom to share as many audios, videos and photos as I feel necessary, without being restricted by publishing norms or the expenses of publishing a book with so many digital extras. With this in mind, in the field, I tried to record and observe as many expressions of Wana culture as possible, from hunting to weddings. This was challenging at the beginning, but it later revealed to be fundamental in developing approaches that allowed me to recognize connections between elements of Wana life that, at a first glance, seemed unrelated.

For this reason and being unable to put in this book all the videos, photos and audio samples we will need, I have created in my personal website an entire section dedicated to Wana people, a kind of virtual *rumah adat*. While reading, the reader will be able to visit giorgioscalici.eu/fieldwork/ where they will find videos, photos and audio recording of Wana culture and life. In this way, I hope the reader will have a more immersive experience of what this work is about and of Wana culture itself. Feel free to roam the website to stimulate your curiosity before continuing with this book.

Disciplined subjectivity and biases

It is widely accepted by now that objectivity is an illusion that anthropology should not accept or aspire to anymore (Bollig and Finke 2014; Spiro 1986). Many works have explored how subjectivity itself is deeply intersubjective (Biehl et al. 2007; Hollan 2001; Luhrmann 2006) and it is not believable that an entire discipline such as anthropology is based on the incredibly rare skill of being able to not have an immediate and subjective responses to what they are observing.

First, then, it is necessary to situate myself as a product of cultural, historical and economic factors, in a similar way to that in which scholars situate the cultures they study.[7] The aim of this is not to reach any kind of objectivity but instead to find an intellectual honesty through which to communicate. I took inspiration from *Bias in the Biography: Bias and Subjectivity in Ethnographic Research* by Margaret D. LeCompte (1987) and decided to practise 'disciplined subjectivity' myself (1987). Outlining my geographic, cultural and academic background may reveal something about the conscious or unconscious drivers of my research. Rather than a separation between the person and the researcher as a modern-day Janus monster, I aspire to the total unification of these two aspects, outside and inside academia. For this reason, I am well aware that some of my agenda, biases and desires have influenced my writing, just as they influence my observation in the field and my wider life. Moreover, I deeply agree with Cowlishaw when she states:

> [A]nthropologists' own 'civilized' nature remains obscure. This is because the anthropologist's professional task depends on over-coming the immediate responses to difference by an act of will and intellect. We cleave to a cultural relativism which turns our attention away from our deepest emotional responses to the radically different 'other', and also limits the cultural understanding to which we are so committed. As anthropologists, we welcome difference but respond as its cool interpreters rather than as interlopers at the site of struggle at the cultural frontier.
>
> (1997: 97–8)

I believe anthropologists' nature shouldn't be a mystery, rather should be shared with the readers. We are not passive and insensitive spectators but we elaborate what we see and, in same way or another, we filter the data, dividing them between relevant or nor relevant and produce analysis that starts and engages with the emic point of view but it remains our research, analysis and writing, otherwise we would not need more than one book or article for each topic but in fact we have many people working on specific topics giving all different analysis, simply because they are different people focusing on different elements of a cultural reality. A glaring example is the almost-total disinterest for the ritual music in the work of Jane Monnig Atkinson, while, as we will see, music is an essential element for a successful ritual. This simple fact seems too often ignored or overlooked, while it should be the first thing we teach to our students, but it is indeed crucial to be aware of ourselves to be good researchers also because, and we should be honest about it, overcoming the immediate responses to difference by an act of will and intellect it is just in-human. Anthropology is a field made by humans talking about humans and we should recognize our emotional response to what we are observing, describing and analysing.

I arrived among Wana people in 2011 through a series of fortuitous circumstances. Since my undergraduate studies in the disciplines of music, I had been fascinated by shamanism and the relationship between music, trance and religion; for this reason, I wrote my bachelor's degree thesis on the role of the drum in Siberian shamanism. Following the idea to conduct fieldwork in Siberia with the purpose of studying shamanism there first-hand, I moved to Rome to study ethnomusicology. The department was more internationally focused than my previous university,[8] with experts in Southeast Asia (Professor

Giovanni Giuriati) and East Africa music (Professor Francesco Giannattasio). During my studies, with a mind to writing my master's degree dissertation on Siberian shamanism, I became a gamelan player in the group called *Gong Wisnu Wara* at the Indonesian Embassy at the Holy See. Thanks to this opportunity, I obtained the Indonesian government's Darmasiswa Scholarship, enabling me to study Indonesian, also locally known as *Bahasa*[9] *Indonesia*, at the university *Sebelas Maret* in Surakarta, Java. Even though my first plan was to go to Siberia, more than 7000 kilometres away from Java, I took this opportunity to visit a new country and to get in touch with a new culture.

I was also conscious that the scholarship provided a unique opportunity to do fieldwork for my master's degree dissertation. It was in the month before travelling that I had to prepare a bibliography for the module 'Methods in Ethnomusicology Research', and while searching for research on shamanism, I found in my university's library *The Art and Politics of Wana Shamanship* by Jane Monnig Atkinson (1989). This was a book that changed my life forever; it was the first book I had ever read in English, and it opened up to me the shamanic reality of the Wana people. My intentions immediately shifted towards travelling to Morowali to study the music of the shamanic ritual called *momago*. This ritual, called *mabolong* in her book, is discussed in depth by Atkinson, but she did not offer much information about music: the word 'gong' is present only eight times, 'drum' ten times, 'sound' four times and 'music' just once. In 2011, after contacting Jabar Lahadji, founder of the Friends of Morowali association, I carried out my first spell of fieldwork, living for six months among Wana people.

During my first period of fieldwork, my ideas on research methodologies changed constantly. I was worried by the state of traditional music and struck by the discovery of the funeral ritual, the *kayori*, and the esoteric shamanic ritual, the *molawo*, since neither had been studied nor documented before. I therefore expanded the aim of my research to include gathering data on how instruments are made and recording and transcribing music for a basic analysis of the musical life of Wana people. The master's degree thesis that followed discussed the uses and characteristics of this music in the three rituals I observed (the *momago*, the *kayori* and the *molawo*), plus the organology and repertoire of Wana leisure music. That experience made me understand that I truly wanted to become a researcher.

Indeed, it is impossible to know if anthropology is our dream career before having experienced the fieldwork, with its ups and downs. Students may often have a romantic vision of ethnographic research. Usually, this impression is supported by the study of old books that may not provide description of the struggles of the task, or by the reports written by post-fieldwork students during fieldwork training given by some British universities (Pollard 2009: 15). In my initial training, I never encountered any studies that acknowledged the solitude one is apt to feel during fieldwork, although it is a common feeling (Pollard 2009: 4); excessive amounts of this state were the biggest problem I faced, even though, strangely, I have rarely been as happy in my life as during that first period of fieldwork. Only later I discovered *A Diary in the Strict Sense of the Word* by Bronisław Malinowski, which contains realistic accounts of his fieldwork experiences. Malinowski, in fact, deliberately looked for opportunities to be alone, noting times when 'I sought solitude' (Malinowski 1989: 283) and had a 'need for real solitude' (Malinowski 1989: 186). He reported feeling 'content with the stagnation and solitude' (Malinowski 1989: 191), while I was still learning to cope with it. By the time I was in my second period of fieldwork, I too found myself in need for solitude; I enjoyed spending nights by myself, watching a movie or playing a videogame on my phone, actions that I could not share with my local friends and informants without becoming the centre of attention. While this desire for a break from active research could be considered quite normal, this thirst for solitude became unusually strong while I was outside the jungle, and I started to actively avoid almost any human contact. In the time spent in Kolonodale or Palu, I had almost no desire to have social interaction with Indonesians. The reason was a kind of culture shock within a cultural shock. While among the Wana I was just *Jojo*, the local name given to me because it was more easily pronounced than Giorgio, outside the jungle I was a *buleh*[10] in an even stronger way than I might have been as a tourist in a big city. I was possibly the only *buleh* for kilometres around, so people screamed at me, took pictures of me while I was eating, touched me and so on. This situation made the time spent outside the forest quite frustrating, and during both my fieldwork periods I spent most of these days in my room by myself, going out only when I had to eat. The time spent alone was divided into work (organizing the data collected) and leisure (watching movies, reading comic books, playing old videogames and reading).

In Italy, the fields of ethnomusicology, anthropology, and religious studies (in Italy, the field is called history of religion) are extensively interconnected. With histories dating to the end of the nineteenth or the beginning of the twentieth century, they established themselves as modern fields of research after the Second World War, after the fascist era. At that time, the major figures in these fields were Ernesto De Martino and Diego Carpitella, who worked together on major research on the phenomenon of *taranta*.[11] De Martino was a key figure in both the fields of anthropology and religious studies in Italy, while Carpitella held the first ethnomusicology professorship in the country. Collaborating with Alan Lomax for many years, particularly in research on Italian music from 1953 to 1954, Carpitella taught a generation of Italian ethnomusicologists, including my former supervisor Giovanni Giuriati. Both he and De Martino were members of the Communist Party, and Italian intelligentsia more generally had strong connections with left-wing ideology. The ideas of Antonio Gramsci, the General Secretary of the Italian Communist party from 1926 until 1927, were particularly influential, as were various theories that experienced revivals in the 1950s and 1960s after suppression from fascism. These political concerns are still partially present in Italian scholarship.

Among the ideas in Antonio Gramsci's *Prison Notebooks* (1948–51), written during twenty years of detention by the fascists, perhaps most useful in anthropology is the concept of hegemony. Hegemony is a form of social order based on a combination of coercion and consent. But while hegemony is totalizing in intent, this is never fully realized in practical situations, where repressed entities are not passive, and they demand some negotiation with the sources of power. Gramsci rejects the division of the world into a passive base and a powerful and controlling structure, but affirms that there is a constant dialogue between the different levels. This idea is particularly important when applied to Wana reality. This is a small 'powerless' community that is constantly negotiating its position in relation to the Indonesian government and the world religions. Gramsci recognizes that cultural activities and products have a key role in the maintenance and reproduction of a social order and in the relationship between powers. With this divergence from Marxist theories, he places topics of concern to anthropologists, such as arts, language, religion, ethnicity and so on, at the centre of understanding power and political relationships. Consideration of factors such as gender, race, religion and ethnicity cast a new light on the community relationships that are a central theme of the present study.

Following Gramsci, the Italian school of humanities studies (including ethnomusicology and religious studies)[12] shows deep connections with the Italian Communist Party (Partito Comunista Italiano), and the aims and the agenda of these fields became interconnected with communist ideologies. Italian anthropology was not born of a colonialist mentality, but instead emerged from a particular attention to the 'problem' of the South of Italy. This area was thought of by Jesuit missionaries in the sixteenth century as 'le Indie di quaggiù'[13] (the Indias of down here) (Sciannameo 2006). Until De Martino, the *Meridione* (the South) was usually only addressed from an economic point of view. De Martino's motivation was to fill a void in the understanding of the unique and complex cultures and worldviews of Southern farmers, breeders, artisans, fishermen and workers in general. These elements made Italian anthropology very different from the anthropology of countries with a strong colonial past, or present. Regarding the anthropology studies in countries like Australia, Elizabeth Coleman warns us that she believes 'that anthropology contributed to the normalization of Aborigines' lowly social position by emphasizing, explaining and defending their cultural difference' (2018: 44), something completely different from the Italian reality.

According to De Martino, the *miseria culturale* (cultural poverty) of the *Meridione* is the representation of a psychological misery produced by historical-social-economic conditions imposed by a regime and created by a relation of plurisecular subalternity. For him, the religious folklore of the *Meridione* was a reflection of the 'non-history' of the South and its continuous repression. Although I would never use the term 'cultural misery', the reality described by De Martino is very similar to Wana realities. This is a small community that has always been in a position of subalternity and that has culture and rituality shaped by this subalternity.

De Martino and Carpitella impacted upon my personal formation as a researcher on many levels. First, they represent a truly interdisciplinarity vision of research. They both took part in one of the most important research expeditions in Italian scholarship, one that produced one of its most significant books, *La terra del rimorso. Contributo a una storia religiosa del Sud* (The Land of Remorse: A Study of Southern Italian Tarantism). The cultural impact of this 1959 book and the project behind it was immense in Italy. Interdisciplinarity is a term that seems to have been rediscovered[14] only recently by UK academia. As well as De Martino (anthropologist) and Carpitella (ethnomusicologist), there was Giovanni Jervis (psychiatrist), Letizia Jervis-Comba (psychologist), Amalia Signorelli (cultural anthropologist), Franco Pinna (photographer) and Sergio Bettini (medical researcher). The lesson that many cultural phenomena are too complex to be approached from a single point of view is crucial in my decision to use many different sources and theories, and to observe Wana rituality with a holistic approach. My own identity as a researcher with training in a PhD in Religious Studies and carrying out an anthropological project stresses the futility of separating these fields. De Martino not only worked on the relationship between music and trance, but he also wrote one of the first major books on death in the Mediterranean area: *Morte e pianto rituale. Dal lamento funebre antico al pianto di Maria* (1958).[15] In this work, he observes that when someone dies there follows a 'crisis of condolences' that can lead to existential collapse. There then emerges the necessity to culturally process mourning inside the socially codified form of the rite. In doing so, the consolation offered by religious beliefs brings the dramatic charge of mourning back to bearable forms. For Wana people, who live a life that they consider wretched, the moral support of their religion and grieving tradition becomes an irreplaceable element for their survival. The coping methods of Wana people are some of the key cultural traits that this work explores.

Having completed my master's degree, I decided to proceed with my academic career and to apply for a PhD. My choice ended up as Durham University, where even though I am an ethnomusicologist, I have found the Theology and Religion department to be a perfect environment for my research. Durham was able to offer something that no other university could offer me, the guidance and the support of two experts on the two main topics of my PhD: shamanism and death. After the discovery of the *kayori*, I decided to go back to an old passion of mine, thanatology (my dream job as teenager), and to find a way to bring together studies of shamanism and death in my current project. That was possible thanks to Professor Douglas Davies, an expert on death studies with training in anthropology, and Dr Simon Mills, an expert on Korean shamanism and music. My engagement with them brought my research into the new areas of emotions and community. These were topics that already existed in my thinking but that I did not have the maturity to conceive them as the central part of this work.

From MA thesis to monograph: Improvements, changes and reflections

Although the research presented is ostensibly a continuation of my MA research, the work is much more than a simple expansion and forms an independent investigation in its own right. In 2011, I was twenty-four years old, and I had no experience of fieldwork. My only information regarding the Wana people was a book based on forty-year-old research, and my initial aim was to carry out an ethnomusicological study on Wana shamanic music and on what it could contribute to wider discussions on music and trance. Five years later, in 2016, I was a much more experienced researcher, with a wide knowledge of Wana culture and rituality and with different aims: I had an MA in Ethnomusicology and now turned towards PhD work in Religious Studies, and I was now most interested in the intricate relationship between emotion, religion and music as a cultural tool. Another fieldwork was planned for 2021 but the pandemics made it impossible.

Indeed, in the five years separating the two periods of fieldwork, my ideas developed as I processed the large amounts of data I collected in 2011 and reflected on my fieldwork strategies and directions. One key factor was that, during the earlier period in the field, I was an ethnomusicology student with only very basic knowledge of religious studies and even more limited English. While the former deficiency forced me to focus on the musical side of my research, the latter ruled out the most recent studies and articles. Improving those language skills in the meantime, though, allowed me access to a wider and more recent pool of research, especially on the topics of emotions (Beatty 2005, 2010, 2014), death studies (Magowan 2001, 2007), shamanism (Winkelman 1990, 2010) and music (Wolf 2001, 2006).

An additional issue emerged in the fieldwork process itself. As I have already noted, the first time I went to the jungle I did so without training or a clear idea of what I would find living among the Wana people. More importantly, the fieldwork was tainted by the uncertainty about my own destiny as a researcher: would it be my first and only fieldwork experience?

Pushed by the urgency of the task, I worked in a 'bulimic' way, trying to collect the widest amount of data possible, not only about Wana music but also regarding almost any aspect of the community's life. Moreover, having to work alone, I had to learn how to take videos, audio recordings and photographs, and conduct interviews – sometimes, all at the same time.

In the five years before returning in 2016, I had time to reflect on my experience and on the data collected, and I had the opportunity to organize a work-plan for my next period of fieldwork. In 2011, I dealt with culture shock and the consternation of finding my research field far larger and complex than I had expected. Studying Atkinson's book, I knew about the main Wana ritual, the *momago*, but much more was waiting for me. I discovered a funerary ritual, the *kayori*, which had never been documented before. There was also another shamanic ritual, the *molawo*, a complex religion and an endangered musical tradition. This all left me feeling overwhelmed by the amount of new information I was learning back in 2011. During my second fieldwork trip, on the other hand, I had the knowledge and the maturity to conduct my research with a clear focus and specific interests. I was no longer jumping from place to place but a researcher returning to the field with a clear mind and considered aims.

These aims involved expanding on some of the limitations of my MA dissertation. The dissertation had a very narrow focus: the ritual and traditional music of the Wana people. The main reason was its position in the field of ethnomusicology, but also my desire to collect a catalogue of Wana music and organology before the disappearance of this culture. This task eventually gave rise to an article dedicated to musical instruments (Scalici 2023), but this turned out to be only a relatively minor section, as the musicology and organology of Wana music gave up space in my thinking to Wana cultural concepts of music and connections with the spiritual world.

Indeed, this book is the evidence of a research that expanded to explore gender relationships, mythology, emotions and much more besides music. In the five years between the two fieldwork periods, I came to the conclusion the only possible path for success in this research was interdisciplinarity: to look at Wana culture in its totality instead of extracting a single element. Of course, in pursuing this I was also helped by an increased knowledge of English and the positive impact of an international environment that kept me up to date with the most recent research and with theories relevant to what I was observing. Thus, while my MA dissertation tackled just a small piece of Wana culture, this work attempts to illuminate connections between different elements of Wana life: music, gender, emotion, death and so on, to offer a more exhaustive study of this culture and world.

During my period of fieldwork, in 2011 and 2016 combined, I collected more than 800 GB of data, in the form of videos, photos and audio recordings. While in 2011 my recording skills were very underdeveloped and my videos lacked technical and aesthetic quality, I gradually improved with experience. Later videos were smoother, there was less camera shake and I learned the best places to position the camera to obtain the optimal shot for research purposes. Nonetheless, light conditions were always a problem. The Morowali reserve is directly on the equator and the darkness of the houses contrasted with the intense light coming from the outside, making good photography relatively easy and good videorecording very difficult. In fact, the night rituals were impossible to film with the camera I had in 2011, and only the night-vision settings of my new equipment for 2016 opened up this possibility.

In 2011, I used a low-budget video camera with DV cassettes, a compact Olympus still camera and a ZOOM H4N audio recorder. In 2016, an important upgrade was an HD video camera with SD-card storage. Being able to transfer video to a laptop computer meant that I was free to shoot far more video; previously, I collected and carried around with me a total of 46 DV cassettes. My still camera was also slightly updated; the Olympus Tough tg-4 was again a compact camera, but this time equipped to work in the jungle, being waterproof, shockproof and incorporating a GPS system. These features allowed me to worry less about the camera during my work, both while crossing rivers and in similar dangerous situations, while also recording. Thanks to the GPS, I was able to record my position and the position of the villages. There is no precise map that shows the positions of Wana villages, partly because entire villages are often moved to new locations, and with the GPS information I obtained, I was able to pinpoint the exact position of each village on the maps I worked with. I continued to use the same ZOOM H4N for audio recording. All of this data gathering relied on a solar panel charger, a lifesaving research tool that I did not have in 2011.

My Wana contacts were all extremely happy to have me photographing and recording their ritual and daily life. In 2011, I avoided filming people crying at funerals, but gradually came to understand that this ethical barrier was entirely of my own construction, and that to do so was not a problem for anyone else present. In this work, I draw upon recordings and other data collected in both 2011 and 2016, and I have indicated that in this work when possible, especially in regard to the interviews with my informers. The ability to call upon data from 2011 meant that I had access to photos, video and audio that was useful in clarifying various points, even if the subject matter was not a primary focus of the main fieldwork for the PhD project in 2016. The decision to include data from 2011 was also based on the unique value of some that I was able to collect on that trip; in 2011 I was able, for instance, to record a *salonde* (female shamanic dance) and a *molawo* (a shorter shamanic ritual), both of which I did not encounter again in 2016 due to the rarity of these events in the area studied.

Material I recorded proved to be important in developing good relations with those I worked with in the field. I showed the videos I made to all those who wanted to see them, and I edited together a video to leave behind in each of the two main places of my fieldwork, Marisa and Taronggo, with both villages owning a television set and a DVD player. I also left photos and short videos of daily life that members of the community had shot while borrowing my camera.

Method

In 2016 I returned to Morowali for a second period of fieldwork, again lasting six months. Without hiring a guide for the first days of research, I decided to directly contact my old informants and to resume our collaboration. The day before I was due to enter the jungle, Indo Jaka (daughter-in-law of Apa Rau, the

Marisa village chief, a former *tau walia*[16] and my dear friend) died and I found myself in the middle of arrangements being made for her funeral. This occasion provided an opportunity to observe funeral preparations that I had never seen before. So far, the funerals I observed were always in places far from where I was based, thus I had previously travelled to the place of the funeral with other people on the last two days. Despite the somber mood, Apa Rau welcomed me as warmly as five years earlier and offered me an empty house in his village. Wana people have a semi-nomadic culture, so it is common for many houses to remain empty for months, or years, at a time. That these houses are opened to travellers already starts to reveal the characteristic *kasintuwu* (sense of community) that will be one of the main themes of this book. After two weeks in Marisa, I went back to Kilo Sembilan for the funeral of Indo Jaka, and then moved with Apa Reilin (Indo Jaka's brother-in-law) to Taronggo. As in 2011, I spent my time between the villages of Marisa, Kilo Sembilan, where my informants from Kaju Poli (including Apa Ingus, a powerful and respected *tau walia* and musician) moved, and Taronggo (hosted by Apa Reilin, son of Apa Rau), a small town just outside the jungle. To move between these places, I joined people already making those journeys. In more than one occasion, I did try to travel by myself, but it turned out not to be the smartest and safest idea. Especially in 2011, travel between villages was a necessity to collect the data I needed about Wana traditional music. In fact, players, instrument makers and the materials they require were all in different parts of the jungle, and it required some effort to bring these three elements together. In 2016, I decided to stay and work with the same people as I had done in 2011, and also to pay a short visit to the village of Lambentana, in a more isolated area of the Wana land, to meet its village chief and to record some mythological tales.

During the five years that separated my two spells in the field, I had ample time to study and review the data gathered in 2011. Following Akhil Gupta and James Ferguson's (1992) discussion on the definition of 'the field', I would consider these six years to constitute a continuation of the fieldwork period. The field is not always a simple geographical place, but it can be any place or activity related to the research, such as a library or the review of one's own notes (Gupta and Ferguson 1992). This previous experience gave me a clear idea of the direction of my research, the needed physical and mental preparation for life in the jungle and a wider experience of the technical elements of the research (audio-visual recording and the basics of visual anthropology).

Having already gained a vivid idea of Wana rituality, in my second period in the field I was able to focus my energies on observing specific elements more than the previous general vision of the ritual. A good example is the time and energy spent in the collection of Wana mythology. My initial approach to this task produced quite disappointing results as the elders of the Marisa area did not remember many tales. Instead, they pointed to Apa Kode, Lambentana's chief, as a knowledgeable man. For this reason, I decided to travel to Lambentana with the help of my guide Lando. The village is one of the most isolated in the Wana territory and its inhabitants speak a dialect of the Wana language not always comprehensible to all others around. Here I found a very different lifestyle in comparison to that I was used to observing. Residents of Lambentana are well known to all Wana people as the most traditional and isolated, and I was able to make useful comparisons between their lives and those of Wana people on the borders of the jungle. Moreover, aware of the constant comparisons drawn between humans and plants in Wana rituality, mythology and songs, I also collected data on Wana botanic knowledge, producing a small catalogue of photographs of plants with their local names and traditional uses.

To transcribe the Wana language I followed the conventions used by Atkinson, whose useful phonetic table (1989: xvii) is the basis for much of the following work. When a vowel is lengthened, I write it with double letters (T*aa*). In Wana language, the sound *n* often precedes names, so *Indo Pino* is actually pronounced *Indo n'Pino*, and I choose to omit this sound in transcription. However, this means it is possible that the name I write as *Ndara* is actually *Dara* with the sound *n* added; when in doubt I transcribe the word as I heard it.

The field research was conducted in several languages. The majority of the time, especially in the villages near the border of the reserve, I spoke *Bahasa Indonesia* (BI) with some brief discussions in *Bahasa Taa* (BT). While in Lambentana, all the interviews were conducted in the only language known by the inhabitants of that village: *Bahasa Tokaju*, also called *Bahasa Maranka*. Knowing only *Bahasa Indonesia* and *Bahasa Taa*, I relied upon a guide, who also acted as translator, to help me with the interviews during the time spent in Lambentana. All interviews I conducted in Lambentana were recorded; my guide translated my questions and, depending on the length of the answer, summarized or translated the replies of my informants. I needed a translator only for the few days I spent in Lambentana while I was collecting information on the local mythology. I am still working on translating the several hours of recorded tales to produce a volume exclusively dedicated to Wana mythology and enriched by a map of all the mythological places.

It is also worth noting that while Atkinson and I transcribe the term 'tau' with a final 'u', Anna Grumblies (2013, 2016) writes the term with a final 'w': 'taw'.

Beyond this, there are no major differences between my transcriptions and those of previous scholars working with Wana people.

My four main field sites (Marisa, Kaju Poli, Taronggo and Lambentana) offered different realities and informants, and gave me a multifaceted representation of Wana reality. A common thread was my collaboration with members of Apa Rau's family, whom I found spread out in Marisa, Kaju Poli and Taronggo. As already mentioned, in Marisa I lived by myself, but shared meals with Apa Rau's family. Marisa is a mayor village 'near', it takes at least three hours to make the journey by canoe, the town of Kolonodale and here Muslim and Wana people live together peacefully. One resident of the village is Om Manggi, who was one of my main informants and who worked with the US anthropologist Michael Alvard in the 1990s. Thanks to this experience, Om Manggi was perhaps the only Wana that understood the reason for my presence there; it is not easy to explain the concepts of universities and PhDs to people who, in some cases, have never been in a school of any kind. Om Manggi was a valuable informant and friend, and this work owes much to his knowledge and help.

The village of Kaju Poli is very small, with less than two dozen people living there, and its Christian Wana residents favour becoming an independent Christian village. Apa Jaka lived in the village, but after the death of his wife decided to move to Marisa with his two children and parents-in-law to build a new house and to start the process of training up towards the possible goal of becoming the new village chief. He is the eldest son of the current village chief of Marisa: Apa Rau. In Taronggo, I lived with Apa Reilin, another son of Apa Rau, who lives with his wife, two teenage daughters and a new-born baby (in 2016). In Taronggo, Christians, Muslims and a few Wana people live together in a particularly interesting social reality. Apa Reilin still follows the Wana religion, but his daughters, who attend a Christian school, have converted to Christianity.

When doing this kind of research, it is always important to be aware of our own status and how the people we are working and living will see and perceive us. Some people perceived me as a rich, white, 'mythical' Westerner,[17] and this status was not a problem, usually. Being a Westerner meant that I had the benefit of the mythical power that the *Tau Baraka* (the mythical people) brought to the West at the end of the golden era. For Wana people, the Westerners live in a mythical space-time. I tried to repay my hosts with gifts (including money) rather than by paying a regular rent. I fixed and bought new parts for Apa Reilin's motorcycle and chainsaw, a piece of equipment that brought his main source of income through his work as a woodcutter. I also bought 'festive' or less common food for his family (chicken, eggs, vegetables, sweets and so on) and gave gifts to his wife and daughters. While in Marisa, I always paid for the petrol when travelling with others to Kolonodale, and there I bought gifts or offered food to my friends and informants. I especially bought gifts and toys for the children. Interesting enough, Leili, one of Apa Rau's granddaughters, asked for a dark-skinned doll and, even considering the Indonesian population, I had to visit many toy shops before finding one. Nonetheless, I never got the feeling, however, that anybody sought after my money; this was especially true of Apa Reilin, and it helped in us forming a bond of friendship rather than one of researcher-informant. While I felt the need to pull my weight and to help my friends as much as possible, they never took advantage of that. Rarely have I felt as part of a family as I did among my Wana friends.

Anna Grumblies, another anthropologist that I met during my first period of fieldwork, reports that the family hosting her sometimes experienced 'jealous neighbours' (2016: 38). Personally, I never noted anything similar during my fieldwork, but possibly because our fieldworks were quite different. While she was stable in one place, thus living with one family, I moved around, changing host quite frequently. Possibly, the lack of a stable link with a specific family avoided the surge of some kind of jealousy or, also possible, I simply didn't notice it. Moreover, I presented myself as a Christian even though I am agnostic, because being known as a person without religion would make the fieldwork, or any kind of work or action, very complicated, if not impossible. In Indonesia, not having a religion makes someone an anomaly and is usually taken as a serious negative trait, often compared to a lack of morality, because 'fifty years on, atheism in Indonesia is still associated with communism and subversion' (Hasani 2022). Even so, I made it clear that although I was born Christian, I do not practise; presenting myself as a kind of 'in pause Christian', a term used by some Indonesians I met during my time there, gave me a label acceptable in Indonesian culture. I often made the point to people around me that I admired the Wana religion over Christianity, and that I strongly supported their culture. In fact, the idea that somebody had travelled from the mythical West to the *Tana Taa* (Wana Land) to study their life, religion and music was a source of pride, and it spread among the younger generations some curiosity regarding Wana traditions. A pride and curiosity that pushed some Wana to follow my research and rediscover their traditional music. Sadly, this desire did not last long, and young people went back to their own hobbies and interests. Although considered beneath the level of a Wana child in my abilities with some common tasks, such as handling a machete (as I discuss more below), generally I was accepted warmly and felt well respected. I like to think the people around me felt my great respect for them and their culture and recognized my desire to help and support them as much as possible. This was the basis of what, in some ways, became a relationship between friends. Despite my position of power (as a rich,[18] white Westerner) I consider myself indebted to the Wana people I met, and I tried to communicate my gratitude whenever possible.

The interviews I conducted were very open and resembled friendly chats more than structured interviews. I opted for this approach for many reasons; first, my interlocutors would get bored very easily if I tried to engage them with a list of questions. I was reminded of Clifford Geertz's warning researchers about 'tormenting intelligent people with stupid questions' (Geertz 1987: 40). Moreover, '*dari pertama*' (from the beginning) was an answer that I encountered many times while working with Wana people. This was the perfect answer for all my questions regarding the origins of something, or as the reason behind a particular ritual action. Everything beyond personal memories was included in the mythical space-time and existed *dari pertama*.[19] To really obtain information, I had to enter into their minds, to truly understand their ways of thinking and relating with the world. In 2011, I had already discovered that direct questions were often useless; once when I asked why traditional songs are four lines long they replied: 'because with three lines it would be too short and with five too long'.[20] This is a reasonable reply for what was perceived as a futile question. As a response, I developed the idea of 'lateral questioning',[21] a method meant to unearth insights that sometimes even the informant is not consciously aware of. I tried to obtain information not by asking directly, but by talking around the topic and looking for alternative ways to obtain information, waiting for the information to be retold as I knew everything while putting together all the pieces I had in an attempt to produce the most faithful puzzle possible. Therefore, considering these difficulties and being aware of the difference between what people do and what they think, I have tried to apply other research method, such as 'situated listening' and 'speech-in-action participant-observation' (Sanjek 1990: 233).

Working in small villages where the majority of people share the same values and generally live in harmony allowed me to avoid many of the problems encountered by Grumblies in Taronggo. Here she found that 'a number of interviews came to an abrupt halt when an uninvited guest came along and, often unintentionally, disturbed the intimacy of the interview with his presence as an other-religious or simply other-ethnic person' (2016: 40). While, in my experience and especially in Lambentana, possibly due to its isolation and heterogeneity, other people loved to join the conversation or to simply sit and listen to it. As Joshua Barker states: 'Where social ties are dense and privacy is not a priority [...] almost all interviews are likely to be group interviews of one sort or another' (Barker 2012: 56). And there is almost no privacy in a Wana village. Indeed, it was not always possible to have one-to-one sessions, and many of my interviews or chats were with groups of people who came to see the novelty of the situation. I generally tried to observe people as much as possible and to learn by observation, as Wana children do, asking questions but accepting that it was a shot in the dark and that it was unlikely to strike gold. Moreover, I tried to chat and talk with as many people as possible and as much as possible, finding this the real way to obtain information. I then asked specific questions and gained deeper insights from my major informants, especially Om Manggi, who was already used to this kind of research.

People of interest

To help with navigation among the great number of names mentioned in this work, I now offer a list of the main informants that helped me during my two periods of fieldwork. Having discussed the ethical issues regarding participation in my research and gained their permission, I use their real names or teknonyms. No one of my informants ever raised any issue regarding their participation in this work. For them it is a reason of pride having a Westerner interested in their culture, and it was a joy to share their culture with an outsider. Moreover, Wana conception of privacy and ownership are very different from the West. Wana are almost never alone, if not actively avoiding being alone, so many of their life is public. At the same time, at the base of this culture there is a desire to share with the others and to help each other whenever possible. Often, my informants were chosen by chance; they were people I shared a journey with or met while bathing in the river. Others I chose according to their social position (elders, *tau walia*, head chiefs). In the case of Apa Kode, the chief of Lambentana, for example, I was recommended to visit him because of his reputation as an important figure in local life. It is easily noticeable that the majority of my informants are male. This was not intentional, but my own gender simply tended to place me more often in situations shared with men rather than women. On top of this, there is the shyness that characterizes Wana women, for example Indo Rau actively avoided to have interviews with me, something I will discuss in detail later. More importantly, this shyness is what stop many women to get in position of power or to become a *tau walia*, thus almost all *tau walia* and village chiefs I met were men. Nevertheless, I managed to create friendship bonds with the wives of several of my informants. This was partly through time spent looking after their children (bringing medicines, sweets and toys, and playing with them while the adults were in the field). It was also partly as a result of my peculiar position within the Wana divisions of the world. As I have already mentioned, my status was lower than that of a child when it came to using a machete; this is a tool used by everybody from a very young age, but it was forbidden to me because of my lack of previous skills. Indeed, the limits of my practical knowledge regarding hunting, farming, building houses or similar tasks placed me at the same level as the children, who were still learning basic skills in these areas. In this respect, I joined the realm of the women who often demonstrated a great patience in showing me their daily duties. Moreover, not drinking alcohol also made me a kind of 'honorary woman' since drinking alcohol outside the rituals isn't well perceived by Wana wives.

When I talk about the Wana people in this publication, then, I am not simply referring to men.[22] Although I did spend more time with men, the people who take the role of elders of the culture and hold power among Wana people, my interest is in the entire community. I engage with the roles of gender in Wana culture in the last chapter. The Wana community first acts and reacts as a single being, and only later divides and categorizes reality into male and female. The exact age of each of my informants is unknown.

Apa Ingus: Powerful *tau walia* and skilful harmonica and *popondo* (single-stringed baton zither) player. In 2011, he was living in Kaju Poli, but in 2016 I found him in Kilo Sembilan and planning to move to Marisa. He lives with his daughter Ingus and her family. They live a modest life. Apa Ingus was one of my main interlocutors, because of both his shamanic knowledge and his musical skills. He was also used to working with researchers having already hosted the French documentarists Gérard Nougarol and Martine Journet (2005, 2007, 2011). A very humorous person, Apa Ingus enjoyed singing badly while I was recording.

Apa Rau: Village head of Marisa and former *tau walia*. I lived in his house during my first period of fieldwork, and I continued to work with him during my second visit. An extremely knowledgeable and kind person, he is one of the few *tau walia* I met to know the *molawo* ritual, and he is one of the best *geso* (one string spike fiddle) players in the area. I often spent my nights listening to him singing while playing his *geso*. We frequently discussed Wana traditions and their value. A very wise man, he was one of my main informants and closer friends. He was always very patient and worked in the past with the French documentarists Nougarol and Journet. He lives with his wife; his daughters and grandchildren live in the village.

Apa Reilin: The son of Apa Rau, he lives in Taronggo village. I stayed in his house each time I visited Taronggo. He was always ready to help me with my research and he taught me about Wana botanic knowledge during our journeys through the jungle. He also lent me his scooter for the one-hour ride to the nearest village with phone signal, so I could contact my now wife. He lives with his Wana wife, and they have a new-born baby and two teenage daughters, who are converts to Christianity.

Om Manggi: A Muslim Wana living in Marisa. In 2016 he lived with Apa Rau and his family. An extremely knowledgeable person, he showed great passion and patience in helping me and answering my questions. Perhaps his previous experiences with the US anthropologist Alvard (2000) contributed to making him a particularly communicative informant. He taught me about Wana botanic knowledge, and we spent many days talking about the Wana people and the world outside the forest while I was treating his injured leg.[23]

Om Suma: One of the most interesting people I met during fieldwork. The son of a Muslim shaman of Wana royal blood, Om Suma lives alone in a large house that he built himself near the big lake. Very respectful of Wana traditions, and perhaps the most knowledgeable and interested person in matters of Wana culture that I met among the younger generation. Extremely skilled guitar player, he has a great love of music and a wide knowledge of Wana songs and music. Having been educated at school, he wrote down for me the texts of many Wana songs and their translations in Bahasa Indonesia.

Apa Kode: Village chief of Lambentana. I worked with him briefly during my time in his village. He welcomed me and spent a few evenings recounting all of the *katuntu* (mythological tales) he knew with patience and joy. He was very pleased by my presence in Lambentana, and about my curiosity about Wana culture.

Apa n'Tongi: Formerly one of the most powerful *tau walia*, who was reported to be even able to walk in the sky, he was starting to convert to Christianity by the time of my fieldwork. He lived in Kayu Poli with his sister Indo Pino during my first period of study. Alongside his religious knowledge, he was also a skilled music player and a fine musical instrument maker. He made me a beautiful *geso*.

Indo Pino: A highly respected and powerful female *tau walia*, one of the only two female *tau walia* I had the opportunity to meet during my time with the Wana. A unique character, she lived with her brother. I worked a lot with her during my first fieldwork trip, partly due to her skills as a flute player.

She died in 2015 but features prominently in the documentary film made by Nougarol and Journet (2011).

Apa Sudin: My host in Marisa in 2011, I spent a great amount of time with him while the younger people were out working in the fields. We talked especially about Wana leisure music, and he made many of the instruments that I brought back.

Apa Main: A powerful *tau walia* living in the Taronggo area. I worked with him in 2011 and met him again in 2016, but by then he was too ill to work extensively. During my first fieldwork period, he was a crucial source of information regarding Wana shamanism and I saw him many times during the *momago* in that area.

Jango: Jango is actually his nickname, meaning 'beard' in Bahasa Wana. He is considered to be one of the wise elders of Marisa. I spent a few nights listening to him telling *katuntu* (mythological stories).

Apa n'Te: Village chief of Taronggo. Always very kind to me, a knowledgeable person and a *tetebua* (a four strings bamboo zither) player, but not a *tau walia*.

Kruyt, Atkinson, Grumblies and other researchers

Over the years, Morowali has primarily attracted scholars of botany, zoology and agriculture rather than anthropologists. At the end of the 1970s, the Operation Drake[74] project visited the Morowali forest, writing a report about the animals and the plants of the forest (1981). Between 1995 and 1996, Alvard carried his research on the Wana swidden culture, focusing on the impact of this agricultural system on the ecological environment of the forest, affirming that the method was not as destructive as declared by the Indonesian government (2000) who considered them 'environment vandals' (Lahadji 1999: 240). In 1999 the US PhD student Cynthia Riccardi wrote a thesis on the indigenous swidden agriculture of Wana people. Finally, Jabar Lahadji, former director and founder of the now-closed *Yayasan Sahabat Morowali* (Friends of Morowali) association and employee of the local office of the forest department, wrote many articles about Wana people, their life in the reserve and their relationship with the government.

Outside of academic fields, the French film-makers Martine Journet and Gérard Nougarol have made a series of films (2005, 2007, 2011) that cover many aspects of Wana culture and provide a rich insight into the life inside the Morowali reserve.

The first ethnographic information about Wana culture can be found in *De to Wana op Oost-Celebes* (On the Wana of East Celebes) (1930) written by the

Dutch missionary Albert C. Kruyt, who spent two months among Wana people. Fifty years later, the US anthropologist Jane Monnig Atkinson arrived in the area. Between 1974 and 1976, she lived among the Wana in the Ue Bone area, in the northern part of the Morowali, studying how the *mabolong*, a shamanic healing ritual known as *momago* by my informants, establishes a political order within the community. She produced an analysis of the ritual lyrics in her book *The Art and Politics of Wana Shamanship* (1989). In addition, Atkinson wrote several articles on other Wana-related themes, in particular the relationship between Wana and the other religious groups that reside inside the Morowali area (1983, 1987, 1988, 1992, 2003).

More recently (2011), the German anthropologist Anna-Teresa Grumblies (a PhD student at the time of my first fieldwork) was in the field investigating the relationship between Wana people and the external world. Her research has since been published: *Being Wana, Becoming an 'Indigenous People'. Experimenting with Indigeneity in Central Sulawesi* (2013). Her essay discusses the concept of *adat* (tradition) and Wana strategies to preserve their independence.

Apart from the more nature-focused work of Riccardi and Operation Drake, the findings of all those mentioned above have offered a great amount of information and data that is used in this book. In various particular ways, due to the closeness of our research, I often rely on the testimonies of Atkinson and Grumblies. Although our work shares a number of key concerns, at the same time, it differs quite markedly and, with time, I have started seeing our work as mutually complementary, existing as a kind of trilogy. While Atkinson analysed thoroughly the political role of the words in the *momago*, she almost completely ignored not only the *kayori* ritual,[25] a very important and unique funeral event, but also the role of music in Wana culture and rituality, and the use of music to get in contact with the non-visible world. I have never had the opportunity to meet or talk to Atkinson, and so have not been able to find out the reason that Wana music is never discussed or explored in her book and articles. In *The Art and Politics of Wana Shamanship* (1989), only a few lines are devoted to music, even though it is a constant presence throughout the *mabolong* ritual. Moreover, her research is almost fifty years old now and it was conducted in an area of Morowali that I never visited. This makes my work partly a window onto how the ritual she studied, and Wana culture in general, has changed over this long period of time.

On the other hand, Grumblies and I met in 2011 while we were doing fieldwork. I was an MA student, and she was a PhD student. I had access to her thesis and her articles, and they were both very useful to me, but the focus of

her research differed from mine. Her aim was to study the Wana conception
of marginality and the people's resilient measures against external forces such
as missionization, government interventions and the work of the palm oil
companies. Although I deeply appreciated her work, and especially her detailed
demonstration of how Wana people have been marginalized by the government
and the world religions, I do not agree with her central conclusions on Wana
emic points of view regarding periphery, centre and marginality. In Chapter 5,
I argue that Wana people have a conception of centre and periphery that is
diametrically opposed to the Western one; they value the centre as a powerless
place while all the power is concentrated at the periphery. For them, Jakarta is
powerful because it is on the peripheries, located far away from the centre of the
world, where they themselves are living.

I believe that the contrast between my conclusions and those of Grumblies
is largely due to our fieldwork focusing on different Wana communities and
geographical areas. She spent her entire fieldwork period outside the Morowali
forest, in the village of Taronggo where Wana people live together with Christians
and Muslims, go to school, have access to medicine and are more in contact with
the periphery (the world outside the forest). I spent some time in Taronggo, but
my main research was done inside the forest. It is possible that, even though
we both worked with Wana people, we are expressing two different points of
view. I am reporting the point of view of the Wana people from the forest, the
people that live in the powerless 'centre' of the world and that define the world
around them from this position. Grumblies, on the other hand, is reporting the
point of view of people living outside of that centre, in a liminal place between
the forest and the periphery of the Wana world, where Wana people are more
strongly influenced and shaped by the point of view of the outside. In Taronggo,
the government, schools and the world religions have a more important role in
shaping Wana identity than in the jungle, and this produces differences in Wana
culture.

Ultimately, I place myself in the middle between Atkinson and Grumblies,
moving from the first and comparing with the latter. This book offers a deeper
exploration of *momago* ritual elements that Atkinson only briefly touched upon
and adds coverage of the *kayori* ritual, demonstrating its important role in Wana
life. At the same time, I both complement and contest the work on marginality
by Grumblies, exploring how forest-based Wana people place themselves in the
world, and how this shapes their power relationships (men–women, visible–
non-visible and centre–periphery).

Structure of this book

During the (too) long gestation of this book, its shape, aims and structure have changed many times. Initially, I planned a tripartite structure exploring the three Wana rituals, the *momago, kayori* and *molawo*. Gradually it became clear that the scope of this plan would have exceeded the possibilities of the work, particularly considering my increasing interests in the roles of emotion, space and gender. Instead, I moved towards a binary division. The idea was to reflect in the structure of the publication Wana divisions of the world according to dyads, and to underline the connection between apparently only loosely related elements with a final part in which I would briefly treat secondary topics of the research. The final structure, though, is to escort the readers through a journey of discovery of Wana rituality. Inspired by my own fieldwork experience and aware of the unlikelihood of readers having much or any knowledge of Wana people, I have decided to present the topic and its complexity gradually, in a manner resembling my own gradual discovery and understanding of Wana culture.

Beyond the Introduction and Chapter 1, which contains a review of literature, this work has a tripartite structure; at the beginning, in Chapter 2, I revisit my first fieldwork period, where there are struggles with culture shock and a great amount of new information emerges from this new reality. Then, in Chapters 3 and 4, the second fieldwork period provides the basis. Here I observe the rituals with the help of knowledge acquired previously and pay attention to details that were obscured before when the task in early fieldwork was to understand the general picture. Finally, in Chapter 5, I present a more extended concluding analysis forged after returning home. This is a deeper consideration of the links between ritual and cultural values, gleaned from careful cross-comparison of all the materials previously collected. In Chapter 2, I offer the basic tools the readers will need to move effectively in this new world. It covers the basic elements of Wana life in the forest, political organization, history, economy and a little on religion. Once this context and prerequisite knowledge is covered, it is appropriate to introduce Wana rituality. Chapter 3 presents the main shamanic ritual, the *momago*. This addresses its basic purposes, Wana conceptions of illness, its structures and development. Chapter 4 is similar in intent, this time focusing on the *kayori*. If the *momago* has already been studied in depth by Atkinson (1989), all the information about the *kayori* is new. This lengthy ritual, almost three weeks long, is described day by day, and some of the key moments are briefly analysed.

Chapter 5 is the point at which the field lines converge and the information from the previous chapters is used to build a wider picture of Wana rituality. Here, I analyse and discuss how the two rituals presented not only reinforce the main Wana values but are sustained by them, in a virtuous circle that allows the survival of Wana culture. Following the divisions of the world made by Wana people, I explore the main dyads of Wana reality: between Wana and others, the centre and the periphery, male and female, centrifugal and centripetal, the individual and the community, dreadfulness and playfulness. I show how the rituals are based upon and reinforce these groups of opposites.

My hope is that, at the end of this work, the readers and I will be able to 'riveder le stelle' (re-behold the stars) (Dante 2005), ending this journey with a clear idea of the values of Wana culture and of how this small community bases its own survival on the principle of *kasintuwu* (sense of community).

It is important to me to clarify that this book has been written with a didactic approach in mind, not only because I hope it can become a pleasant reading for many students but, due to its interdisciplinarity, I am aware of the possibility that somebody who is reading it for its shamanic content could not be an expert on the anthropology of emotion, or a death scholar could be outside their comfort zone when discussing indigenous cultures and so on. Whoever will be the reader of my work, please know that I did all I could to make it as user friendly as possible, because we are first and foremost teachers before than researchers. Research without a clear dissemination and communication, inside and outside the academia, is just public onanism: a bunch of confusing people around the only person who is having a nice time.

Theories and themes

The Wana people are at the ethnographic core of this work, and the book explores, in particular, their rituals as a window onto many important cultural elements, such as emotions, shamanism, death and the relationship between centre and periphery. This chapter will discuss past and recent theories on the topics underlying this entire research. Still, considering the vastness of the topic and the interdisciplinary nature of this work, this chapter will not cover all the theories used; a few smaller topics will be discussed at appropriate moments in the analysis where they might add more without interrupting the flow of these main chapters.

Emotions

It is hard to offer any definitions concerning emotions that apply cross-culturally, let alone to take on the commitment necessary to understand the emotional world of people culturally distant from the researcher. It is particularly intriguing to consider how emotions can differ so much from culture to culture, and also how facets of culture such as music and religion can be so influential. Despite the difficulty of this task, my goal is not to understand what emotions are but how culture shapes their expression. Often in the course of ordinary life, there can be a schism between what we feel and what we can or want to externalize. Feeling emotions is a human ability, although work as early as Darwin's (1872) already demonstrated that other animals also have the ability to feel emotions. For Darwin, emotions have a role in the survival of the individual; they were described as deeply related to and influenced by the environment, and as primarily used to signal intentions to others. The kinds of emotions we feel and how we express them are influenced by culture. Events that can arouse anger or fear in certain cultures can lead people to feel happiness or enthusiasm in others.

To study this parlous field, I will focus on the emotional and ritual life of Wana people. I choose rituals as an arena of study because they occur in situations of extreme emotions; as Geertz has noted: 'we must know how we feel about things and to know how we feel about things we need the public images of sentiment that only ritual, myth and art can provide' (1973: 82). In these situations, there is not just a mixing of different feelings: fear, sadness and agitation bound up in the facing of death or illness, but there is also happiness and exalting associated with wedding parties and the playfulness of the rituals. Fiona Magowan's account of an Australian Aboriginal funeral, in which a great range of emotions is shown, could easily be describing the *kayori* (Wana funeral):

> [T]he ritual structure provides a framework for creating community through ancestral song and dance [...] Although the funeral will give rise to a variety of inner emotions during different phases such as anger, fear, grief, longing, compassion, sympathy and feeling of illness or wellbeing amongst others, the phases of funeral performance are couched in strings of performative emotions which join participants together.
>
> (Magowan 2007: 102)

Emotions are a powerful fuel for humankind but at the same time, if not properly orientated to the cultural setting, they can create cracks within a person and hence the community. Sometimes emotions can become so powerful that they cannot be controlled, and they may cause someone to become lost and no longer to be a productive member of the community, creating or widening a void with other members. The more dangerous being overcome by emotions is for the community, the more severe the cultural rules tend to be.

First of all, I want to clarify that in this work I will use the term 'emotion' in full awareness of its limitations. The term is deeply culturally linked to a sphere of Latin-rooted languages, and it is often impossible to translate it into other languages. For example, the Indonesian word *rasa* is usually used to translate the term 'emotion', but it has a series of different meanings in Indonesia, such as 'flavour' and 'opinion'. Rather than searching for a perfect definition, potentially only to see it become outdated a few years later, my approach is to acknowledge the limitations of my imperfect terminology and to focus my energies elsewhere. I will use the term 'emotions' for convenience while acknowledging that it does not carry objective validity. Moreover 'without a neutral scientific terminology, what justifies our beginning with the concept of *emotion* rather than *sentimiento* or *rasa* or *Gefühl*?' (Beatty 2005: 18). More importantly, I am not interested in what emotions are, 'but how feelings are related in human lives with thinking and wanting, and also, with what happens in human bodies' (Wierzbicka 2009: 10).

Until the 1980s, the most common approach to emotions was a materialist one. Emotions were seen mainly through the lens of externalized indicators: facial muscle movements, raised blood pressure, hormone levels and other bodily expression. For example, Paul Ekman (1980) believed in the existence of a core of universal emotions (anger, disgust, fear, happiness, surprise and sadness) expressed universally with the same facial muscle movements. This mind-body dichotomy was clearly evident in the 'two layers' approach, where on one side there were pre-cultural emotions and on the other, there were cultural emotions (Kleinman 1980; Lévy and Rosaldo 1983).

At the same time, researchers such as Vincent Crapanzano (1980) started exploring in more depth the implications of considering emotions to be shaped by socially constructed categories. This different approach to emotions stressed the role of the relationships between people in its study; the negotiation of emotions must be considered to involve not only the relations among the people scholars work with but also those between the researcher and the informants (Briggs 1970; Crapanzano 1980). By this time, emotions were seen as constantly mediated by language and culture. Researchers such as Lutz Jäncke (1985) and Naomi Quinn and Dorothy Hollan (1987) were interested in how emotions vary in different cultures, and they considered emotions as more 'socially validated judgment than an internal state' (Lutz and White 1986: 408). For this reason, they focused their efforts onto the translation of emotion concepts and related social processes.

In more recent years, ideas from Andrew Beatty (2005, 2010, 2012, 2014) about the narrative description of emotions are particularly interesting. Beatty suggests that a narrative approach is the best way to successfully describe, study and report the emotions of the people we work with: 'emotions might be *third-person constructions*, a collective product, but they are *first-person experiences* and not reducible to any of their ingredients. [...] Unlike most other things that are in some sense culturally constructed – norms, values, cultural models – their *sine qua non* is their personal reference. [...] Emotions are particular or they are nothing' (2014: 551).

I partially agree with Beatty, but I am also concerned about the emotional response of the community, looking beyond its single members. For this reason, in my research, I have tried not only to describe the individual's emotional expression but also to give a sense of the wider history and the collective narrative behind it. In general, I have focused on the entire community precisely because I consider it an emotional being in itself. It is my intention in the future to extend this focused description to grasp the complexities behind the experience of that single Wana person. Indeed, various scholars believe that emotional work blurs the separation between the individual and the community (Leavitt 1996; Parkinson 1995; Svašek 2005; Svašek and Skrbiš 2007).

While working with emotion, one of the biggest issues we face is our empathy and how this may or may not help in our work. How can a researcher really know or understand someone else's emotion, especially if that person comes from a radically different background? John Leavitt states that 'the problem with empathy is not that it involves feeling but that it assumes that first impressions are true' (1996: 530). But, although I agree that empathy brings many perils, there is also much to be said for the stance of Bonini Baraldi (2013) and also of Beatty: 'without it we have a very thin sort of understanding and no possibility of sharing lives' (2019: 263). Although Owen Lynch rejects 'empathy as a naïve and ethnocentric practice, a form of Western imperialism over the emotions of the Other' (Lynch 1990: 17), I argue that empathy, as the capacity to understand what another person is experiencing and to place ourselves in another person's position, could actually be an important foundation of anthropology. Beatty separates narrative empathy from intuitive or automatic empathy, defining the former as 'correctly following the threads of an emotion episode, situating oneself, in fact or imagination, inside the hurly burly, the thick of it' (2019: 263).

In the Wana context, I will show that although people consider the violent 'grief-expelling procedure' (Mills 2012: 154), called *mandeke*,[1] that characterizes their funerals a form of play and not a bodily enactment of real emotions felt by the actors (Harré 1991), behind these ritualized forms emotions are actually felt (Kapferer 1979: 153). Just as Emile Durkheim explains with the idea of the *homo duplex* (1915), Wana people split their identity between expressing personal pain and social pain. According to the sociologist:

> [M]ourning is not the spontaneous expression of individual emotions [...] Mourning is not a natural movement of private feelings wounded by a cruel loss; it is a duty imposed by the group. One weeps, not simply because he is sad, but because he is forced to weep. It is a ritual attitude, which he is forced to adopt out of a respect for custom, but which is, in a large measure, independent of his affective state.
>
> (Durkheim 1915: 397)

Indeed, in the last part of this work exploring the controlled violence during the *kayori*, ideas about surface and deep acting in the expression of emotions will be important; these come through strongly in Arlie Russel Hochschild's *The Managed Heart: The Commercialization of Human Feeling* (1983). In this book, the author explores the performance of emotional labour, and the dissonance experienced by workers who must display emotions in exchange for economic rewards. In the Wana context, there is no economic reward, but there is certainly a social obligation and opportunity associated with expressing certain emotions in ritualized and non-spontaneous ways. Moreover, as Wikan points out, 'Sorrow is experienced and expressed in ways intricately linked with popular conceptions of health and sanity that are systematically inculcated in the young and receive persistent social backing' (1988: 455). Furthermore, according to this theory, social actors that adopt surface acting (by just externalizing an emotion and not really feeling it) experience more emotive dissonance, while those deeply acting an emotion experience only minor emotive dissonance.

We should not forget that avoiding the expression of strong feelings is a common trait in many Southeast Asian cultures. And this attitude to emotions can create the need for a ritualized expression of pain and sorrow. Indeed, Wana people believe that strong emotions can be dangerous for a person; it can lead to illness of the soul and the need for shamanic treatment. A similar attitude is found among the Toraja people of Sulawesi, who 'believe that emotional upset has an adverse effect upon one's health' (Wellenkamp 1988: 492).

Death

It is particularly important for emotions to be controlled while people are coping with dangers related to the death of a member of a community. My work is based on the idea that emotions are shared trait among humans but that their expression is closely controlled by culture, especially in situations when there is so much at stake as to risk emotional annihilation (Davies 2002). It is exactly to explore these issues that a large part of my study focuses on the *kayori*, the funeral ritual for Wana people, and I draw upon several of the most important works on death. Though it is commonly assumed that funerals are designed to honour the deceased, it is primarily the living that are targeted: to negotiate the non-meaning of death, to overcome it and to put it at the service of life and of the survivors. In the 1970s, Louis-Vincent Thomas, the founder of thanatology, asked: 'Is it not topical to note that where the mourning is a general institutionalized and codified practice it is hard to find "pathological mourning," contrary to what happens in the West where everything is being done to prevent it?' (Thomas 1976: 342).[2]

While exploring the need to balance the negativity of death with an excess of life, the work of Maurice Bloch and Jonathan Parry, two of the most important scholars of death studies, will have an important role. There are many similarities between Wana funerals and those in Madagascar studied by Bloch (1971), where the round dance expresses the vitality needed to overcome the dangers of death. Moreover, the ideas behind Parry and Bloch's edited volume on *Death and the Regeneration of Life* (1982) are at the base of my research. Here, funerals are approached as the occasion to reinforce the social relationships of a community through an extreme expression of life energies. While this is not a new idea, having also been explored by Richard Huntington and Peter Metcalf (1991), it is still poignant, especially now that Western culture seems to consider the role of playfulness as something antique or exotic, while it was something normal in a much closer past (De Martino 1958).

Although Michelle Rosaldo is right in pointing out that 'the emotional force of a death, for example, derives less from an abstract brute fact than from a particular intimate relation's permanent rupture' (1989: 1), a funeral is not only a way to help individuals face a loss, but it is above all a reaffirmation of the totality of those individuals, the community. Death is about solidarity, and Bloch's ideas about the expression of solidarity during funeral rituals are crucial: 'Death is the time when the solidarity of the local community should be most manifest' (1971: 139). For this the concept of *communitas* (Turner 2011) will also take a pivotal role in this work, especially since Wana people do not conceive of life outside of the community. We will later explore the importance of *kasintuwu* (sense of community) as the moral centre of Wana life. Shamanism goes even further, fostering feelings of *communitas* to a point that the boundaries between the self and others are dissolved, and the individual becomes one with the community, achieving a level of transpersonality (Peters 1989). I agree with Unni Wikan's idea that 'because suffering is not individual but afflicts members of the community, emotional expression is too crucial to be left to an individual's devices' (1988: 457). At the same time, I will follow Rosaldo's advice: 'Rather than speaking of death in general, one must consider the subject's position within a field of social relations in order to grasp one's emotional experience' (1989: 1). This balance between loss as group experience and the one's emotional experience is the great challenge of this century of cultural and social changes, where on one side many people don't find support in the traditional ways of grieves, but at the same time feel loss in the individuality of their experience and pain.

The theories behind secondary burial, initially studied by Robert Hertz (2004), but explored impressively by Metcalf and Huntington in *A Borneo Journey into Death: Berawan Eschatology from Its Rituals* (1982) and *Celebrations of Death: The Anthropology of Mortuary Ritual* (1991), will also emerge in observations about the Wana funerary ritual. In fact, as testified in various places in the edited volume *Journey of the Soul: Anthropological Studies of Death, Burial, and Reburial Practices in Borneo* (Wilder 2003), second burial is a common ritual in Indonesia and it brings the opportunity to make the death of a loved one a less abrupt event, giving mourners an emotional guide to successfully transforming a negative event into an opportunity to re-create the community and to promote fertility, both of the land and of the community. The relatively long mourning period helps the community to slowly accept the idea that one of its members is dead. The separation from a friend or a relative is not an immediate event but a slow assimilation of the idea that the person has passed away. Inside the Catholic culture we can think about the masses for the dead that are celebrated thirty days after the funeral. In fact, in Italy those are called *trigesimi*, literally meaning 'thirtieth'. Long mourning periods are widely present among many different cultures, for example in Mongolia where 'the mourning period lasts seven, twenty-one, or forty-nine days' (Stuart 1994: 99) and in Japanese culture, which presents some similarities with the *kayori*: 'After the forty-ninth day service, the spirit of the deceased is expected to have arrived at the other world, and this signals the end of the end of the initial mourning period' (Kim 2012: 246). Meanwhile, among the Temiar of Malaysia, with their culture closely resembling that of the Wana people, there is 'a mourning period of a month or more during which musical activities have been prohibited' (Roseman 1984: 427). This long mourning period offers an opportunity to gradually accept the separation from a loved one, making death a less traumatic event.

It is no coincidence that the *kayori*, like the *momago*, is one of the main opportunities for expressing *kasintuwu*. As in the *momago*, it is the family alone that takes care of the expenses of the ritual, but friends and relatives help in the construction of the ritual hut, in the preparation of food, and also with their presence. They are there not only for themselves, enjoying the feast and saying goodbye to their friend or family member, but also so that the community can continue to live. This is because 'the stability and continuity of the social structure depends on the strong solidarity of the local group' (Radcliffe-Brown 1965: 168). Funerals are, as Bloch (1971) and Parry (1994) note, an opportunity to reaffirm the values of a society. As Radcliffe-Brown points out: 'the stability and continuity of the social structure depends on the strong solidarity of the local group' (1965: 168), and without it the negative energies derived from death could impact on the core values and rules of a culture. The *kayori* is there to make sure that these values are reinforced, and that the community works together to overcome death; as Durkheim states, 'if the idea of society were extinguished in individual minds, and the beliefs, traditions and aspirations of the group were no longer felt and shared by the individuals, society would die' (Durkheim 1915: 347). As Douglas Davies points out: 'Behaviour surrounding death is often exciting in the physiological sense that it intensifies the emotional dynamics of individuals and their communities, even if that excitement is prompted in people circling those who are immediately bereaved and in the opposite state of depression. A social group often comes alive as one of its members dies' (Davies 2015: 37). It is fascinating how similar this situation is to that in Madagascar described by Bloch:

> Some of the men have perhaps already fortified themselves for the night with liquor. When they have all gathered there may be a short prayer and hymn singing led by a senior man or by a pastor if there is one present. Once this is over everybody settles for the night. The local family sit inside the house around the corpse and mourn. The women neighbours carry on with the preparation of the meal. The men sit all around the house but especially on the side where the windows and doors are, namely the west. There they pass the night playing dominoes or betting, or whiling away the time as best they can. From time to time they sing and generally have as good a time as possible. Admittedly the songs are often Church hymns, but they are sung in a boisterous way which contrast with the way they are sung in church. Hymns are the accompaniment of all social gatherings.
>
> (Bloch 1971: 141)

Clear commonalities are also evident in Richard Wolf's account of funeral practices amongst the Kotas of India: '[The] sadness participants experience during a funeral, for example, is accompanied by ancillary feelings, transient modes of emotionality that include (in the Kota case) poignant joy, intoxicated abandon, reverence, and fortitude' (Wolf 2001: 380).

Among the Wana, this sadness is also expressed with a violent 'grief-expelling procedure' (Mills 2012: 154) called *mandeke*. These episodes are reminiscent of 'running amok syndrome', a phenomenon of Indonesian and Malaysian culture in which a person (often male) suddenly assaults people or objects with a weapon, usually a *kriss* or machete (Winzeler 1990). It may well be that there is a cultural commonality between this and the *mandeke*, especially given that, in both episodes, violence hides a lucid act; in the Wana context this is the expression of personal and community pain, and in running amok it is a desire to end one's life (through being killed by the police, considering that this takes place in a culture that stigmatizes suicide) (Winzeler 1990). However, a key point of difference is the presence of an undercurrent of play in the Wana case; other Wana bystanders told me '*mereka bermain*' (they are playing), meaning that those doing the *mandeke* were 'playing', with the rest of the community also participating as active observers. Indeed, while the *mandekers* are acting like people possessed by their pain, the bystanders pretend that the actions of these individuals are dangerous for themselves and for others; in truth, everybody knows that it is a controlled expression of violence and that there is no actual danger. De Martino's observations about episodes of violence during funerals are pertinent here: 'this behaviour is not only the ritualistic and symbolic equivalent of an attenuated pulse of total annihilation, but it also sets the measure to be observed in their execution' (de Martino 1958: 186).[3]

Although these tightly prescribed and controlled emotional contours might shock a Western audience, even in Western funerals, where well-mannered calmness, seriousness and undisguised sadness prevail, 'mourning is not the spontaneous expression of individual emotions' (Davies 2002: 16). 'Besides expressing sincere sorrow, crying during a funeral is perceived as a social obligation' (Guggino 2004: 350) because emotions are cultural artefacts and 'affects [...] are no less cultural and no more private than beliefs' (Shweder and Levine 1984: 141).

In the control of this pain and the other emotions associated with it, humour plays a crucial role. As noted by Wikan, sadness is dangerous and it can be controlled with humour, because 'the laughter pains, and it erodes self-respect and presumably also social respect' (1990: 97). If a member loses their self-control and expresses their emotions in a way not recognized by the community, the ritual risks failing in support of the idea of unity, and the 'density' of the community is in danger (Gilsenan 1973: 170–5). For this reason, Wana people, who shun violence, use humour to control the behaviour of the community.

Indeed, like Wana people, the Balinese 'naturally' link 'laughter to sadness in a nearly spontaneous response of self-protection and self-value, and also a sane expression of compassion and care' (Gilsenan 1973: 124). As I will show in the following chapters and in the photos presented in this work, Wana people cope with the wretchedness of their lives with humour and laughter. Moreover, laughing is not only contagious, like sadness, but it is release of aggression and anger, two common elements of grief among many cultures (Marris 1974; Osterweis, Solomon and Green 1984; Rosenblatt, Walsh and Jackson 1976).

In the end,

> Comic events and trance behaviour in healing rituals are expressive of certain mental perspectives and emotional attitudes to realities created through ritual performance. As such they can be the means for the release of tensions produced by the social and psychological state of the individual. But such events set within the processional form of a ritual have transformative significance for the ritual form as a whole.
>
> (Kapferer 1979: 167)

This directly relates to Thomas's observations regarding the underlying functions of funeral rituals: 'The funeral rites, in fact, celebrate life […] This is not to deny death, but to accept it as a condition of regeneration' (Thomas 1976: 473–4).[4]

Shamanism

Shamanism has a strong connection with death, because as Praet states, 'There is no clear distinction between activities of curing and those of mourning' (2014: 137). The idea that the death-related rituals and the shamanic healing rituals are similar will be explored later in this work. It is clear, though, that both rituals aim to heal the entire community and to transform a negative event into a re-creative energy that might allow for survival not only of personal suffering but also of the entire community. Moreover, shamans have always had an important role in engaging with the therapeutic transformation of emotions (Walsh 1980). Thanks to their liminal status, they cover the role of mediator not only between the non-visible and the visible worlds, but also between humans and their emotions. Walsh's declaration that shamans were the first to do so may be arguable, but their role is certainly important.

Another important theme of this work is the relationship between centre and periphery and the way Wana people's perceived powerless position has shaped their vision of the world. Wana people express their agency over the external powers that constantly pressurize them, forming a 'counter hegemonic discourse' (hooks 1990: 341). For bell hooks, marginality is not something 'one wishes to lose, to give up, or surrender as part of moving into the centre, but rather as a site one stays in, clings to even, because it nourishes one's capacity to resist' (hooks 1990: 341). Of course, marginality is derived from a theoretical hierarchy and power relationships that are extremely complex and express a multifaceted condition (Dennis 2007: 2763). In fact, if from the point of view of Indonesia more widely Wana people are marginal, from the Wana point of view they are at the centre of the world. Of course, they do not have great power in either position, but while being marginalized does not give them any particular hopes for a better future, seeing themselves as at the centre gives them the hope for coming rewards. Ultimately, the idea of marginality is 'a material force as well as an ideological concept and a description of social reality' (Perlman 1976: 15).

Said's idea of the 'Orient' as a mere projection emanating from the West (1978), and the power relationships contained in this delineation, will be particularly useful while exploring how Wana people characterize the West. It is a homogenized place that encompasses everything outside of the Wana Land, even places to the east.

In Michael Winkelman's article *Shamans and Other 'Magico-Religious' Healers: A Cross-Cultural Study of Their Origins, Nature, and Social Transformations*, the author tries to clearly define and distinguish between the diverse denominations used in academia: shaman, healer, medicine-man and medium (1990). Even with the assistance of his systematic tables in which he clearly labels each denomination and its characteristics (Winkelman 1990: 316–17), it is hard to place Wana shamans into a specific category.

There are a number of authors that have been particularly inspiring during my research and the writing of this book. Their ideas will not necessarily be discussed explicitly in this work, but their approaches have inspired and guided my own. First, Marina Roseman's work on the Temiar of Malaysia (1984, 1990, 1993, 1998, 2008) has fascinated me since my first research on the Wana people. The Temiar have many cultural similarities with the Wana people, and her attention to their music (1990) and her study of their emotional world in relation to their performance (1993) offer great insights.

The incredible research offered by Douglas Hollan (1988, 1994) and Jane Wellenkamp (1988, 1994) on the emotional world of the Toraja has offered a large amount of useful data for comparison between the two cultures. Their work on both death and emotions (Wellenkamp 1988) and the cultural regulation of emotions (Hollan 1988) has proved to be an extremely useful resource in studying a culture that is as closely related as Wana culture is. Avoiding strong emotions is a central topic in the Wana approach to life, and especially in their ways of expressing power even in a powerless situation. More importantly, Hollan and Wellenkamp's book *Contentment and Suffering* introduced me to the concepts of suffering, grieving and self from a psychological point of view. Combined with an excellent anthropological approach, this work pushed me towards exploring the role of the *mandeke* in Wana funerals.

Wolf's research on the Kota of India (2001, 2006) has also had a profound influence on my work, even if its presence is not always clearly externalized. In particular, there is the relationship between centrifugal and centripetal forces, and between the village and the forest, and also the role of music as a unifying factor with central socio-religious value in bringing people together (2001, 2006: 141). Finally, there is Winkelman's research (1990, 2010), which offers theoretical material that brings structure to reflecting on the role of the *tau walia* among Wana people, and on their important links with the economic and ecological life of the community. This scholarship also introduced me to the world of medical ethnomusicology (2010) and pushed me to explore cultural conceptions of illness.

I am aware of the many scientific studies on music and healing (Crowe 2004; Panksepp and Trevarthen 2009; Vaitl et al. 2005) and of Winkelman's fascination with the psychological implications of music and trance on shamans themselves. However, I move the focus to the wider community. In fact, the *tau walia* will not have a central position in this work, and I will not focus on trance and the role of music in inducing trance. I am more interested in exploring the cultural values and powers that Wana culture attaches to its ritual music. Rather than focusing on altered states of consciousness (ASC) in shamans, I will consider the wider community, with a particular interest in how the community manages to shift from negative emotions to the playfulness of the ritual. Thus, I apply theories previously developed about shamans to understand the experience of the entire community. This approach is suitable here because Wana people themselves are more concerned with the community than with the individual member, and shamanic rituals and funerals do not only need shamans and patients but also the active participation of the community (Ohnuki-Tierney 1981: 171).

We should not forget, the striking idea from Winkelman's approach to shamanism, the idea that the power and success of a shaman is based on their ability to give hope. He calls this the 'biology of hope' (2010: 185). This notion fits very effectively in discussions of Wana culture, where the community accepts the wretchedness of life because they have hope in a future reward. The shaman has the duty to keep this hope alive with a periodic immersion in the power of mythical reality.

As Crapanzano notes regarding the Moroccan Hamadsha: '[Saints, jnun, and Baraka] are elements in which I would call the participational mode of explanation of illness and therapy. They may be considered *signs* of psychic states and *symbols* of socio-cultural processes' (1973: 213). Moreover, Larry Peters notes among the Tamang of Nepal that 'the curing activities involved in shamanic healing are not exercises in the treatment of organic disease but attempts to treat disturbing emotional states and interpersonal relations' (Peters 1978: 65). The shamans grasp at the air, as if to catch and retrieve the escaped soul, and gesture to restore it to the owner's head. 'Shamanic texts are best described as dramatic dances [...] in non-literate cultures religion is always a performing art, and the sacredness of religious stories or prayers resides not in the words of the texts as they have been or could be transcribed but in the power invested in them through performance' (Porterfield 1987: 726). Sometimes, the shaman's job is to reinsert the patient's lost soul. This process is also dramatized. The shamans grasp at the air, as if to catch and retrieve the escaped soul, and gesture to restore it to the owner's head. With their power and chants, the shamans bring back the lost golden age, the space-time when everything was possible, and humans were complete. This return to the golden age has a beneficial effect on the patient; it is a return to the space-time when everything was full of power and nobody was sick. Every myth is a quest for the mythical era (Lévi-Strauss 1958) and each ritual is the repetition of a myth. For example, Mircea Eliade refers to customs among Australian indigenous people saying how medicine-men restore the mythological temporarily using the 'bridge' between Heaven and Earth, which in the past was available to all humans (1971: 57), or

> being *real* and *sacred*, the myth becomes exemplary, and consequently *repeatable*, for it serves as a model, and by the same token as justification, for all human actions. In other words, a myth is a *true history* of what came to pass at the beginning of Time, and one which provides the pattern for human behaviour. In imitating the exemplary acts of a god or of a mythic hero, or simply by recounting their adventures, the man of an archaic society detaches himself from profane time and magically re-enters the Great Time, the sacred time.
>
> (Eliade 1971: 18)

The Wana rituals deal with the beliefs, traumas, culture and memories of patients, so shamans are working on a patient's psyche. Actually, the shamanistic cure seems to be the exact counterpart to the psychoanalytic cure, but with an inversion of all the elements. Both cures aim at inducing an experience, and both succeed by recreating a myth which the patient has to live or relive. But in one case, the patient constructs an individual myth with elements drawn from his past; in the other case, the patient receives from the outside a social myth which does not correspond to a former personal state (Lévi-Strauss 1963: 199).

Some researchers, such as Sherzer (1983), have criticized the 'talking-cure' analogy made by Lévi-Strauss, pointing out that the Kuna patient does not understand or hear all the words. In a similar way, Nathan Porath calls into question Atkinson herself and her description of the *momago* where she describes the songs of the *tau walia* as 'embellishments', just as during the *semanget* shamanic ritual among the Orang Sakai they are of 'little therapeutic importance' (Porath 2013a: 12). I take issue with this stance and argue that Atkinson was ethnomusicologically deaf to the incredible musical world of Wana people, giving almost no space in her work on the *momago* to the incredible musical and sound world of the Wana. Among the Wana, although they might describe them as 'embellishments', the shamanic songs have a crucial role in healing the patient and in helping them understand their pain and illness. Dramatization is crucial for the success of the ritual; it helps the patient to understand what is happening to them, especially considering that people in this context do not have an extensive understanding of contemporary medical science. Shamans are, in effect, making something frightening and incomprehensible simpler and relatable to the worldview of the people involved. Again, the example of the Tamang of Nepal illustrates the prevalence of this phenomenon in other traditional cultures:

> [T]here is also the influence of cultural expectations of disease and the belief in the efficacy of the puja. Through these elements, the illness is placed within a conceptual framework. The patient's symptoms and all the mysterious and chaotic feelings of distress were organized and their causes identified by the shaman during diagnosis, both prior to and at the time of this puja.
>
> (Peters 1978: 82)

This process has been recognized by the psychiatrist Edwin Fuller-Torrey, who considers this 'naming process' a 'universal component of psychotherapy which is used by both witchdoctors and psycho-therapists alike'. Fuller-Torrey believes that once the illness is put into a suitable cultural frame, the patient can empathize with other people previously cured of the same complaint, with identification helping to reduce anxiety and to put the patient in a more serene state of mind (1972: 16). A similar theory was expressed as early as 1944 by Kluckhohn who underlines how the identification of the illness helps the patient and their family to make order from the chaos created by a previously unlabelled complaint. As Peters explains, 'the diagnostic process through which illness is identified makes a transformation from chaos to order in the eyes of the patient and those concerned for him, and that has therapeutic effectiveness' (Peters 1981: 135).

Of course, all this happens in the subconscious of the person, because ritual symbols may refer to extensive and complex ideas of value, structure and transformation, whose verbal statement requires considerable time. Consequently, the symbolism of ritual is often obscure, since it refers to intentions and beliefs that are complex and, in part, unconscious (Wallace 1966: 237). The battle between shamans and illness is played out on a symbolic plane, where words, music and action build a powerful world around the patient. The shaman 'holds a dialogue with the patient, not through the spoken word but in concrete actions, that is, genuine rites which penetrate the screen of consciousness and carry their message directly to the unconscious' (Lévi-Strauss 1963: 200).

Geertz not only underlines the power of the shaman to create meaning, but also the role of the chant in these processes: 'a sing [*sic*] is mainly concerned with the presentation of a specific and concrete image of truly human, and so endurable, suffering powerful enough to resist the challenge of emotional meaninglessness raised by the existence of intense and unremovable brute pain' (Geertz 1973: 105) because 'As a religious problem, the problem of suffering is, paradoxically, not how to avoid suffering but how to suffer, how to make of physical pain, personal loss, worldly defeat, or the helpless contemplation of others' agony something bearable, supportable – something, as we say, sufferable' (Geertz 1973: 104).

Music and trance

A study on shamanism also requires, willingly or not, a reflection on trance. These two phenomena are often studied together because shamans must enter a state commonly referred to as trance to travel between worlds and to contact their spirits. Indeed, trance is a highly complex term to explain. At the origin of the word *trance* is the Latin term *transpire*, which means 'to die', 'to go beyond', 'to pass from one state to another'. In the shamanic context, this refers to moving from a physical reality to a spiritual one. Beyond the etymological explanation, though, this phenomenon does not carry a univocal definition covering the entire spectrum of phenomena encountered by researchers. These phenomena can go from hypnosis to deep listening, passing through *the zone* spoken about in sport, and many other examples that could fall under the umbrella term.[5]

Michael Lambek (1989) and Roberte Hamayon (1993) note how the people studied by anthropologists usually do not have a homologous term for 'trance', but just as in the cases of 'emotion' and 'shaman', they use they own terminologies and conceptual representations of the phenomenon.

The vastness of the phenomenon has prompted researchers from different disciplines, such as anthropology, psychology, ethnomusicology, neurology and others, to study trance since the beginning of the twentieth century. Despite this multiplicity of approaches, the phenomenon is not yet completely explained. Ronald Shor (1959) described trance as a state of functional non-awareness, a separation from the common awareness that supports, interprets and gives meaning to our experience. Arnold Ludwing considered trance 'any mental state(s), induced by various physiological, psychological, or pharmacological manoeuvres or agents, which can be recognized subjectively by the individual himself (or by an objective observer of the individual) as representing a sufficient deviation in subjective experience or psychological functioning from certain general norms for that individual during alert, waking consciousness' (Ludwing 1968: 79). Charles Tart (1975) defined an altered state of consciousness, a more general term used instead of trance, as a qualitative alteration in the overall patterns of mental functioning so that the experience is felt to be radically different from ordinary functioning. More recently, Judith Becker defines trance as 'a bodily event characterized by strong emotion, intense focus, the loss of the strong sense of self, usually enveloped by amnesia and cessation of the inner language' (2004: 43). Finally, Van Groenendael considers 'trance as a mental state, induced by a variety of factors, which creates a distance between the person concerned and his surroundings and now renders him totally self-absorbed, now produces exceptional or abnormal behaviour, of which he would be incapable in his normal state, and which gives him a sense of liberation' (van Groenendael 2008: 134).

I am attracted by two elements of Becker's and Van Groenendael's definitions: the 'intense focus' and the 'distance between the person concerned and his surroundings'. Observing Wana rituals, I started to understand it as that the trancer[6] is hyper-focusing on a specific element, and in a certain way is hyper-present in the ritual. At the same, though, they are absent and away from the ritual context. In Wana rituality, shamans leave their bodies to travel between worlds, leaving the void of a soul inside them. They focus their attention upon one or a few objects or phenomena (such as the ritual cloth, the music or the smell of a plant) to help them enter trance, generating this hyper attention and making them seem absent when, actually, all his mental presence is concentrated on a different plain of existence, the spiritual one.

Some scholars, like Gilbert Rouget (1985), tend to separate trance and ecstasy, placing these two phenomena at the two opposite poles of ASC. Trance is described as a physical phenomenon and ecstasy as a mental one. Becker 'prefers a generic category of "trance" that includes meditative states, possession trance, shamanic trance, communal trance, aesthetic trance and isolated moments of transcendence' (2004: 45). I prefer to use the more general label 'ASC' to avoid limiting the meanings evoked with the term 'trance'. On the other hand, I recognize that 'ASC' can be too generic, that the word 'trance' already carries a strong connection with the shamanic world, and that (despite its imperfections) it is more indicative of the emotional, physical, and mental situations that shamans face during their flights.

Cardeña proposes labels for a range of possession experiences: (1) 'transitional possession' with occasional changes in depth of involvement rather than a fixed state of consciousness, (2) 'alternate identity possession' in which an alternate identity, human or otherwise, takes over the usual identity of the individual and there may be co-occurrence of the usual identity of the individual along with the alternate one and (3) 'transcendent possession' in which the individual is totally immersed or 'surrendered' and the individual does not perform the acts, songs or movement but becomes 'him/herself, the act, the song and movement' (1989). These labels, although highly useful in many respects, cannot cover all elements of trance. Trance is not only difficult to define but also to analyse phenomenologically, particularly in regard to how states are obtained. Evidence from the Wana context suggests that trance states are not simply induced by a single factor and that they do not have an on/off switch; to enter trance, Wana shamans need different impetuses (darkness, ritual music, religious beliefs, memories and many others) that together allow them to leave this world and to return to mythical space-time. Of course, music often has a crucial role in instigating trance; it must be remembered that, above all, trance is a cultural phenomenon, and it therefore needs certain culturally specific triggers. If an Indonesian shaman were exposed to Siberian shamanic music, it would seem unlikely to expect the shaman to enter a trance, because that music does not possess the configuration of attributes that have become internally linked to the shamanic trance state through repeated experience over many years.

As early as the eighteenth century, Rousseau understood that 'as long as we choose to consider sounds only through the commotion they stir in our nerves, we shall never have the true principles of music and of its power over our hearts. Sounds in the melody do not act solely as sounds, but as *signs* of our affections' (Rousseau quoted in Rouget 1985: 168). Also, Rouget (1985) and Bastide agree that 'It is not a stimulus [music] that determines trance [...] it is the total situation that acts, [...] it is the total situation that causes music to lead to trance' (Bastide 1972: 73). And Friedson clearly states that 'The same basic music would sometimes elicit a wild and potentially violent spirit possession in a novice or layman and other times the controller, remembered divinatory trance of a *nchimi* [...] The change is in the healer's relationship to the music' (1996: 28).

I include social environment as one of the trance triggers because shamanic trance is always a social event. 'The group acts as a unit. Ritual practitioners, patient (if there is one), trancer, musicians, onlookers, even hecklers in some situation become part of a larger, ongoing, largely predictably event. [...] Trancing, though experienced in a particular body, seems never to be bounded by that single body' (Becker 2004: 124). I saw among Wana people evidence to support Turner's interpretation: 'an increase in the level of social arousal, however produced, is capable of unlocking energy sources in individual participants' (1986: 43), energies that help not only the individual patient but the entire community to heal and re-generate stronger than before. As Friedson also writes, 'Coming together in the musical experience creates a powerful source of cultural energy. [...] This form of musical communitas may have important healing proprieties' (1996: 125) that destroy the distance between the members and create a 'we-relation' (Schutz and Luckmann 1973: 63). Also, Margaret Kartomi writes:

> [T]he music serves primarily as a communication of mood (from musician to trance dancer) through the music's associativeness and mesmeric continuity; not only does it assist a subject into a trance state but it lends colour to and is part of the traumatic experience itself. It builds up and sustains a state of undifferentiated emotional excitement. Music has become one with the ritual and is not a separate aesthetic category. For its purpose, Central Javanese trance music is highly potent and effective.
>
> (1973a: 166)

Becker (2004: 148) associates the profound emotional response to trance with 'the production and release of certain hormones and monoamines' that lead trancers to 'feel themselves to be in the presence of spirits'. It is fascinating how both Becker and Kartomi, but also Erika Bourguignon (1979), underline the emotional element in trance events. Put simply, 'trance behaviour may serve as a psychological safety valve; it affords occasions upon which it is unnecessary to control the passions' (Kartomi 1973a: 165). It offers an opportunity to express extreme emotions or desires in a 'safe' environment. In his fieldworks during the

1950s, Ernesto de realized that trance is used by the most marginalized social groups in order to, at least for a short period of time, voice their frustration and suffering (1961: 243). Ioan Myrddin Lewis (1972) arrived at similar conclusions around ten years later in his work on ecstatic religion.

Furthermore, as Wier intelligently notes, 'trance restricts primitive chaos or chlinthonic[7] [*sic*] energy and helps us to harness that energy. [...] In restraining the chaos, energy may be focused into creation. Trance, therefore, has something to do with energy utilization and the potentiation of creation' (Wier 1996: 23). When shamans enter trance, they are living in and, at the same time, creating mythical time, and by doing this they legitimize their power.

Many people ask if trance is genuine or faked, but this question is trivial. Often coming to mind is the image of magicians and con artists whose tricks are aimed at stealing money from people. In traditional cultures, shamans do not create a mythical world in order to cheat people; instead, they use a mythical world that has already been created and shared by the community to help people at their own expense. The life of the shaman is dangerous; it involves fighting demons, travelling between worlds, and coming into contact with diseases, all with the purpose of helping the community and of ensuring its survival. In Wana society, all *tau walia* live normal lives; they have to work like everybody else, but they must also be ready to help others in exchange for very little reward.

Becker also writes that the predictability of trancing and the stereotypicity of trancing, conforming to community expectations, is not, I am convinced, a result of fraudulence, of chicanery, but of skill. Trancers and deep listeners have more control over the activities of their minds and bodies than most of us. They are not 'out-of-control' but, rather, more fully able to modulate and enhance what are normally autonomic bodily responses than most people. They are profoundly in control of themselves (2004: 68).

This control does not mean that they are 'awake', but just that they are able to be *clearly absent*.[8] When shamans enter trance, they are following a pattern; they cease to be normal members of the community and they take on the shaman's role. 'Even in trance, the individual holds strictly to the rules and expectations of his culture and his experience is as locally patterned as a marriage rite or an economical exchange' (Benedict 1934: 77). 'As a matter of fact, the shaman does nothing other *than respect the model of behaviour prescribed for his function. He takes up his role* as a shaman, a role that consists of portraying his contact with the spirits' (Hamayon 1993: 29). This model to follow is possible because the members of the community have witnessed trance behaviour from childhood; this early experience encourages familiarity with, and acceptability of, dissociation, in turn making the transition into possession easier (Kiev 1961; Mischel and Mischel 1958; Pressel 1974). Indeed, as shamanic trance overlaps with dreams, 'the power of a healer rests in this ability to gain access to, and maintain contact with, the non-visible world of the spirits. To dream and to dance are essential to a *nchimi's* healing art' (Friedson 1996: 22), and equally important to the Wana healing art.

Ultimately, as for the study of emotion, we should not look for commonalities but for singularities: 'Through comparative studies we may indeed find universal aspects of health care, but in the final analysis, all healing is local because it is personal' (Friedson 1996: 100).

Marginality

The last key element important in understanding Wana culture is how people cope with their marginality regarding the world outside of the jungle. This is a world represented by the Indonesian government, the Christian missionaries, other communities, and the few tourists visiting the Morowali forest. The power relationships important in the lives of Wana people are truly shaped by their geographical situation, particularly as the position of the community in relation to others has a crucial influence over their access to mythical power. From an external point of view, they occupy a peripheral position, but they experience and narrate this as an active choice that in fact places them at the centre of the world. This is an expression of power – perhaps the only one – that reverses the power relationship between the Wana people and those who are more typically understood as their more powerful neighbours. As Harms et al. point out, 'remoteness is never fixed; it is not a predetermined and enduring place but a process situated in dynamic fields of power. The condition is always infused with the edgy feeling experienced by people living in a world where the relations of inside and outside, near and far, proximate and remote are always contested' (Harms et al. 2014: 364). It is clear that the concept of marginality is a complex one (Dennis 2007: 2,763). The centre is generally understood as a realm with a dense concentration of power, while the periphery is where the energies, power and control of the centre is looser. Edward Shils, in his *The Constitution of Society*, suggests that every society considers the centre to be a point of reference because it establishes 'the order of symbols, of values and beliefs, which govern the society' (1982: 93). He concludes that 'It is the centre of the order of symbols, of values and beliefs, which governs the society. It is the centre because it is the ultimate and irreducible' (Shils 1982: 93). Shils seems to overlook the fact that for every centre there is a periphery, and vice versa. The field of mobilities will play a crucial role in the analysis of Wana relationships of gender, space, power and movement, because 'at the center of constellations of power' we find 'the creation of identities and the microgeographies of everyday life' (Cresswell 2010: 551).

Myth

Myth has been one of the key themes of the study of religion since its beginning; it has often been considered the 'oral literature' of preliterate societies. For Edward Tylor and James Frazer, myth was an explanation of the world. For Tylor, myths were rational explanations for all the phenomena of the world (1871), while Frazer relegated mythology to simply being explanations behind the practices in rituals (1889). From this point of view, myths were considered true and 'historical' events. Lucien Lévy-Bruhl (1985) believed that indigenous people (or, in his outdated words, 'primitive people') rely on religion and myth to understand the world, while modern people have science. According to this view, mythology is not logical, as Tylor and Frazer believed, but an expression of a 'primitive mentality' that contrasts with the mentality of the modern man. According to Lévy-Bruhl, for those with a 'primitive mentality', mythology is used not to understand the world but to re-create the communion that indigenous people attribute to the golden era they describe in myths. For Rudolf Bultmann (1985), myth is still an explanation of the world, like it was for Tylor, but it must be read symbolically and not literally; myth must be demythologized so that it stops being about worlds and becomes about the human experience of the world. In this way, it can become a universal experience: 'The real purpose of myth is not to present an objective picture of the world as it is, but to express man's understanding of himself in the world in which he lives. Myth should be interpreted not cosmologically, but anthropologically, or better still, existentially' (Bultmann 1985: 10).

Eliade, who attempted to affirm the compatibility of science and myth, states that 'Every myth shows how a reality came into existence, whether it be the total reality, the cosmos, or only a fragment – an island, a species of plant, a human institution ... [it] becomes the paradigmatic model for all human activities' (1987: 97–8).

For Eliade, a myth does far more than explain the reality around us, it regenerates it. And it is in this way that myth offers something that science cannot, having a simply explanatory and not a regenerative function.

In 1984, both Alan Dundes and William Bascom offered two definitions of myth with truth at their centre. Dundes argued that 'A myth is a sacred narrative explaining how the world and man came to be in their present form' (1). Bascom highlighted in particular the idea of truthfulness, which he saw as separating folklore from myth. The latter, he argued, are 'considered to be truthful accounts of what happened in the remote past', and this is in direct contrast to his concept of folklore, which he regarded as 'fiction' (9).

Ninian Smart offers a definition that is particularly useful. Although it is incomplete, it covers what I consider to be one of the key characteristics of myth – identity – calling myth 'A story which forms the identity of an individual, his/her fellows, and/or the cosmos in which they inhabit' (1981: 26). Indeed, I will go on to consider Wana mythology as part of the identities of these people. Developing from Smart's formulation, David Leeming also focuses on the ability of myth to define a person. In fact, for Leeming, a myth is 'the expression of a social ethos' or the 'basic assumptions that define a person, a family, or a culture – with the informing reality that resides at the centre of being' (1990: 4).

In Australia, scholars such as Gillian Cowlishaw have approached myth in a very particular way, expressing a desire to 'explore the intense contention that is concealed behind a particular mythopoeia in everyday public life' (2010: 210). This project is strongly related to the colonial history of the country and the problematic elements linked to aboriginal culture and its political role in the nation. Although extremely interesting, Cowlishaw's approach is of limited use in this work due to the deeply different history of Indonesia, its very different colonial past and its current situation.

Ultimately, it is important to remember that to study mythology is to study the stories of the other while being aware of their point of view. In this work, I use the term 'myth' to refer to stories that may be considered either true or fictional by my informants; once again, the point of view that matters is the one of the people we work with. Myths play a pivotal role in the meaning-making process of Wana people. Wana people differentiate fables from myths, but it is an impossible task to ascertain how many people actually consider their mythology to be true stories and how many do not. Aside from this issue, though, years of stories and rituals mean that mythology certainly has an important place in Wana cultural and emotional identity, and it helps them understand the world around them. Lévi-Strauss (1955) stated that what 'we' call history is a myth by another name; although this may be a problematic statement in several respects, it is certainly an important issue if we consider the real impact of history on the average citizen of a metropolis. One might ask: does history have an impact on the identity of a citizen of, say, Manchester, even if that person has no knowledge of Britain's colonial past?

Sacred and profane

In this book, the classic dichotomy of sacred–profane gives way to a more pertinent dichotomy of visible/non-visible. The visible is the human world, a power-less world that might in some senses be equivalent to the profane sphere, while the non-visible world is the power-full world, one linked to spirits and mythology, and thus aligned with what elsewhere has been called the sacred. Although I frame the issues in these different terms, elements of the sacred–profane relationship remain important and must be explored. First of all, I am aware that in general, drawing distinctions between the sacred and the profane is never an easy task (Bascom 1984: 12).

Durkheim was the first to propose the sacred–profane dichotomy as the central characteristic of religion: 'religion is a unified system of beliefs and practices relative to *sacred things*, that is to say, things set apart and forbidden' (1915: 47). According to the sociologist, sacred things have a unifying power, as they are represented collectively as things that transcend everyday life, while the profane encompasses all mundane individual concerns. Indeed, Durkheim suggests that this dichotomy might be universal. Jack Goody criticized this stance in 1961, noting that many societies do not have words to translate terms such as 'sacred' and 'profane' and hence they must be products of European religious thought. On the other hand, even Edward Evans-Pritchard (1956) argued that in Neur rituals cannot be found a sacred–profane dichotomy. If on one side it is true that translating specific terms into other languages is a problematic task, it is also true that even without directly equivalent language, ideas such as sacred and profane can still be present in different cultures, although they might carry different characteristics. For example, although Wana people divide the world into visible and non-visible domains, this division overlaps to a large extent with the sacred–profane dichotomy.

For Eliade, sacred–profane distinctions were rigid, with the sacred being something that 'does not belong to our world' (1987: 11). For Jonathan Smith, who critically engaged with Eliade's theories, the sacred is a social construct, and the sacred place is a place of clarification (a focusing lens) where men and gods are held to be transparent to one another. It is a place where, as in all forms of communication, static and noise (i.e., the accidental) are decreased so that the exchange of information can be increased [...]. The ordinary (which remains, to the observer's eye, wholly ordinary) becomes significant, becomes sacred, simply by being there. It becomes sacred by having our attention directed to it in a special way.

(1980: 114–15)

With this approach, sacred and profane become situational categories and not inherent categories; they become categories of emplacement (Smith 1992: 104).

But in more recent times, the dichotomy of sacred–profane has more often been couched in the terms 'sacred-secular', or 'religious-secular'. Scholars such as Talal Asad argue that the secular 'is neither continuous with the religious that supposedly preceded it (that is, it is not the latest phase of a sacred origin) nor a simple break from it (that is, it is not the opposite, an essence that excludes the sacred). I take the secular to be a concept that brings together certain behaviors, knowledges, and sensibilities in modern life' (2003: 25).

Ultimately, I do not think it is possible to make a clear distinction between the sacred and the profane. These are qualities that are assigned by the subjects we observe, so something can be both sacred and profane at the same time, depending on the point of view. This became particularly clear to me when I considered my own status in the field. As someone from the West, I myself carried extraordinary, almost sacred, qualities for my Wana informants, but at the same time I struck them as extremely human in my clumsiness to adapt to life inside the jungle. For these reasons, in this work, I will focus more on the visible/non-visible distinction, where the visible has human qualities and the non-visible has spiritual ones, and where the shaman, as a liminal being existing between the two worlds, can have access to both.

A cultural framework of the life and reality of the Wana people

Indonesia in general, and the island of Sulawesi specifically, has attracted significant numbers of scholars from the fields of anthropology (Belo 1960; Geertz 1973; Mead 1942; Wellenkamp 1988) and ethnomusicology (Aragon 1996; Kartomi 1973a; Rappoport 2004), some of them became key figures in their respective fields. Unlike the Toraja and Bugis of Sulawesi or the Dayak of Borneo, the Wana people are not among the best-known cultural groups in Indonesia. Moreover, very little academic research exists on their cultural and religious life and the information regarding this community is not extensive or widely known.[1] To compensate for the reader's possible lack of existing knowledge about the Wana people, and to facilitate understanding of the rituals proposed in Chapters 3 and 4, the following discussion I present will provide an overview of some of the key topics arising in the present work: Wana social order, religion and cultural values. In doing so, I will also equip the readers with the tools that will guide them through the rest of this work. I will explain who the Wana are, how and where they live, before explaining their relationships with colonial empires and why this is important context for the research. I believe that a culture is shaped by and, at the same time, shapes the world around it. For this reason, I will offer a brief description of Wana history and economy, although little information exists about both. Many elements of Wana culture can be illuminated through understanding the past of this group of people, their modern situation and their relationships with other cultures. In particular, I will reflect on key topics such as conceptions of space-time among the Wana people, their music and their religion.

The Wana, people of the forest

The Wana people are an indigenous community that lives inside the Morowali nature reserve in Sulawesi, Indonesia. In 1980, a World Wildlife Fund report estimated that there were about 5,000 Wana people living in Morowali (Lahadji 1999: 238).[2] However, like many other ethnic groups that inhabit the Indonesian archipelago, they are not present in the 2003 census (Permanent Committee on Geographical Names 2003) or the 2010 census (Badan Pusat Statistik 2010). This is indicative of the Indonesian government's dismissive attitude to local ethnic minorities, as I discuss below.

The natural reserve of Morowali, with its 2,250 km[2] of equatorial forest (Lahadji 1999: 238), has been home to the Wana people since the arrival of the Indian kingdoms (Alvard 2000: 59), and possibly even before. The Wana people speak their own language, called *Bahasa*[3] *Taa*, an Austronesian language which seems to derive from the Pamona language (Noorduyn 1991: 89). The Wana language itself is then divided into four dialects: *Bahasa Taa* (Marisa area), *Bahasa Untunue* (Uewaju area), *Bahasa Kasiala* (an area near Uewaju) and *Bahasa Tokaju* or *Maranka* (Lambentana area). The difference between these dialects can be so wide that a *Bahasa Taa* speaker could not understand somebody speaking *Bahasa Maranka* and vice versa, forcing me to hire a guide to go and visit the Lambentana village. The Morowali forest is in the central area of Sulawesi Island, and it extends from the Kolonodale gulf to the Bongka Tojo bay. On 24 November 1986, the Indonesian Ministry of Forestry (MoFor) declared the forest a nature reserve due to its great diversity of flora and fauna. Twelve per cent of the entire world's bird species can be found in the forest, and it has several rivers, the most important being that which gives its name to the reserve: the Morowali (Lahadji 1999: 238). The area is also characterized by its considerable number of caves, and this has an enormous influence on the mythical world of Wana people. While in the field, I heard many stories surrounding these caves, including one that identifies a particular cave as a passage to Mecca, one in which there is talking water, and another about a cave hosting a mythical war drum (*kratu*) that was transformed into stone by the Wana gods. In the past, the Wana people used these caves as shelters and, up until a few years ago, Wana groups from the Lambentana area in the north of the forest hid in them when foreigners approached their villages.

Wana territory

The Wana territory is divided into ten areas, each ruled by a community leader, called *kepala suku* (literally head-clan), who is chosen by the elders. There is no official information about the different areas, their leaders and economy; the following list is based on my personal knowledge of the areas I visited and on the information I managed to obtain from my informants.

- The area around the Marisa village is ruled by Apa Rau, and it is here that I spent the majority of my fieldwork period. It is located in the southern part of the reserve and due to its vicinity to the sea is the only area with a maritime tradition. The economy of this area relies on the trade of dammar gum, wood and rattan with the town of Kolonodale, which is situated outside of the forest (Map 1). Due to this active trade with the outside world, knowledge of the Indonesian language is widespread among inhabitants, and outsiders are accepted. In the area, there are both Muslims and Christian populations, the latter concentrated in the village of Kilo Sembilan.
- The Taronggo area is ruled by Apa n'Te. This area straddles the central-eastern border of the nature reserve. The village of Taronggo, which is outside the forest, is one of the largest in the whole Wana territory, and it has a church, a primary school and a medical centre. Families have electricity, running water and houses made of brick, and they come from different ethnic and religious backgrounds. The economy is based on the cultivation and trading of cocoa, coconuts and palm oil. Due to its position, knowledge of the Indonesian language is widespread among the inhabitants of this area too. Grumblies spent her entire fieldwork period in this village, so I will use her words to describe it:

> Given the various religious affiliations found in Taronggo, the village is home to a Christian Protestant church – the largest building in the village – which belongs to the Central Sulawesi Christian church (*Gereja Kristen Sulawesi Tengah*, BI), the main Christian church formation in Central Sulawesi. There is also a small mosque in the Southeastern entrance to Taronggo and a Pentecostal church building that is currently in expansion planning, although the Pentecostal community is marginal in numbers. Plans for the erection of a *rumah adat* (BI), a house for Wana local custom, are irregularly discussed but so far have not been realized. Taronggo is also home to an elementary school, the *sekolah dasar* (BI), also called SD, where the village's children, regardless of their religious

profession, can go to school. For medical care, the government has erected
a stationary medical center, a small house supposed to function as a home
for a nurse. In case of medical need, people also turn to one of the three
local kiosks to buy medication.

(2016: 30–1, emphasis in the original)

- Apa Kode rules the Lambentana area, which is located in the northern part
of the forest. This area is considered by the Wana people to be the most
'primitive' area of the territory. I heard stories of how, up until a few years ago,
inhabitants did not have modern clothes and it was here that people used to
hide in caves when foreigners approached their villages. My impression from
visiting the area was that it is indeed very different from other parts of the
territory, but that many of the things I had heard about it were exaggerations;
I was warmly welcomed, and I did not notice any major differences from the
other areas. The mountains that form the area isolate the villages from the
outside world – almost nobody speaks *Bahasa Indonesia* – and the houses
are built in the traditional style, on stilts and without walls, but with pits for
fires on the side of the mountains. The area is famous for the great abundance
of rice and for the bitter cold of the night. People here produce machetes to
sell, and they also breed pigs, animals that I did not see in other villages. In
the Marisa area introduced above, wild pigs are hunted and eaten regardless
of the fact that there are also Muslim inhabitants. However, that they are not
bred here could possibly be due to the presence of Muslims.
- The Uewaju area is situated on the *Tunda n'tana* mountain, the mythical
land said to have been placed on the primordial waters by *Pue*, the Wana
god, and called the navel of the world. This area possesses a mythical aura,
and almost all Wana people believe that their traditions are strong and well
preserved here. The reality is perhaps more questionable, and the overriding
perception may be due to an indigenous cultural bias that considers
everything related with the mythical mountain as something extraordinary
itself. Uewaju is also the biggest Wana village, with perhaps hundreds of
inhabitants. They do not speak Indonesian and the economy is based on
dammar gum[4] and the trading of handmade machetes and blowpipes.
- Posangke, which is ruled by Apa Dimes, is in the centre-north of the
reserve. This area is considered poor but with plentiful rice, and people here
collect and sell dammar resin and trade machetes and blowpipes.
- The Langada area is situated in the south-western part of the forest.
Inhabitants trade with the outside world, walking to the Tambayoli village to
sell dammar resin rather than using canoes.

- On the edge of the region, the Wuata area (ruled by Apa Jusi), the Lemo Walia area (ruled by Apa Jupi), the Uempanapa area (ruled by Koyu) and Solobiro (ruled by Apa Ida) are all outside the natural reserve and the majority of the population is Christian. They trade cocoa, coconut and rattan.

Wana villages can range in size from a dozen inhabitants, in the case of Kilo Sembilan, to hundreds, in the case of Uewaju. Although the Wana people have almost completely transitioned from a nomadic tradition to a settled culture, they still roam from village to village, meaning that the number of people living in one village varies constantly. Proof of this can be found in Atkinson's observation in the 1970s that 'Wana typically reside in their rice fields, not in their kampung [village]' (Atkinson 1989: 2), while between 2011 and 2016 many Wana people were settled in villages and considered the houses near the rice fields to be resting houses used during breaks from work. Sometimes, an entire village can move to another part of the forest, such as when, in 2016, the whole population of Lambentana moved away to escape the Christian mission in Uetuwu, a few hours away from where they were living. Due to this constant movement of people, it is common for individuals to have relatives and friends in different villages, or to be living in places far away from where they were born. The village chief of Marisa, Apa Rau, was born in the Uewaju village, for example. The powerful *tau walia* Indo Pino was born in Posangke, lived in Kaju Poli, and eventually died in Kilo Sembilan, while Apa Ingus was also born in Uewaju but was living in Kilo Sembilan by 2016 and was planning to move to Marisa.

A remnant of their original nomadic culture, the Wana people still adopt a slash-and-burn method, meaning that after a few years of exploiting the land they move to another part of the forest. Just as in various other cultures (Hertz 2004; Metcalf 1991; Scarduelli 1992), following the death of a member of the community, entire villages used to move to new areas to avoid any contact with death and the polluted ground. Once they found land suitable for cultivation, the Wana people used to make sure that the spirits of the forest were in favour of them using it. For this reason, they would hold a chicken sacrifice in which the animal's blood was spread together with some rice onto the ground (Atkinson 1987: 345). During my fieldwork, however, I did not see any surviving rituals of this kind. The Wana people's slash-and-burn agriculture has led the Indonesian government to consider them 'environmental vandals' (Lahadji 1999: 240). It might be argued, though, that these techniques have been used for many centuries and, furthermore, studies from the American anthropologist Michael

Alvard suggest that this method does not have an excessively negative impact on the flora and fauna of the reserve (2000: 438). To better understand the bias behind the position of the Indonesian government, we must consider that, as a whole, Indonesia is the world's second highest contributor of plastic waste to oceans (*Jakarta Post* 2015), the third for the emission of greenhouse gasses and, in 2007, it became the country with the highest rate of deforestation, surpassing Brazil (Vidal 2014). These unflattering records cast a light on the complicated relationship between the Indonesian government and indigenous cultural minorities.

From my base in the Marisa village, it took one hour by canoe to reach the sea. It is faster and more comfortable to travel by canoe when carrying the large amount of dammar gum or wood that the Wana usually bring to Kolonodale. On arriving at the point where the Morowali River enters the sea, Wana travellers move to a larger canoe that is better adapted to these waters, and a further three hours in this vessel are needed to reach the Kolonodale town outside of the forest. Kolonodale is the principal town of the North Morowali Regency (which was established in 2013); while until 2004, it was the capital of the entire Morowali Regency. This town is a crossroads for local travellers, especially those who travel from the two major cities of the area, Luwuk and Palu, and its hospital is the only healthcare institution in the area. Kolonodale is one of the main trading centres for those living in the southern part of the Wana territory; here they cannot only buy everything they need, from televisions to sugar, but they also sell wood, rattan, dammar resin and cocoa.

Engagement with capitalist economic systems is changing Wana traditional life and disrupting patterns of ritual activity. In the large village of Taronggo, casual work in palm oil plantations has introduced a weekly work schedule that makes it harder for people to actively participate in rituals such as the two-day long *kayori*. Many people cannot be present any longer for the full two nights because of their work commitments. This 'urban' settlement outside the forest contains new and expensive desires and needs: rent, electric light, television, motorbikes, furniture, clothes, new foods and so on. The increasing consumer possibilities have amplified the reliance on money and work.

Life inside the reserve, on the other hand, is less economically demanding and more relaxed. People have the tough work of collecting rattan, dammar resin, coconut and similar materials, but the constant presence and support of the community brings a discrete autonomy and removes the necessity of working every day, and especially when sick. My friend and informant Om Manggi did not work for weeks due to an infection in his leg but, nevertheless, he knew that friends and family would support him during his convalescence. Moreover, in the jungle, the main basic needs are covered by the raw materials available there; unlike outside of the forest, people do not have to pay for housing, and there are no schools or motorbikes[5] to bring economic pressures.

Indeed, the Wana people have a particular conception of 'need' that it is useful to understand because it relates to a vision of themselves and the world that will be central in this work. A conversation that I had with Indo Rau, the wife of Marisa's village chief and my host, while I was packing to go back to Italy in 2011, perfectly illustrates this approach to life:

> G. S.: Do you need my tweezers?
> Indo Rau: Only if you give it to us, otherwise not.[6]

This was not an isolated episode. I had similar discussions over other objects of common use and modest price, such as mirrors, pots and shoes. I will explain later how, in Wana culture, people consider themselves to be living in poverty and the need for something exists only when the object is already in their possession. People tend to adapt to what they have at hand and do not get frustrated by dwelling on things that they cannot obtain in their economic or wider lives.

The diet is also based on what the forest offers. Often plain rice is the only dish in a meal, only occasionally supplemented with wild pig meat, bats, *biawak*[7] or fish, mostly smoked to preserve it. More often, people add produce that is cultivated in their gardens or the plants that grow wild in the forest, such as tapioca, papaya (which is also used to treat malaria), bamboo and rattan (which has a taste similar to artichoke). An alternative to rice is the *gata*,[8] a food of gelatinous texture and white-grey colour that is derived from the processing of sago.[9] It does not have a strong taste and is eaten with meat or fish broth. Wana people can buy salt, dried fish or *kecap manis* (sweet soy sauce), crucial to enrich the taste of the plain rice or *gata*. In all Wana houses, coffee is always present, and it is served with a great quantity of sugar that is bought in from Kolonodale or extracted from the sugar canes that are present in the forest.

The Wana people and colonial empires

Like Atkinson (1989) before me, I was struck by the widespread sense of inferiority that Wana people seemed to show during my time with them. More than once, I heard people call themselves or their ancestors *miskin* (poor) or other negative epithets.[10] Apa Rau, who I suppose was around aged sixty-five at the time, told me that his grandfather fought in wars between tribes and that he was so *miskin* that he had to dress himself in leaves and coconuts.[11] In his words, 'We did not have clothes because we were *miskin*.'[12] Atkinson's observations are strongly worded: 'Wana are fully aware that they are at the bottom of an ethnic ladder, dominated and despised by their neighbors – Bugis, Mori, Pamona, Gorontalo, and others – who subscribe to one or another world religion. Wana represent themselves as poor and degraded' (Atkinson 1990: 55).

It is possible that this tendency to deprecate themselves originates in a cultural predisposition related to the myth of the fall that is central to Wana mythology, combined with the effects of a subordinate power relationship with foreign powers such as Indian, Muslim, and Dutch colonizers. The relationship between the Wana people and outsiders seems to have shaped their vision of themselves and their reality and is possibly pivotal to this negative self-evaluation. This self-evaluation is, however, certainly one of the factors influencing people, when they marry someone of another religion, to undergo religious conversions to their spouse's religion, and in an increasing trend for conversions to Christianity, a religion seen by many Wana people as superior because it is strongly related to the 'powerful' West.

By the fifth century CE, commerce between Indians and the population of the Indonesian archipelago was already flourishing, although the Indians never obtained control of the hinterlands of the main islands of Java, Sumatra, Borneo and Sulawesi (Scarduelli 1992: 42). It is likely, then, that the Wana people living in the hinterland mountains did not have much contact with the sultanates of Central Sulawesi, while it is documented that the Wana of the coastal settlements paid tributes to the sultans of Ternate and Bungku around 1257 (Alvard 2000: 59). The name Wana itself derives from Sanskrit and means 'forest' (Ibid.), and this confirms that there was contact between this group of people and Indian culture. 'The Wana may have taken as a name for themselves a term applied by outsiders to the inhabitants of the rugged forest interior' (Atkinson 1989: 182).

The indigenous name of the Wana is *Taa*, meaning 'no' or 'not', and it is used rarely nowadays. In this work, I have decided to use the term Wana instead of *Taa* for three reasons: (1) it is the word used in the few existing academic works about this population; (2) it is the label used by Indonesians; (3) it is used more frequently than the term *Taa* by Wana people themselves. I will use the term *Taa* only when referring to the Wana land, because my informers exclusively call it *tana Taa*. Many other Wana words derive from India too, such as *suruga* (paradise), which seems to come from the Sanskrit *svarga* (Atkinson 1989: 38), or the term *naga* that is used instead of the Indonesian *ular* to refer to the snakes that inhabit the Morowali forest and Wana mythology.

Between the fifteenth and seventeenth centuries, the Kingdom of Luwuk of South Sulawesi extended its interests through Morowali and Poso regencies into Wana territory. Central Sulawesi was under the control of the kingdoms of Makassar, Mandar, and Ternate (Sangaji 2007: 325). According to Atkinson, the influence of the latter was so important that Wana people consider the Raja of Tenerate their first king (Atkinson 1989: 335). Around the year 1450, Islamic traders started their expansions into Indonesia (Wagner 1961: 87) and many of these kingdoms began to transition from Hinduism to Islam.

Like the Hindus before them, Muslims could not impose themselves on the hinterlands. The difficulties encountered into penetrating into inner areas (especially in the big islands: Sumatra, Borneo, Sulawesi) do not allow us to define the process in terms of conversion: what happened was a gradual absorption of Muslim religious principles, a partial and selective assimilation within the indigenous cultural context (Scarduelli 1992: 46). Li points out how 'in economic and political matters the relationship between upland [internal] and lowland [costal] systems has long been marked by tension' (Li 1999: 8). The relationship between the costal kingdoms and the inner community was not egalitarian and the latter were considered 'inferior and treated in a derogatory way' (Hauser-Schäublin 2013: 13).

Clear traces of these historical episodes can be found in many mythological stories, such as that which explains the good relations between Muslims and Wana as resulting from the fact that they are descendants of two brothers. In the story, the elder brother is Wana and the younger one Muslim. The latter was unhappy because his brother liked to eat pork, so he went to *Pue* to complain, but the god found the complaint baseless. Atkinson noted how, on one side, many Wana converted to Islam, temporarily or permanently, while on the other side, Islam had a substantial influence on Wana culture (Atkinson 1991: 45). This continuous assimilation of cultural elements from external sources demonstrates that Wana religion 'is not an ossified survival of a Palaeolithic past, but instead a dynamic system that has developed and adapted to cope with changing circumstances' (Atkinson 1989: 48). Indeed, also the so-called traditional cultures are flexible and idiosyncratic, facing conflicts and resolutions as part of their everyday social dynamic (Hiatt 1965; Myers 1986). An important question is: at what point has a culture adapted so much that it becomes something else? While rituality seems to have remained more or less stable during the last forty years, the world around it has changed a lot, and so has the Wana relationship with the wider world. Atkinson's reports are perfect points of comparison in understanding how the *momago* has changed, and they reveal that although the ritual elements themselves have not altered drastically, clearly fewer people are now taking part in them, or taking part in them differently, as a result of work-related needs. New forms of entertainment are emerging that could soon replace the shamanic ritual as the main festive moment in the life of a Wana person. The Wana world is experiencing obvious changes and it is likely that the situation in forty years from now will be more different from the present day than what Atkinson found forty years ago is. As I observed, rituals are starting to fail, and they do not have the same authority that they had in the past; I even saw Wana people confused about what the correct ritual procedure at any given moment was. In 2016 – much more so than in 1974 – the jungle was becoming less isolated day by day, with many people travelling outside the jungle each day, and televisions bringing representations of the outside world into their huts every night. It is likely that Wana daily and economic life will be impacted upon far more than their rituality is, but it is also possible that the Wana religion will eventually disappear, leaving behind just a few *scaramantic* gestures and fables. Ultimately, Wana culture, like all cultures, is definitely adapting to new circumstances. One day – perhaps not in the too distant future – this culture will have become something very different.

Going back to Wana history, the first communities of Dutch missionaries started to populate the Morowali area around the two World Wars. Atkinson writes of a contact that ended in armed conflict between the Dutch and the Wana in 1942. The latter tried to evoke their mythical hero, *Pololoisong*,[13] to fight the invasion (Atkinson 2003: 145), but the hero did not show up and, with their rifles, the Dutch army easily won the battle. Relations with Christian missionaries, already recorded by the missionary Albert Kruyt in the 1920s, increased in 1979 with the arrival of the New Tribes Mission, an evangelical missionary group from the United States and Canada (Atkinson 1991: 45). Kruyt built a missionary school in Poso. The two aims of the mission, supported by the Dutch government, were 'civilizing' the natives, transforming the 'savage' head-hunters into people that could be accepted by Europeans, and countering the advance of Islam in the area (Coté 1996: 93). A new wave arrived in 2015, just before my second period of fieldwork.

While the presence of Hindu and Muslim cultural elements does not create any serious social conflict, and the relationship between Muslims and Wana is peaceful and friendly, the arrival of Christianity has created social division and clashes. In the area of Marisa, for example, Wana Christians living in Kilo

Sembilan want to establish an independent Christian village. They are boycotting community rituals like the *kayori* (Wana funeral), undermining the *kasintuwu* (sense of community), and taking economic advantage of other local people by using their canoes for economic purposes without paying to hire them or giving owners money for maintenance or petrol. By doing so, they are taking advantage of the kindness and desire to help these other people. The situation is considered so problematic that, in 2016, some people came to me asking for advice. They were hoping that, due to my supposedly more extensive knowledge of the world, I would be able to advise them about the best way to manage the situation. Sadly, the only advice I was able to give was to be aware that the Christians are there to stay and perhaps to wipe out the Wana religion, as had already happened in the past with other indigenous religions. Henceforth, they cannot simply go away and leave the land to them; rather, they must stand up and make it clear that all religions are welcome, but that respect and support between each other are the base for a peaceful co-existence. Some communities in the north of Morowali have resolved to relocate to the inner part of the forest to avoid any contact with the Christians.

Considering that the evangelical Protestantism missionaries[14] (Clark 2019) themselves possess a mythical aura, as the West is considered a mythical place, they have a considered superior white skin and arrive by helicopter,[15] Wana people are facing an unbalanced confrontation. It is unclear to me how the Christian missionaries are allowed to land their helicopters inside this national nature reserve while I, for example, required the permit from the Indonesian government to conduct a research in Indonesia (permit that required nine months to obtain), the permit from the Indonesian Ministry of Forestry to live inside a natural reserve and the permit from the local office Kolonodale to enter inside the Morowali forest. Missionaries are, though, some of the few, if not the only, windows on to the outside world for local people. The impression of the outside world is, as might be expected, filtered through the agenda of the missionaries. This can give biased information to a community that has almost no knowledge of the life beyond their own situation. This was illustrated clearly to me once when talking with Apa Sudin:

> Apa Sudin: All the people believe in the same Pue.
> G. S.: Does everyone believe in the same Pue?
> Apa Sudin: Yes, everybody. Everybody except Israel.
> G. S.: How do you know about Israel?
> Apa Sudin: The missionaries told me about it.[16]

This and other similar experiences helped me to understand that the effect of the missionaries' proselytizing is enhanced greatly by Christian and Western identities, the two being synonymous in some respects. For some Wana individuals, becoming Christian means to become somewhat Westernized, hence they can feel superior to others around them. Atkinson reports strong evidence of this complicated relationship between Wana people and Christianity already emerging in the 1970s: 'Some report having been told to their face that they lack the personal worth of a dog or a chicken because they have no religion' (Atkinson 1991: 46). I also experienced first-hand Wana Christians treating non-Christians as 'savages', and looking down on them for still believing in spirits. In villages such as Taronggo, Wana Christians often show an attitude of superiority towards their relatives from the jungle to the extent that the latter might be banished to an isolated space during a wedding feast. My guide Ajeran confirmed to me that this was exactly the case on one particular occasion I witnessed, and that the family was ashamed to have relatives commonly considered 'primitives' by Wana converted to Christianity. In her thesis, Grumblies perfectly describes that event:

> He [Apa Ele, the father of the bride] invited those guests who stand or sat close to the dining tables to the big buffet. Then he turned to his *keluarga dari gunung* (BI), his family from the mountain, and explained to everyone that there was not enough space for every guest to eat from the dining tables and not enough chairs. And because his mountain relatives were not comfortable with sitting in chairs or eating from plates, he invited them to take their meal in the nearby town hall around the corner, where they could sit on the floor and eat with their hands as they prefer to; instead of plates the food would be served in banana leaves. But the food, he insisted, would be the same, here and there; they would make no difference between people. Then he wished everyone a great celebration.
>
> (2016: 168)

Thanks to this vivid narration, we see how the discriminations against the Wana are manifest. The 'town' people take advantage of their position and, artfully, reserve for the Wana people a second-class service, writing it off as doing them the favour of allowing them to follow their usual 'habits'. Grumblies then corrects her statement about the same food being served to everybody:

> [Wana] generally are believed to dislike beef (a fact that is simply not true; my interlocutors stated they indeed like beef, but they rarely get the chance to taste it). 'They are happy with chicken, why should we serve them cow?', one of my

Christian interlocutors replied when I asked about this circumstance. Wana usually were not always aware of such acts or processes of (symbolic) violence as directed towards them. Some distinctions were internalized relations people were not actively recognizing as actions of differentiating.

(2016: 169)

In the documentary *Gods and Satans* (Journet and Gourdol 2004), there is another episode that is illustrative of the complexities of these relationships. In the Marisa village, the presence of a Wana Christian did not create any problems until he began to attempt to convert other people to his religion. This forced the village chief Apa Rau to expel him as a way of defending the traditions of the village. I have already noted that, as early as the 1970s, when Atkinson was in the field, similar conflicts with the Christians were already occurring, while the relationship with Muslims was friendly. According to her, Islam accepts and permits Wana shamanistic practices, while Christians completely refuse them and consider them sinful. Christianity is considered a religion for powerful people and in the 1970's more than now, it gave access to Western comforts (hospitals, schools and medicines). 'Christianity puts a poor Wana in a bind, people say, for either one must sit by and watch loved ones die or one must commit a sin by calling on traditional forms of aid' (Atkinson 1988: 53). Nowadays the situation is slightly changed, with few schools, medical centres and pharmacies available to the Wana, but the power relationships did not change. As Atkinson and I observed, the Christian identity is strongly interconnected with ideas of class and status. Atkinson follows up with a stark illustration: 'People tell of being told [by the Christians] their necks will be cut like chickens, their genitals split open and rubbed with salt, for their human worth is less than that of dogs refusing religion' (Atkinson 1979: 32). Nowadays the situation is less violent but nonetheless tense. Christians and Wana remain two separate words, both culturally and socially, with the Christians in a position of power, due to their relationship with the powerful West, and an intolerant or haughty attitude towards the Wana life, considered a shameful trace of the past. In the end, the following testimony from my time in the field seems to reinforce this idea of a sense of incompatibility between Wana and Christian belief systems:

Om Todi: I would like to convert to Christianity but then I will not be able to go to the shaman. Who could cure my 'inner illness' if not a shaman? I also have a woman that I could marry, but she is Christian.[17]

The Wana people and their neighbours

As I have just discussed, the relationship between the Wana people and foreign powers has always been one where the former is in a role of inferiority and submission. A similar attitude is also present in their relationships with the other ethnic groups of the Morowali area, such as the Mori or the Bugis.

The Wana people have an ancient relationship with the Mori, and, in the past, the two groups were firm rivals. Currently, there is active exchange between the two; weddings between members of these two ethnic groups, for instance, are very common. However, it is notable that it is usually the Wana partner that converts to the religion of the other because the latter is invariably perceived as more economically and socially advanced. Usually, they do not live in the forest, are assimilated into the great Indonesian culture and, more importantly, are Muslims or Christians. Many young adults look at the Mori as a model encouraging them to move away from Wana traditions. Apa Rau once criticized this admiration to me in strong language:

> You know how the Bugis dance, how the Mori speak, but you do not know what the Wana do. How can you say that you are a Wana?[18]

The Wana relationship with the Bugis is different, however. This group is also considered a kind of enemy, but they are looked down upon on moral grounds. They are believed to be people quick to anger and always ready to use their machetes. From the other perspective, though, the other inhabitants of the area generally seem to treat the Wana with indifference. I had a few opportunities to travel with Apa Rau or other Wana people outside of the forest, and on these occasions, they seemed to pass totally unnoticed, maybe because my presence changed the normal dynamics, or perhaps because they were considered strange people for still living in 'primitive' jungle conditions. Anyway, many people in Kolonodale hold friendly relationships with Wana people and treat them as peers. It was difficult, however, to find evidence of anything other than the kind reception typical of Indonesians more widely.

Finally, it is worth noting that the Chinese population in Kolonodale seems uninterested in the existence of the Wana people. The owner of a restaurant I often went to in Kolonodale, Mrs Liang, once asked me:

> Mrs. Liang: Who is that man without shoes?
> G. S.: He is a Wana. His shoes must have split during his journey.
> Mrs. Liang: Wana?[19]

While I was trying to explain who the Wana are and how they live, I noted Mrs Liang's blankness at discovering that an entire cultural group of people was living without electricity just on the other side of the bay.

The Wana people and the state

I have already briefly outlined the relationship between the Wana people and the empires. At this point, it is important to note also that Wana spiritual life does not fit within the foundational philosophy of the Indonesian state, *Pancasila*, being considered *adat* (customs) rather than an *agama* (religion) (Schiller 1996). The use of the term *adat* underlines a certain ethnocentric, superficial and discriminating approach and a lack of proper understanding of Wana religion, which is often mistakenly considered by the government to be based on animism. Michel Picard stresses how 'today "religion" [*agama*] tends to be countered to "tradition" [*adat*] – particularly in those societies which have been Islamized or Christianized' (2011: 6).

The term *pancasila* derives from the combination of two Old Javanese words, themselves derived from Sanskrit, *panca* (five) and *sīla* (principles). The five principles that have been placed at the heart of the Indonesian state and of Indonesian life are: (1) belief in the one and only God, (2) a just and civilized humanity, (3) an unified Indonesia, (4) democracy and (5) social justice for all (Prawirancgara 1984). The first and, therefore, most important principle is monotheism, a religious idea brought to Indonesia along with Islam. Religion among the Wana people might itself be considered monotheistic, and one that is free of ethnic boundaries. Wana people believe that anyone can follow the Wana religion and become a shaman, and the existence of *Pue* (the Wana god) does not exclude the existence of other gods. The Indonesian government, however, uses the absence of a sacred text as a reason to exclude Wana practices and beliefs from religious regulation. In fact, in Indonesia six religions (Islam, Christianity, Protestantism, Buddhism, Balinese Hinduism[20] and, recently added, Confucianism) are recognized by the government. To join this list, three conditions must be fulfilled: (1) the religion must be monotheistic, and this casts aside all religions that cannot be reconnected with the one true God of Islam; (2) it must not have ethnic boundaries, thus keeping Judaism away from Indonesia;[21] (3) it must have a sacred text, another condition that recalls the Islamic religion, the centrality of the Quran,[22] and a cultural distinction between literate and illiterate religions and cultures (the latter represented by the Wana).

It might be argued that religious laws in Indonesia are discriminatory on many levels. An individual's religion is recorded on their ID card, and those without a religion are likely to encounter difficulties obtaining these identification documents. This can have serious knock-on effects and cause numerous problems in negotiating bureaucratic systems. Thus, the declaration of a person's religion can be a political statement in Indonesia. In the Wana context, 'Religion, as an institution set apart from the rest of cultural life, appears to be an introduced idea' (Atkinson 1991: 47). Indeed, the Indonesian word *agama* (religion) cannot even be translated into the Wana language, and people directly use the Indonesian form when talking about other religions, those of the country's rulers. When interrogated on the matter, Wana people always replied to me that they do not have a religion; religion is a matter of the government, Islam, or Christian missionaries.

During my fieldwork, I witnessed a small clash between Wana people and the government. During district elections, a government unit came to the Marisa village to convince Wana residents to vote. After a long discussion, Apa Rau pronounced the collective decision to abstain from voting due to continued indifference of the government towards their problems. Distaste for politics and politicians is so deep in Wana culture that it has found its place in mythology:

Apa Rau: Abunawas[23] was smart, the first politician. He was not a good man.[24]

This problematic relationship with the government has led to the Wana people isolating themselves, under the motto: 'no government, no religion, no village' (Lahadji 2008: 23).[25] This motto expresses a rejection of following the rules of a government that demands that they follow a recognized religion and embrace a sedentary culture. Indeed, this motto is truly representative of Wana ways of thinking that I encountered often; they consider themselves to be a group without religion, and this is an attitude that that can be dangerous in Indonesia, where atheism is not considered normal (Osman 2012).[26]

The Indonesian government considers the Wana people to be a 'backward' (*terkebelakang*) community (Lahadji 1999: 243). Part of the focus of this idea is the problem of illiteracy and the sparse knowledge of the Indonesian language among Wana people. Nathan Porath explores a similar issue in his *'They have not progressed enough': Development's negated identities among two indigenous peoples (orang asli) in Indonesia and Thailand*, where he explores how the Sakai of Sumatra 'wish to progress' to avoid being considered 'wild people who did not wear clothes […], living an unhygienic […] life deep in the forest […] and shunning the rest of the world through fear' (2010: 271).

Very few people are able to send their children to schools outside of the forest, relying on the hospitality of friends or relatives living in Kolonodale or Taronggo. Formalized learning is, though, having a strong negative impact on the survival of Wana culture; not only are the children sent to school in areas where the majority of people do not know Wana traditions, but a key feature of the national curriculum is *Pancasila* (Kuipers 2011). Missionaries have also translated the Bible into the Wana language, making it the only written text in this language, and so forcing anyone curious to read in their own language in this direction (Journet and Nougarol 2005). Curt Sachs's warning about the impact that literacy has on traditional societies is relevant here: 'the backbones of a scriptless culture are tradition and memory; both vanish under the impact of general literacy, and with them fade the imagination and creativeness of uneducated performers. Literacy and folk art bloom in inverse ratio' (1962: 46–7). I do not totally agree with Sachs, and I do not wish to suggest that a traditional community should be forced to live in isolation for the benefit of Western scholars, but instead that the processes of formalizing education can be detrimental if not properly controlled, especially if there are other religious and political groups ready to exert undue influence. There is much evidence of similarly problematic developments in other cultural contexts, such as the education of American Indians in missionary schools, where Native Americans were forced to accept the Christian belief (Denvens 1992).

Kasintuwu

Possibly, in an attempt to contrast the negative and complicate relationship with the other cultural and religious groups, the Wana have placed the *kasintuwu* (sense of community) at the core of their culture. *Kasintuwu* is a key concept to understanding Wana culture, and it will be a constant theme throughout this book, especially in the discussions of rituals, where I will explore the values expressed in them. Atkinson translates the term as 'mutual support' (1989), while I prefer the phrase 'sense of community'. Regardless of the translation, *kasintuwu* permeates all aspects of Wana life. Many told me that without *kasintuwu* 'it is impossible to wake up in the morning', and that life outside of the community would be meaningless. Thus, I argue that *kasintuwu* stands for a lot more than mutual support; it is a constant expression of the awareness of living inside a community and of the precedence of the community over the life of any single member.[27] *Kasintuwu* is expressed through people supporting each other, but I conceptualize it not only as a relationship between members but also as a relationship between members and the totality itself, the community. It is a clear example of the 'mechanical solidarity' theorized by Durkheim, but without the presence of a repressive law that controls the people (1997). Wana people do not rely excessively on rules; they have a more relaxed approach about what people can or cannot do. This approach could be the product of a lack of need, since I never saw a Wana person going against the rules. It could also be that the humour used to shape people's behaviour is more than sufficient to control the community. One day, talking with Apa Reilin, I asked what the punishment was for a thief, and he told me that he had never seen anybody being punished for such a crime, or indeed for any other crime. He also told me, that theoretically, if someone would be caught stealing something, like a banana, he would have to walk around the village with a banana on the shoulder and all villagers would have to give him or her a banana.

Atkinson says that the term *kasintuwu* comes from the word *tuwu* (to live) with the prefix *sin* – (together) (Atkinson 1989: 26). I rather think that the term is composed from the words *kasi* (spinning top)[28] and *tuwu* (meaning both 'to live' and 'to spring') with the *n* an oral addition, like in Wana names such as Apa *n*Tongi and many others. It is possible that this word derives from one of the many mythological tales that I heard and collected.

> At the beginning of time, there were two kasi, one made of gold and the other made of wood. On the top of each kasi there were 1000 people and the kasi were striking each other. At one point, the golden kasi broke and the people on top of it decided to go to the West. These people were the ancestors of the Dutch and of Western people as a whole, while the people of the wooden kasi were the poor Wana that remained in their land.[29]

My interpretation of the word *kasintuwu* is that it actually indicates the community formed of people sprung (*tuwu*) from the wooden spinning top (*kasi*). In this way, *kasintuwu* expresses a strong sense of unity and commonality. Thus, I believe that the best translation for the word is 'sense of community' rather than 'mutual support'. In the following section I will explore the concept of lost density or plenitude related to similar myths and to a re-creation of this primordial density (having 1,000 people on a single spinning top).

Rituals such as the *momago* and the *kayori* are the most palpable expression of *kasintuwu*, but it can be found almost everywhere in Wana life, from the sharing of food to the nights spent watching television all together thanks to a single person offering the petrol to generate electric power. *Kasintuwu* will be the key used to understand Wana rituality and culture as this book unfolds, since it is expressed in almost all Wana actions.

Primordial density

Related to *kasintuwu* and the myth of the spinning tops, each time Wana people officiate a ritual, they re-enact the primordial density of the golden era – a state of initial plenitude. A mythological background provides the foundations for the construction of a Wana person's identity, distinguishing them from all other people of the world. Earlier, I described the myth of the spinning tops, but a second myth also tells of Wana people being descended from the mythical couple, Santoto and Delemontu. This story might be at the heart of the 'we are one family' idiom. Any further efforts to understand the origins of Wana kinship is beyond the scope of this book, but it is certainly my intention to emphasize how unity among Wana people has these deep roots and a huge influence.

Wana mythology narrates how all Wana people come from the same place, either the mythical couple or the wooden spinning top, depending on the myth. Put differently, it might be said that Wana people all come from a very small space, the womb of a woman or the spinning top. From this point, like a cultural big bang, they spread and multiply in space, ending mythical space-time. According to the tales, the golden era ended after many big bangs, although it must be kept in mind that in mythological space-time, events do not follow a linear succession. There are five events that marked the end of the golden era and the loss of primordial density: (1) the fracture of the vine uniting the ground and the sky, (2) the breaking of the golden spinning top, (3) the dissemination of the holy land all over the water, creating the continents, (4) the departure of Poloisong with the *kayu paramba* (the money tree) and (5) the departure of the *tau Baraka* from *Tana Taa*. All these events see a rupture and a centrifugal movement that either sends away mythical power from Wana people or scatters actual pieces of the Wana land away from where they are, decreasing both the density and power of their land. In the same way, when the soul leaves the body for too long, the owner loses its plenitude and gradually dies. In songs and mythological tales, Wana people often compare people to trees and plants, and likewise, it seems possible to compare the *Tana Taa* (Wana land) to a person who has lost their soul, and therefore their integrity and all their power. This explosion or rupture is well represented by the destruction of the vine that connected heaven and earth, and by the destruction of the mythical spinning top. These two fractures began what Wana people see as the beginning of their life of wretchedness, and the division of the initial Wana community into clans and villages. This correspondence between unity and mythical power can be found again in the rituals.

More than unity, though, I suggest it is useful to talk about density. The high density of the beginnings is contrasted by the sparsity of current times, where even the people of myth are at the edge of the world. To reaffirm and recreate density, the people of the village gather in a small hut to treat the illness of a single member. Hundreds of people gather for the death of a person, since a more serious crisis requires even greater density. In both rituals, a great quantity of people is forced for a night or two into a space that is not truly suitable for them all. These rituals do not only reaffirm the unity of the community and its power, but they also reaffirm the physical density that brings this power. They are a quest to bring back the perfection of the original state: a return not only to mythical space-time but to the mythical centre, one that is synonymous with power and regeneration.

Moreover, the first Wana people lived together on a spinning top until the day it fractured, and they moved all around the Wana land. With the passing of time and the increase in their number, they lost the mythical power of their ancestors. It is reasonable to note a direct connection between the unity or density of the mythical space-time and a loss of power related to the decrease of that original density, the dilutions of the state of perfection. There is perhaps a similarity in the Bible, where the life span of humans becomes shorter and shorter with the increasing distance of humans from Adam moving towards Noah.[30] In some ways, the fractures of the mythical vine and of the spinning top can be compared to the explosion of the big bang, which saw an originally dense mass expand and decrease in density, and a weakening of gravity. Wana society, despite being at the centre of the world, has lost all its mythical people, and those left behind consider themselves the poorest people in the world.

Wana religion

As I have already suggested, atheism is not highly regarded in Indonesia, if not explicitly opposed. At the base of this attitude is the pivotal role that religion has in Indonesian culture and the common correlation between atheism and communism, which is now illegal.[31] For this reason, I had to pretend I was a Christian during all my permanence in Indonesia, otherwise it would have been extremely difficult obtaining permits or simply having a positive relationship with the people around me. Even if the Wana describe themselves as a people without religion, they have a complex and ancient system of beliefs, rituals and gods. They have been forced by history and oppression to define their religion in contrast to the religion of the cultures that have set out to rule them: 'Indeed, their concept of *agama* represents the transformation of a traditional religious system provoked by challenges from representatives of world religions' (Atkinson 1991: 48). They have come to the point of considering *agama* to refer only to the religion of the rulers and not to their own system of belief.

At the foundation of Wana religion is *Pue*, the creator god. Even if nowadays Wana religion presents itself as a monotheistic religion, there are various elements that testify to a gradual shift away from animism, or the veneration of the spirits of animals.

> Apa nTongi: Once, when people went hunting, the *tau walia* used to pray to *Pue Binatang* (Lord of animals) to avoid upsetting him.[32]

There are testimonies of a past belief in two principal divinities: *Pue Ri Arantana*, god of the underground and the benevolent dispenser of rewards and punishments, and *Pue Lamoa*,[33] god of the sky and of lightning, with which he can transmit illnesses to humans. Om Suma once told me:

> There is a *Pue* that lives in the underground. He is very benevolent and if we want something, he will give it to us, but if we behave badly, he will punish us.

Atkinson offers a useful testimony about these two divine beings:

> Like Kruyt, I was told of two beings, Lai and Ndara, who were siblings when the earth and sky were still connected by a vine. Also like Kruyt, I heard accounts of Lai and Ndara that included a third sibling, Koni (the name means 'eat'), whom his siblings murdered for devouring people. Koni, I was told, was the first liver-eating demon (*measa*). When the vine holding heaven and earth together was severed (one of Kruyt's accounts holds a mouse responsible for gnawing through the vine), Lai managed to grasp the vine and climb upward. Lai became the *pue ri wawo yangi*, the Owner above the Sky, while Ndara went down to become the *pue ara ntana*, the Owner beneath the Earth.
>
> (1989: 197–8)

During my residency, I also encountered *Koni* being referred to by another name, Inkoni (also meaning 'to eat'), being called a giant (*tau rumbi*) or, according to other versions, a *measa* (demon) with many siblings: *Pauvumbagna*, *Indara* (Atkinson's Ndara), *Inpide* and *Ilai* (Lai). Myth characterises *Inkoni* as a man-eater, and his siblings despised him for this. One day, *Inkoni* tried to eat *Indova* but after a fight with *Inkoni* where the demon cut off one of her gluteal muscles, she managed to escape. Later, *Indara* killed *Inkoni* by slashing him from one shoulder to the opposite armpit.[34] This myth shows how *Lai*, *Ndara* and *Koni* are extraordinary beings that are also known in the area I researched, though with slightly changed names and having been downgraded from the status of gods to that of giants or demons. The 'i' added to the beginning of the name by people in this area could simply be a difference of dialect.

The female *tau walia* Indo Pino believed in three gods. The existence of these three gods (one of the sky, one of the ground, and of the spirit world) could be indicative of an intermediate phase between belief in the *Pue Binatang* only and the ditheism involving both *Pue Lamoa* and *Pue Ri Arantana*. Nowadays, the most common idea is that Wana religion is monotheistic, and that it has just one *deus otiosus*, *Pue*, who dwells in the sky. As Atkinson observes:

> Aspects of their cosmology assign roles to two lords, one above the earth and one below, and certain healing rites involve a vengeful lord of thunder. These dual roles are subsumed by the unmarked Wana term Pue (Owner or Lord), the creator and overseer of the world. It may very well be that Pue has assumed a more central place in Wana discourse as a result of contact with Muslims and Christians.
>
> (Atkinson 1983: 691)

Of course, the structures described in these passages are not clear and definitive, and it is possible to find contradictory information that complicates interpretations. Indo Pino once told me about the existence of many small *pue*, the *pue* of rivers, animals and plants, and this clearly suggests an animist period.

> Indo Pino: There is a small *pue* in the river.
> G. S.: Is there a *pue* in the trees?
> Indo Pino: There is a *pue* in the trees and in animals too.[35]

Indeed, the presence of divine beings who act as protectors of the natural elements is found in many other shamanic religions in which there is a 'lord of animals' (Balzer 1997; Eliade 1972; Müller 2001). This kind of belief is typical of nomadic cultures that base their survival on hunting and on the benevolence of nature. Of the young people I interviewed, none was willing to confirm the existence of these small *Pue*, and this leads me to suspect that belief in the spirits of natural elements is a remnant of an archaic state of the Wana religion. Indo Pino was already aged when I met her, and since she was born in one of the inner villages, Posangke, it is possible that her early education came from people who had experienced little contact with the Dutch, and with world religions, and thus had maintained ancient beliefs.

To understand the Wana religious system, it is necessary here to present the basics of Wana mythology. During fieldwork, I tried to collect as many mythical tales as possible, including through meeting the village chief of Lambentana; Apa Kode, a man famous for his mythical and musical knowledge. I have since cross-referenced the stories recounted to me by Indo Pino, Apa Rau, Jango and Apa Kode with scarce bibliographic sources on the topic. I have tried to organize the stories into a linear and sequential order, but this task is very hard when faced with the complex logic of the mythical. When not stated otherwise, the following stories are a mix of the different versions I have collected from my informants during my two fieldworks. For Wana people, mythological stories are something that must be told sparingly and almost never in a complete form since they believe that the narration of the entire mythology could bring the world to an end. Apa Rau[36] and other shamans told me that the only way to avoid this danger would be to make a great sacrifice of chickens that would calm the spirits and *Pue*, allowing the complete telling of the mythology over seven days and seven nights. I will explore these ideas further at a later point, while discussing Wana ideas of space-time.

According to the stories I gathered, in the beginning there was only the sea. One day, *Pololoisong*, the Wana trickster, asked *Pue* to create the world. *Pue* placed the first land onto the world in the form of the holy mountain/axis mundi *Tunda n'tana*,[37] and continued his creation following the requests of *Pololoisong*.[38] *Tunda n'tana* was connected to the sky, *suruga*, through a vine called a *vaiansivangu*, but the *vaiansivangu* was gnawed at and severed by a mouse, causing the separation of the sky and the earth. This ended mythical space-time and signalled the definitive departure of *Pue* from humanity. It was also an event necessary for the survival of humanity, since the nearness of the sky to the ground made the temperature too high for all living beings. The separation from the *suruga* and the subsequent end of mythical space-time is a pivotal idea in Wana culture; it marks the start of what they consider to be their wretched life. The myth of the broken vine or a more general *axis mundi* can be found in other cultures too (Eliade 1972; Geertz 1973). Since the end of mythical space-time, this link between the ground and the sky has remained accessible only to certain kinds of beings (spirits and shamans).

At the beginning of time there was no night. One day, due to the extreme heat, a man called *Pue Bunku*[39] struck the sun (*eo*) with his blowpipe (*sopu*), breaking the sun into thousands of pieces that became the moon and the stars. Finally, there was the night (*wuri*), and humankind could rest from the daily heat.

At the request of *Pololoisong*, *Pue* began to create the animals. First, he created chickens, and this led to no significant changes on Earth. Then he created pigs, which started rooting around and spreading earth into the water around *Tunda n'tana* and, while the mountain became smaller, landmasses and islands were created. On another day, *Pue* created trees when *Pololoisong* asked for something to help avoid the heat. Among the trees was the special *kayu paramba*, on which money grew instead of leaves. If the *kayu paramba* had been cut down in a proper manner, it would have brought riches to the Wana people. However, *Pololoisong* did not care about the money and did not follow *Pue's* instructions for sawing down the tree. Thus, he did wrongly, allowing it to fall into the sea. *Pololoisong* used the fallen tree as a canoe to travel with the money to the West, perhaps the Netherlands, while condemning the Wana people to a life of poverty.[40] Grumblies reports that one of her interlocutors commented on the presence of the *kayu paramba* in the West in this way: '[the West] where white and rich people live. If the tree had landed on the earth, maybe you would now be poor and Wana people would be rich' (2016: 102). This quote is particularly interesting considering Aberle's idea (1970) that the motivation behind millennial movements is not poverty per se but the awareness of having much less than other people.

Pololoisong is also the creator of the first man, *Tau Santoto*. To put an end to the loneliness of *Tau Santoto*, Pue waited for the man to fall asleep then took a rib from which to create the first woman, *Delemontu*. The Islamic and Christian influences in this myth are extremely clear, but the Wana people managed to adapt it into one with highly local meanings. According to Wana thought, 'women possess "enough" ribs, but men are missing two. Whereas women have a complete set, nine on a side, men have only eight on a side. For this reason, it is said, men strap on a knife' (Atkinson 1990: 81). Therefore, the missing rib means that men are in a state of lacking, while women are complete and therefore superior. Moreover, the number of ribs possessed by each gender plays a central role in the funeral ritual *kayori*, and this will be explored in a following chapter. *Santoto* and *Delemontu* had sixteen sons, eight male and eight female, each the archetype of a human action; they were the first farmer, the first hunter and so on. Among them was also *Dungola*, the first musician, entertainer and shaman. These mythical children are called *tau Baraka* (the people of mythical space-time) and were so powerful that they could make anything appear in front of them just by closing an eye and pronouncing a spell: 'Adi adi of mother and father, mine is the truest (knowledge); I just have to open my eyes' (Atkinson

1989: 43). *Pololoisong*'s departure to the West ended this golden era in which these mythical people lived, as they also left to go to *Joe n'tana* (the place at the end of the world). One day, however, they will return to begin a new mythical era. This belief seems clearly linked to the myth of the eternal return, explained in detail by Eliade (1971), and found in many cultures.

Powerful numbers

Based on the mythical tales and always present in Wana religious life and in all the rituals are the powerful (because they are related to the power of myth) numbers three (*togo*) and seven (*pitu*). We will find them appearing often in descriptions and analyses of the rituals, and the reader should keep in mind that, due to their power they use in the rituals, it is no coincidence. Three is a powerful number in many cultures, including Christianity (with the Trinity and Jesus being resurrected on the third day after his death), Judaism (with the Three Patriarchs and the Torah being divided into three parts) and Buddhism (with the Triple Bodhi and the three jewels). *Dungola*, the first shaman, was able to continue a healing ritual for three nights in a row, and Atkinson testifies to the fact that the largest shamanic ritual, which was celebrated together with the harvest festival, the *salia* (also called the *masalia*), used to last three, or more rarely, seven nights.[41] Three is a number also present in the *molawo* ritual and in the *kayori*. Humans possess three souls, there are three mountains balancing the world (which Wana people believe to be flat), and there were three Wana gods at a certain point in time.

Likewise, seven is a powerful number present in many shamanic cultures, including for the Khanty, Tatars and the Samoyedic people (Eliade 1971). The number seven is also present in Buddhism, where seven steps led the Buddha to the top of the cosmic world (Eliade 1971), and in Christianity, with the seven gifts of the Holy Spirit and the sacraments, while there are seven Great Holy Days in the Jewish year. Elsewhere, the traditional Menorah has seven branches.

For the Wana people, seven days are needed for a complete telling of the *katuntu* (mythology), and the same number of days spent in the jungle is needed for a new *tau walia* to gain their powers. Similarly, a feast is organized for the deceased in the afterlife seven days after death. According to myth, seven springs created the two lakes near Marisa, there are seven worlds of spirits, and seven mythical chickens. Most importantly, the number seven symbolizes the entire life span (Atkinson 1989: 160), and for this reason it has a central role in the *kayori*. In contrast, the successive numbers of eight and nine are often related to death.

It is not the aim of this section to offer an exhaustive list of all the times the numbers three and seven recur in Wana life and rituality, especially because they appear so ubiquitously and in aspects as diverse as medicine preparation and mythology. My intention is to make the readers aware of their importance and to prepare them to recognize the value of these numbers every time they arise as this book progresses.

Tempo

Another important element of Wana culture is time. It is strongly interrelated with mythology and the people's current state of perceived wretchedness, and it is an important factor to consider when seeking to understand Wana culture. In fact, for Wana people, the concept of time is a weak concept; they usually measure time with spatial terms, causing an overlapping of space and time. When asked about the time required to go from one village to another, a Wana person might reply by listing the number of *gunung* (hills and mountains) and rivers there are between the two villages. Moreover, Wana people do not keep time; traditionally they do not have birthdays, years, months, weeks or names for days of the week. All of these are concepts that have been incorporated into Wana life recently. The term used as an equivalent for 'time' is clearly borrowed from the outside, and from the Christians in particular. Instead of the Indonesian term *uaktu*, Wana people use the term *tempo* (from the Latin *tempus*). Understanding the way Wana people conceptualize time, especially mythical space-time, is central to understanding Wana worldviews.

In Western cultures, people usually think about time as a linear and measurable entity. This is illustrated by the arrow of time, which was developed by the British astronomer Arthur Eddington (1948). Time is depicted as an arrow in which the past moves to the future, passing through the present. In this way, an event can be clearly placed on the arrow, and the idea of cause-effect is clearly shown.

Wana time, on the other hand, is cyclical and past and myth often overlap. Wana time can be divided into mythical space-time, the present and the return of mythical space-time. With also a liminal status when the memory of the past gradually becomes mythological space-time. The golden era of mythical space-time ended with a traumatic event, the separation of the human and the spiritual worlds, and with the *tau Baraka* (the people of myth) leaving Wana land to go to the edge of the world. Since that moment, the Wana people have lived in an eternally wretched present, in which every day is the same, and years, weeks and months are not counted. There is no continuity between the present and the past or future. Even if there is a clear separation between the present and the mythical era, the past is gradually absorbed by it, and what is not directly witnessed anymore becomes an event of mythical space-time. For example, when researching the arrival of the gongs in the forest – musical instruments that are used prominently in several forms of ritual – my informants told me that they were present *dari pertama* (from the first time), even though it is much more likely that the gongs arrived in the forest 'only' 100 years ago. After the end of mythical space-time, Wana people started to live in the present, but it is a wretched present that will end only when another event occurs, the return of the *tau Baraka*, marked by a cataclysm that restores mythical space-time and closes the circle.

Alfred Gell affirms that for indigenous people profane time 'is concrete, immanent and process-linked' (1992: 17), but this is completely untrue for Wana people. For them, profane time does not have any value and is not counted. Indeed, human-scale measures of time are not considered significant at all. As mentioned before, Wana people do not count years, and they do not have special time markers to distinguish normal days from special ones, such as annual festivals or birthdays. Women return to work on the same day that they give birth, as they are not inclined to attach particular value to that day, and recording a person's age is quite a new practice, making it almost impossible to know the age of many of my interlocutors. When during our period in the field together, Grumblies and I celebrated her birthday, our Wana friends did not completely understood what we were doing and were puzzled by our practices. The only recurrent event in Wana life is the *patunku*, a harvest festival. But its frequency is not stable, depending on how successful the harvest is, an element that could not happen for entire decades, and it is not held systematically in the same month. Combined with the fact that not all village areas celebrate the festival on any given year and in the same period of the year, this means that it is difficult to keep track of the passing of years in Wana life.

This all means that Wana people live in a kind of eternal present. It is important to consider that Morowali is located just one parallel south of the equator. Thus, each day has the same amount of daytime and night-time of all the other days;

roughly twelve hours. Days are essentially not culturally distinguished from each other until the special one that that will mark the return of the *tau Baraka*, thus restoring mythical space-time and closing the circle. This particularity of the Wana culture reminded me of how people use to say '*moviti ddocu*' (move on the spot) to mean 'don't move' in certain parts of Sicily, Italy. Wana people move because they get older and see new generations grow up, but nothing truly changes; history does not become part of their story. Ultimately, it is as if they are simply moving on the spot, occupying an eternal present. The situation seems to fit the fourth variant of time theorized by Gurvich: the cyclical time that has a 'motionless' or 'static' quality (1961: 21). According to Leach, a better definition would be 'alternating time' instead of cyclical time (Leach 1961: 125). He observes that this kind of time is not a cycle but 'a sequence of oscillations between polar opposites: night and day, winter and summer, drought and flood, age and youth, life and death' (Leach 1961: 125). Indeed, Leach's idea is partially useful in describing the Wana situation. The alternation, through the rituals, of mythical and profane time creates this oscillation between polar opposites, an alternation that will end only when mythical space-time returns to the *Tana Wana*, its original and rightful place. Ultimately, the situation seems to reflect a combination of cyclical and alternating ideas of time, with micro-reality (profane space-time) formed by a cyclical repetition of days, seasons and years, but interrupted by macro-reality (mythical space-time), and thus creating an alternation between the two.

The phrase *moviti ddocu* also raises the possibility that, for Wana people, the concept of time is more akin to Western ideas of space. Apa Kode told me that the French documentary makers Journet and Nougarol spoke the language of heaven, the same language that is spoken in mythical space-time, because that is where they live. In other words, mythical space-time has not ended but has been moved to a simultaneous existence somewhere else. This brings about the wretched time in which Wana people live nowadays, a time that seems almost coterminous with the *Tana Taa*, a spatial notion. The time experienced by Wana people is considered qualitatively different from the time experienced by people in the West; the latter are considered to be living in mythical space-time. They believe that due to the arrival there of the *kayu paramba* (money tree), all the people who live in the West are rich and free of problems. All the objects I carried were considered special because they were possessions of someone from mythical space-time. For example, my phone was thought to have special functions and capabilities (being waterproof, unbreakable, usable in the forest and so on) because it was a possession of a mythical Westerner.

Rituals

The Wana people have many religious rituals. Some of them are disappearing and have become rarer than others, and I attempt here to outline how they are organized. In doing so, I will compare Kruyt's data from the Taronggo area in 1928 with Atkinson's from the northern part of the jungle in 1979, and my own, from the Marisa, Taronggo and Lambentana areas in 2011 and 2016.

During his stay of just two months among the Wana people, Kruyt, a missionary from the Netherlands, was exposed to different expressions of shamanic power. He attempted to organize these expressions in order of their power and importance. The first was *walia mangepe*, which Atkinson calls 'the lowest level' (Atkinson 1989: 207); this is a type of cure that I also encountered. In these small domestic rituals, the *tau walia* extracts objects[42] of a size not visible to normal people from the bodies of patients, by sucking them out or through cleaning the patient with the *pompolonzu* (the ritual cloth) while reciting one or more *do'a* (spell). Atkinson explains that Kruyt's next level is *walia mantende* (Atkinson 1989: 207), a ritual in which, through a long chant (*patoe*), the *tau walia* requests Pue Lamoa to remove the hooks (*mata mpea*) that are afflicting the patient but are non-visible to normal people. While Atkinson knew this ritual by the same name, in the area in which I researched, it is called *molawo*. This is a dangerous and rare ritual that not all shamans are able to perform; Atkinson identifies this ritual by the name of *molawo maneo*, the 'crooked' *molawo*. The term indicates a ritual in which the performer travelled to the place of *Pue Lamoa*, while a journey to *Pue* (the benign god) was called *molawo manoto*, or 'straight' *molawo* (Atkinson 1989: 199). The next ritual outlined by Kruyt is *walia moganda* (Atkinson 1989: 207), which Atkinson encountered as *mabolong*, and I knew as *momago*. The term *momago* was used by the communities studied by Atkinson to refer to all shamanic rituals (Atkinson 1989: 211), while the ritual I explore in this book is *mabolong* or *moganda*. These three names all seem to describe the same ritual, which I will analyse in next chapter. Finally,

At the top of Kruyt's hierarchy are *to walia mamparada woto ntongku*, 'the priests who climb the mountain slopes (where the walia-spirits live) along a ladder.' These priests thus do not await the arrival of the helping spirits, but seek them out in their habitat. Kruyt does not mention traveling to the Owner (*Pue NdA.*). He goes on the explain that the spirit familiars let down a ladder for the shamans to use to reach them. This mediation takes place in the *mosalia*, a great ritual performed at most once a year to promote the health and well-being of a community.

(Atkinson 1989: 207)

Table 1 The description of a Wana ritual and, when applicable, the term used by each source to indicate that specific ritual

Kruyt (1928)	Atkinson (1974–6)	Scalici (2011–16)	Ritual
Walia mangepe	*Walia mangepe*	*Walia mangepe*	The shaman, without recourse to the spirits, ejects objects from the body of the patient
Walia mantende	*Walia mantende*	*Molawo*	Ritual in which the hooks, whose presence in the body is caused by *Pue Lamoa*, are removed from the patient
Walia moganda	*Mabolong*	*Momago*	Shamanic night ritual, accompanied by the sound of the gongs and drum (*ganda*)
Walia momparada woto ntongku	*Walia momparada woto ntongku*	N/A	Ritual over three or seven nights, during which shamans heal the whole community
N/A	*Molawo*	N/A	Mother of all of the rituals. A one-night ritual, during which the *tau walia* travels directly to *Pue*
Molawo	N/A	N/A	Shamanic chanting during the *walia mamparada woto ntongku*

Neither I nor the two scholars who came before me managed to see this ritual. The scheme that follows summarizes the similarities and differences found by each of these three scholars at different periods in time and in different geographical areas.

The *molawo*

One of the most intriguing details highlighted by Table 1 is that the term *molawo* is used to indicate a different occasion in each period of study and in each area studied. For Kruyt, it is simply a chant that is part of a larger ritual, and for Atkinson it is the mother of all rituals. For my own informants, it is a rare ritual, in which one *tau walia* chants for a whole day (in keeping with Kruyt's observations), enacting a journey to *Pue Lamoa*. This is considered the most powerful ritual of all, and not all *tau walia* know it; perhaps in this powerfulness, there a link to the mother-of-all-rituals status described by Atkinson. The *molawo* is quite a rare event; in a full year, I had the opportunity to attend this ritual just once, and even on that occasion, I couldn't assist it in its integrity. I have seen no indications that either Grumblies (who carried out one year of fieldwork) or Journet and Nougarol (who have worked with Wana people for twenty years) ever managed to observe one. On the occasion that I did so, I was walking in the jungle with my guide and our friend, the *tau walia* Apa Ingus, and I was unprepared to record the entire ritual. Fortunately, though, the *molawo* consists of four repeated parts, and I was able to record at least one iteration of each of these four parts.

There are three reasons that make this ritual not as common as the *momago*. First, it is considered only as a last resort. It is only when the *momago* and the Western medicine have failed that people organize a *molawo*.[43] Second, not every *tau walia* is able to officiate this ritual, but only the most knowledgeable, making it harder to find a *tau walia* able to perform it. Finally, this ritual is dangerous. The *tau walia* engages directly with the vengeful god *Pue Lamoa*, and the illness of the patient could end up being transferred to one of the few participants, or to the *tau walia* themselves. The absence of instrumental music, playfulness, a large participation and food create a severe atmosphere unique among the Wana rituals. In fact, there were only eight people present on this occasion: the *tau walia* Apa Danto, the patient, the chief-village Apa Ede, a woman and her child, my guide Ajeran, Apa Ingus and I. This means that only five of the eight people presents were actually expected at the ritual, and three of them were central participants, the *tau walia*, the patient and the *tau walia*'s assistant. It is not only music that is forbidden during this ritual, but all loud noise is taboo, perhaps as it recalls the thunder sent by the vengeful god *Pue Lamoa*, god of thunder. At the same time, music is not required because the core purpose of this ritual is not to call the spirits but instead to mediate between the *tau walia* and *Pue Lamoa*. During the *molawo*, the *tau walia* meets *Pue Lamoa* and asks the god to free the patient from the hooks that are pulling at his or her flesh. Disease is imagined as something concrete, as an 'illness' that can be spat away or that takes the form of hooks that can be removed.

The *molawo* takes place during the day in small huts in the forest that are usually used to give refuge to travellers and workers in the paddy. Inside the hut, I witnessed the sick person lying on the floor – he had a respiratory problem – with the *tau walia*, Apa Dende, on his right side and Apa Ede on the left assisting the *tau walia*. Sitting close to the patient, the *tau walia* held two tied-together green sugar canes perpendicular to the floor and began chanting while moving the sugar canes back and forth. Occasionally, he took a break to breathe again and to chew some betel leaf, while the other people chatted. The *tau walia* seemed embarrassed to have me around, and the ill man seemed to be asleep, for he did not speak or open his eyes.

Once the first part of the ritual was complete, the *tau walia* took a chicken, and spat into its anus to cleanse it. Sadly, I was not able to elicit an explanation for these actions. Meanwhile, the woman covered the patient with a long cloth, and the chicken was covered with a t-shirt. Any contact between the man and the chicken must be avoided as the ritual would fail if the two touch each other in any way; the purpose of the ritual is to transfer the illness from the patient to the ritual tools, and any contact between the man and the animal would break the flow of the disease from one being to the other. After the ritual, the chicken cannot be touched, killed, or eaten because touching it would mean contracting the life-threatening illness that has been extracted and that the chicken now carries.

The *tau walia* sat beside the patient, behind his back, passing the bird in circular motions over the patient's body while singing. During this ritual, the *tau walia* sang the same chant three times while moving the animal from the patient's head to his feet and another three times while moving it from the feet to the head. Near the end of the chant, the singing and the movement became slightly faster. When this part of the ritual finished, the chicken was put away and the length of cloth was removed from the patient's body.

The *tau walia*, still sitting near the patient, began to pat the patient with the sugar canes, starting from the head and moving slowly down to the feet. He continued to sing while doing so and there was a clear connection between the rhythm of the song and the *tau walia*'s movements. A little more time was spent patting the feet before the *tau walia* patted the canes on his own hand. This patting was repeated three times, going from the head to the feet, and another three times going from the feet to the head.

After these six passages, the *tau walia* put away the cane and took out a piece of cloth. This was passed over the patient's body, the action accompanied by the *tau walia*'s chanting. He did this three times, each time starting from the head and finishing on the feet, and each time placing the used cloth inside a larger one and then picking this up to continue. Again, this action was repeated three times from the head to the feet and three times from the feet to the head. The movement from the head to feet and vice versa could be a representation of time; dramatizing the path of the sun could be a way of helping the *tau walia* to obtain control over time and thus to restore mythical time. Likewise, the disposal of the ritual instruments at the end of the *molawo* is strongly linked to the sun and the sky; one sugar cane is buried pointing in the direction of the rising sun, while the other is placed on the patient's roof, pointing towards the setting sun. The cloths are placed on the roof, halfway between the patient (on the ground) and *Pue Lamoa* (in the sky).

Unlike in the *momago*, taboos and vows play an important role in the *molawo*. In the seven days that follow the ritual, the patient is not allowed to do certain things:

(1) Leave the house. More generally, it is forbidden to touch the ground.
(2) Touch metals. This is linked to the fact that metal attracts lightning, and *Pue Lamoa* is the god of lightning.
(3) Eat meat.
(4) Become exposed to loud noise, such as music or the sound of scooters. Apa Ede told me that loud noises are also connected with thunder, and also that during the ritual a loud noise could shock the patient.
(5) Speak inappropriately – in other words, to gossip or swear.
(6) Work.
(7) Touch fire or get too close to it. The heat can also be linked to lightning.

The *tau walia* too must avoid certain actions and circumstances, depending on the type of disease that the sufferer was inflicted with. For example, in the case of rheumatism, the *tau walia* cannot eat spicy food, and in the case of chickenpox or measles, they cannot eat food of a red colour. The *walia* (spirit) indicates what a *tau walia* can or cannot do at the end of the ritual. It is clear how these prohibitions and vows are strongly related to the characteristics of the illness, becoming a perfect externalization of the ideas behind the sympathetic magic theorized by Frazer (1889),[44] in which resembling or the symbolic association between object, events or people can be used to influence an event. This kind of thought will play an important role in exploring the relationships between the non-visible and the spiritual world and will be discussed in later chapters.

Music[45]

Music will be another key topic of this work, reflecting its importance to the Wana people themselves. There is no ritual without instrumental (*momago*) or sung music (*molawo* and *kayori*), and due to its peculiarities, music is the perfect medium to control spirits and emotion.[46] The relationship between music, spirits, and emotions and how it intertwines with the visible and non-visible will be explored in a following chapter. In this section, my aim is to lay out basic information of a music culture that has never been documented before, providing a basis for understanding the roles of music in Wana life and rituality.

Wana leisure music is experiencing a period of great crisis; currently traditional music is a matter for a few elders, who still own and use the few musical instruments in circulation. The young are great music lovers but are much more interested in Indonesian pop music. The passion for this music is so strong that they buy mobile phones just to listen to MP3 recordings of it, there being no telecommunications signal in the jungle; the phones are given to them by friends and relatives from outside the forest. Playing the guitar is very common among young people, and they mainly use the instrument to play pop hits. I received many requests for new strings from my trips to Palu. It seems that music is maintaining its importance in Wana society, even though the traditional forms are being replaced by modern mainstream ones. Indeed, after centuries of vitality and presence in the community, Wana traditional music seems to be approaching the end of its time, and documenting and safeguarding this treasure has been a major motivation for me.

It has not been easy to approach this tradition. This is not because of a lack of Wana interest in sharing their music with me, but because of the difficulty in finding and reconstructing musical instruments and, ultimately, finding players. Often, people do not dedicate much care towards their instruments; they are, in fact, placed in the corners of their houses or between roof inlets and are often abandoned there for years. Usually, an unusable instrument is not replaced (again reflecting the idea of that which is not needed is also not being wanted), effectively reducing the number of specimens and the possibility of their discovery by new generations. During my stay, I found with difficulty only two *geso* (spike fiddles), two *popondo* (chest resonators) and three *tulali* (flutes); for the other instruments, I had to find people able to make them. Even if traditional music is disappearing, the strong cultural connection between music and the non-visible is still strong and crucial to understand Wana rituality and human–spirit relationships. As Steven Friedson notes 'music makes translucent the boundary between human and spirit' (1996: 100). As we will see, a few of these instruments have a direct connection with the non-visible world, and they are able to affect material, emotional and spiritual realities with their sounds.

Wana people have a great awareness of the sound quality that an instrument must possess, and the choice of materials is always aimed at achieving the best possible result. Even when forced by the lack of materials, for instance by building resonance boxes from plastic containers, the Wana always want to obtain the desired sound. They are also very careful and critical about the musical instruments built by other people; I encountered some instruments that had been built by people considered not up to the task, and these people were widely criticized for their sloppy work.[47]

Many Wana people have great practical knowledge about music but do not possess a specific vocabulary; in fact, there are no words for 'music' or 'rhythm', while they do clearly distinguish instrumental music (*krambangan*) from that for single voice or for voice and instrumental accompaniment (*linga-linga*). In addition, words do not distinguish clearly between the intensity and the pitch of a sound; the word *malangan* means both 'high-pitched' and 'strong/intense', while the term *rede* is used to indicate a low-pitched and a low-intensity sound. Each note is simply called *soo* (sound), thus a note, any note, played on an instrument is called 'name of the instrument' *soo*. For example, a note on the flute will be simply called *tulali soo* (flute's note). The lack of specific names for the different *soo* has practically forced me to use Western terminology to indicate Wana musical intervals and sounds. It is extremely important to note that from the Wana point of view, the timbre is a way more important musical parameter than the melody. In fact, the same melody played by different instruments, or even different versions of the same instruments, is perceived as different. Indo Pino played the same melody for hours on different flutes while explaining to me that they were different music because played on different flutes. The term for something in tune is *matino*, while something out of tune is *ta matino*. *Ta* meaning 'no'.

This linguistic approach to their traditional music has created some issues regarding the classification[48] of their musical instruments. Unfortunately, I wasn't able to find a shared concept of instruments classification, this doesn't mean that certainly Wana people don't have any, but that if they have one, I wasn't able to understand and extrapolate from my experience among them. It is possible that the instrument classification was simply given from granted by the Wana, how it happened for many other elements of their culture that they didn't feel the need to tell me about or to explain to me because they were obvious to them, they were an intrinsic part of their life, and like we don't feel the need to talk about our breathing when we talk about our day with a friend, because we give it for granted, they didn't feel the need to explain to me some elements of their life because they were how they were *dari pertama* (from the first time. From the beginning of time.). In other words, they simply are, and everybody should know about them because they have always existed and will always exist. For this, no explanation is due.[49] A possible classification of them according to the Wana would be too fragmented and not very practical for the reader. A division by material would be almost pointless because the Wana never even mention such categorization and too often their instruments are made of makeshift tools, such as plastic bowls instead of coconut, fishing rod instead of horsehair or *enau* bark instead of skin. It could be possible to put all the flutes, *tutali*, in the same family, but at the same time, the *tulai* and the *popondo* (single-stringed baton zither) are usually presented as a couple due to their link to courtship and gender. But this division would leave out all the other instruments that do not have a direct connection with the invisible world of emotion and spirits or to a specific gender. We saw before how the Wana value the timbre over the melody, but classify their musical instrument based on their timbre would also be difficult because even two models of the same instruments are considered to produce different music because they have a different timbre, and it would be impossible to divide them into groups. Due to the lack of a better, or an indigenous, way to organize their musical instruments, I have decided to use the classical Sachs and Hornbostel (1914) system of classification (idiophones, membranophones, chordophones and aerophones), widely familiar to the academics, and to indicate, when present, the relationship between different instruments.

The reader is kindly invited to visit giorgioscalici.eu to take advantage of the possibility of not only being able to see the instruments, but also being able to listen to them and learn how they are made. I am actively working on this cultural archive to allow both Wana and not Wana an easy access to a precious but endangered heritage. While preservation often brings its challenges, including the imposition of a predetermined criteria (Churchill 2006; de Jong 2007), it is an important task that must have at is core the point of view and the desires of the community. Indeed, the Wana deeply believe in sharing what they have, they even arrived to invite all the unemployed Italians to go live in their land because there is enough land for everybody, so they are both glad and proud to share their knowledge to everybody who is eager to learn from them.

Thus, the Wana musical instruments are as follows.

Idiophones

Yori is an idioglot, mouth harp, with a case made to carry it safely while travelling.[50] Similar instruments, even with the container, are present among the Hmong of Vietnam, *dan moi* (Ó Briain 2018), the Lahu people of China and

Thailand, *ata* (Fairfield 2018), or among many communities in the Philippines (Maceda 1998), just to name a few. The instrument is made from the palm of the *enau* tree; from the plant, they obtain a thin rectangle in which the *gila* (lamina) is obtained and this acts as a vibrating body. Small holes are made on the sides of the instruments, through which two thin chords of bark are passed and fixed. These strings are used both to hold the instrument (with the left hand) and to make the blade vibrate (when the other is pulled with the right hand).

The rhythmic pulling of the string causes the vibration of the foil, and consequently the emission of the sound. The case, called the *tonga yori*, has a tubular shape and is made of bamboo. Once the *yori* is stored in its case, strings are tied around the outside to secure it and to allow it to be safely transported. Apa Sudin once told me: 'We played this when we did not have the guitar.'

Although in the past this instrument was very widespread, the use of the *yori* now seems to have completely disappeared. Because of bad eyesight, the man who made the instrument for me had to be helped by his son, who had never seen the instrument before (this happened in 2011). As might be expected, the long period of obscurity for this instrument also meant that I could not find any skilled players. People I interviewed knew how to make the instrument sound, but they did not have the knowledge to play whole melodies.

Tulalo is a friction idiophone. A bamboo tube is partially carved, so as to obtain from the tube two long tongues of cane, joined at the handle (*konkonya*), which maintains the natural cylindricity. Two *suru* (small holes) are made in it on the opposite side of the handle. The sound is produced by the hitting of one of the two tongues on the palm of the free hand; the supporting hand acts on the holes, in order to modulate the heights of the sound produced.

My informants told me that the instrument was exclusively used to provide accompaniment to the other instruments. This instrument has almost disappeared and is no longer used.

Ngonngi – the gongs, or in the Wana language *ngonngi* – are a 'recent'[51] introduction into the religious and musical practices of this culture.[52] 'In many cultures, gong ensemble music in ritual is seen as the actual medium through which the human and spiritual worlds merge' (Pugh-Kitingan 2012: 149). An essential element in a *momago*, the main shamanic ritual, is the ensemble of ritual instruments: two gongs, one big and one small, and a wooden drum. A similar situation has been observed for the rituals of the Taman of Borneo, where the ritual music is played with drums, gongs and bowls (Bernstein 1997: 89).

The smaller of the two gongs used during the ritual has an average diameter of 26 cm, while the larger has a diameter of around 41 cm. The instruments are not made locally; village chief Apa Rahu and other people told me that the large gong of Marisa village was brought into the village of Kayu Poli around 30 years ago by a man called Nyole. The small gong in Taronggo was brought in 2010 by Anna Grumblies, who had purchased the gong in Bali.[53] The large gong in Taronggo village seems to have been present in the jungle for at least 40 years.

(Scalici 2019: 132)

In earlier times the *tetebua*, or its variant *tamburu*, was used during the *momago*. The gongs, that are also considered a community's good, are usually guarded by a *tau walia* or village chief. Female *tau walia* Indo Pino used to keep the gongs of the Marisa area when she was alive.

Membranophones

Ganda indicates an hourglass drum, about 50 cm high, with double membrane; on one side, with a diameter of about 18 cm, *biawak*[54] or snakeskin is stretched out, while the other membrane, also about 18 cm in diameter, is made of deerskin or couscous.[55]

For the *momago*, the *ganda* is hung from the ceiling between the two gongs and played by two people positioned on either side of the drum. The reptile skin is struck with a bamboo strip knotted at the end, while the mammal skin is struck with two wooden drumsticks.

In the central part there is a decoration and a small hole, less than a centimetre in diameter, used to improve the sound of the instrument.

A dry corn grain is inserted inside the instrument. It is usually put inside the drums to increase the sound produced; it is reasonable to hypothesize an apotropaic function of this small detail. As Jules Combarieu observes, musical instruments place in the magician's hands 'des parcelles de tous les règnes de la nature: ils sont faits de roseau ou de bambou, de coques de certains fruits, de métal, de bois dur, de pierre (sonore), de peaux d'animaux, de carapaces, d'os, de cornes évidées, de soies, de rafia tordu, de crins, de boyaux … ; ils constituent un résumé du cosmos'[56] (Combarieu 1982: 260–1). Just as wood represents the plants of the forest, animal skin represents animals in their entirety, oviparous and mammals, and corn represents the cultural world of the village. Dried corn is also used as a unit of measurement to indicate the amount of the fine that must be paid in the event of not completely lawful marriages and was used, in the past, also for a variant of the *kayori* (funeral) in which grains were placed inside a coconut and shaken. A grain of corn was placed inside a small rattle, called *diodio*, which was tied to the warriors' machetes to attract women.

Like the *tau walia*, the drum is also a common good and it hasn't a single owner because the *momago* tends above all to reaffirm the *kasintuwu* (mutual support) and the importance of living inside a community.

The Wana also told me about the *kratu* (the war drum), but I never saw one. It is tall and narrow, with a single membrane made of *rusa* (deerskin) on the upper and wider side of the drum while the other side was open, similar to the Filipino *dabakan*. Possibly derived from the container used to beat the rice. The *kratu* was used for the *tongkepuno tau tau* (war call). According to the tales, it seems that a mythical *kratu* is kept in one of the caves surrounding Uewaju but has been turned into stone in the mythical space-time. It was also used to accompany the *mamose*, a war dance dating back to when the Wana were head-hunters.

Chordophones

Popondo is a single-stringed baton zither, equipped with a bamboo connection element to the coconut rigid resonator.[57] This does not act as a bridge. The string is tensioned by a sagittal peg and runs on the narrowest side of the rectangle fitting on the sides of the support, of which the tuning seems to vary between a quartertone below and a quartertone above F3. With one hand, the player strikes the string with their fingertips, while the fingers of the other hand are used to modulate the sound. It consists of a sound box made of half a coconut that rests on the player's chest, a wooden part, parallel to the chest, on which one string is fixed, and a piece of bamboo that connects the coconut to the wood. In the past, the string was made from the *enau*, the same tree from which the *yori* is made. This kind of instrument is extremely ancient and widely present in the Southeast Asia. We can still find Bar zither player among the Khmer of Cambodia, *kse diev* (Sam-Ang 2008), and Vietnam (Nguyễn 2008).

As in many other Wana musical compositions, melodies played on this instrument are limited in range to the interval of a fourth (F-B)[58] and, like many other Wana compositions, the player alternates linear melodic intervals and repeated notes (the initial F and the final G). Similar melodic structures can be also found in their songs. The melodies of this instrument are very repetitive and, again, the timbre is the main feature of this instrument; in fact, it has a particularly evanescent sound.

A masculine counterpart of the *tulali* (flute), these two instruments are present in the origin myth of death and in courtship practices. Also, like the flutes, it can be decorated with the same geometric patterns that are meant to attract the attention of the opposite sex. In fact, these are the only two decorated instruments in the Wana tradition, and their uniqueness again points to a powerful love call. As Apa Ingus told me: 'There is a woman in Taronggo who, caught in jealousy, has burned her husband's *popondo*.' Indo Pino added: 'When a man plays the *popondo* under a woman's house, she will know what the man wants to drink or eat.'

Atkinson discusses how these instruments are connected to the world of spirits: 'It is not uncommon for one who is skilled at playing a musical instrument such as flute or stringed chest resonator to play haunting and plaintive songs to attract hidden beings' (Atkinson 1989: 54). There are strong connections between Wana music and the non-visible; ritual instruments recall the spirits, the *balo pombongo* evokes war, while the *tulali* and the *popondo* call up love.

Tetebua – This is a four strings bamboo zither, like those present throughout Southeast Asia, including in Malaysia (Roseman 2008: 318) and Vietnam (Nguyễn 2008: 300).[59] Before the arrival of the gongs, this was the shamanic instrument par excellence, and its use in shamanic rituals can still be found among the Temiar (Roseman 1993: 131). The connection between the bamboo zither and the gong can be found in many other Southeast Asian populations such as the Jarai of Vietnam: 'The sophisticated Jarai version (gong) is played polyphonically to imitate the gong ensembles' (Nguyễn 2008: 300) and the Philippines (Canave-Dioquino et al. 2008: 433). Among the Wana people, the instrument is more closely linked to drums; in fact, Wana people talk about the *tetebua* as a drum, and they use the word *tamburu* to refer to a slightly different version of this instrument. Apa Ede told me: 'With a big bamboo it sounds like a drum.'

The instrument is made of bamboo, preferably a short and wide piece that is conducive to obtaining a strong and deep sound, although I saw a variety of shapes and sizes ranging from 30 to 100 cm in length. On the bamboo there are four strings that are raised by placing small bridges under them. Between two of these strings a hole is made that is covered by a bamboo lamella. This lamella has its ends carved into the shape of a beak so that it can be hooked onto the two strings that support it. When struck, the lamella emits the same note as the two strings to which it is attached.

A side hole is engraved to improve the sound, but it is also used to store the sticks when the instrument is not being played. These sticks are the *votu*, which is made of bamboo and used to play the two lower strings, and the *tumbai*, which is made of wood and used to beat the central lamella and the two strings to which it is attached. The instrument can be played by two people at the same time, each with two sticks, and it can also be played with the fingers in a pizzicato style.

In the northern area of Morowali, there is a variation called *tamburu*, which has the two strings on which the lamella is fixed replaced by a single large band made from the bamboo itself. The repertoire of this instrument is much more varied and broader compared to those of the other instruments, even if the melodies are composed of only two notes.

This instrument is tuned to reproduce two notes: C3 (the lamella and the two strings attached to it) and F3 (the other two strings). It is possible that this two-note tuning is due to its ancient shamanic function, it offered the rhythmic entrainment that 'increases emotional excitement and may facilitate the experience of a different self' (Becker 2004: 147).

Geso is a single-string spike fiddle, generally tuned a quarter of a tone under C3 and almost certainly of Arabic derivation.[60] Many other stringed instruments in the Indo-Malaysian area, such as the *rebab*, are said to have been introduced in Malaysia with Islamization (cf. Schaeffner 1978: 247). It consists of a coconut resonance box, covered with lizard (*kenbosu*) or snakeskin. The wood of the *ba-a* tree is used for the handle, and much attention is paid to the personalization of this part of the instrument. A similar instrument is known as *tro* among the Khmer of Cambodia (Sam-Ang 2008) and as *erhu* in China (Thrasher 2000), but spike fiddles are present in the entire Asian Continent.

In the past, the strings were made from the fibres of the *enau* palm, but now fishing line or wire is used. The bow is made from bamboo, while the strings are still made from the fibres of the *enau* palm, which are cooked before use in order to make them more resistant. A long time ago, the bow's strings were derived from the mane of a horse (*jaran*). A fundamental accessory for the *geso* is the dammar gum that is passed on the string of the bow to increase friction.

This instrument is used, in particular, to accompany the singing of the player. Unlike many Wana musical expressions, the songs for voice and *geso* seem to demonstrate greater inventiveness and freedom. The melodic range of these songs exceeds the limit of the interval of a fourth. Usually, the same note opens the first and the third line, while another note begins the second and fourth line as well as closing all the lines and so serving as a tonal reference point for the whole piece. The instrumental music and the voice follow the same melodic structure, but it is performed by the instrument at an octave above the voice. The instrumental music dominates the text and not vice versa; in fact, Wana music adapts, through vocalic additions, a potentially infinite number of texts to a finite number of instrumental bases.

Aerophones

Balo Pombongo is a war horn made of bamboo. The distal end of the bamboo cane is cut off; the proximal one is instead closed by the natural knot of the cane. On the side, a *woro* (large hole) is made to act as an embouchure.

The instrument was not usually played outside of its war functions for fear of recalling war and other misfortunes. Wana people believe that the sound of something can recall whatever it signifies, so the act of playing war music outside of war times can bring about war.

Tulali is a bamboo ring flute with three finger holes and a mouth opening (*pagoma*)[61] similar to that of the Thai flute *khlui* (Miller, Sam-ang 1995), or the *suling* of Sunda (van Zanten 1994). It is considered a purely feminine instrument and it is closely connected to life and death; in fact, the instrument appears in the myth surrounding the funeral ritual along with its masculine counterpart, the *popondo*. It is also considered a powerful instrument of love, and it was mentioned to me several times, 'When you play the *tulali* men come to you.' Indo Pino, a powerful female *tau walia*, told me, 'Once I was playing the *tulali* in my house, my husband came, and he already knew what to do.'

As Sachs notes, 'Owing to its tubular shape, it represents the penis' (Sachs 1962: 95). This connection between flutes and sex is present in many cultures, although usually the flute is considered a masculine and not a feminine instrument, the flute seems to have charming powers everywhere. 'Among American Indians, the flute belongs greatly to lovers and love [...] Among the Sioux, young men in love learn the flute so they may woo their girls in the proper way' (Sachs 1962: 95). Likewise, the Temiar of Malaysia use the instrument in courtship (Roseman 2008: 320).

Use of the *tulali* is disappearing among Wana people; only a few old women still know how to build and play it, but most no longer have the breath to play it fluently. However, one particular melody for this instrument seems to be well known. In fact, Indo Pino, who was considered the best Wana flute player, mainly played that melody, although she told me that she played different music when played it on different flutes. This indicates that for the Wana is the timbre the musical element which gives the sense of diversity instead of the melody.

Tulali can be decorated with *rando* (decorations) of geometric patterns. After engraving, they are coloured white with a powder derived from molluscs.

Two other flutes and a clarinet are considered part of the same family as the *tulali*: the *lolove* (a three-hole spout flute that is played with the nose), the *poloi* (a three-hole transverse flute) and the *kukua* (a three-hole idioglot clarinet).

The fact that I spent four months of my fieldwork before I learned of their existence indicates these instruments have as good as disappeared. There are very few people who still know how to make these instruments, and those that were made for me were almost completely unplayable, except for one *kukua*. Even with a well-constructed instrument, it was an even greater obstacle to find anyone still capable of playing it.

This instrument is used, in particular, to accompany the singing of the player. Songs called *linga-linga* are improvised on a fixed structure of four lines (*togonjaya*) that must all end with the same vowel. In the end, we have Wana songs.[62] These songs, called *linga-linga*, are improvised on a fixed structure of four lines (*togonjaya*) that must all end with the same vowel. I once asked why a song must be four lines long and this is the answer I got: three would be too short and five too long.

The shape of these songs seems to have an Islamic influence, since the structure is very similar to that of the Malaysian *pantun*, which is of Arab derivation. The latter is a very common strophic form in the Indo-Malaysian area, formed by a rhymed quatrain (Matusky and Chopyak 2008: 234–5). It seems that the documented example of *pantun* closest to that of the Wana area comes from the Bugis people: 'After a day spent working at sea or in the fields, some Buginese and the Makassarese like to spend their evenings singing quatrains (*pantun*), sometimes improvising humorously in reply to each other's contributions. These performances are accompanied by a local zither (*kacapi*)' (Kartomi 2008: 403). *Pantun* is usually of eight syllables (Matusky and Chopyak 2008: 242), and with some exceptions it seems that it also follows this poetic structure in the Wana context. If, on one side, this poetic form gives some limitation in terms of length, on the other side the subject of these songs is extremely free and can range from love to mythology. Even if there are some songs who became widely known by many Wana or are often performed by some players, there is always space for new songs created and sung on the spot. In the past, they were used for marriage requests; in a continuous improvisation, the girl's suitor and parents argued about the possibility of a marriage.

Given the critical situation the Wana culture is going through, I decided to collect as many Wana songs as I could hear or came across, so that this art form does not disappear without leaving traces. It is fascinating to notice how in Wana songs humans are usually replaced by plants or birds. Besides the existence of seven mythical birds, giant chickens, and the theoretical link between the shamanic dance, *motaro* and the movements of the chickens,[63] the Wana culture currently does not seem deeply linked to these animals. On the contrary, plants are still one of the main sources of medicine and nutrition, and play an important role in all Wana rituals, especially the *molawo* in which a betel nut represents the patient themself.[64]

Om Suma even composed a song about me:

U'ngka nja Italia	From Italy
Jelah re Indonesia	He came to Indonesia
Ratah re tana Marisa	In the village of Marisa
Damam pali linga-linga	To look for songs

Unlike many Wana musical expressions, the songs for voice and *geso* seem to demonstrate greater inventiveness and freedom. The melodic range of these songs exceeds the limit of the interval of a fourth. Usually, the same note opens the first and the third lines, while another note begins the second and fourth lines as well as closing all of the lines and so serving as a tonal reference point for the whole piece. The instrumental music and the voice follow the same melodic structure, but it is performed by the instrument at an octave above the voice. The instrumental music dominates the text and not vice versa; in fact, Wana music adapts, through vocalic additions, a potentially infinite number of texts to a finite number of instrumental bases.

Conclusions

Within this chapter, it has been my intention to emphasize that Wana culture is not an isolated unchanging entity but an ever-adapting reality that has been shaped by the ecology, history and the relationships with the other communities and the colonial empires; it has proved itself to be a highly active, fluid and resilient culture, with many distinctive elements enduring even in the face of the strongly oppositional stances imposed from outside by laws and world religions. For Wana people adaptability has become a necessity for survival in a life that they consider wretched, but that is rich in friendship and sense of community. Wana people often told me that they are 'satu keluarga' (one family), indicating more than the literal kinship they have with the many relatives around them, they feel that all the members of the community are part of the same family: the Wana people.

At the same time, this chapter has sought to provide a cultural grounding as a foundation for understanding the two rituals which will be explored over the course of the next two chapters, the shamanic ritual *momago* and the funeral *kayori*. Mirroring my own first period of fieldwork, it has taken on the initial 'culture shock' of encountering new ways of thinking and behaving, offering a general picture of Wana culture and guidelines for becoming orientated to Wana rituality. Wana people's understanding of their own history, relationships with other groups, conceptions of time, understandings of numerical symbolism, and musical practices are key areas of concern in this work, since they deeply inform how the focal rituals unfold and the complex array of meanings communicated through them. With this knowledge, the rest of this work unfolds in much the same way as I experienced my second period of fieldwork – with a deeper level of awareness to focus on the details, to recognize focal points, and to see the connections between different elements.

The *momago*

The previous chapter gave the opportunity to the reader to encounter the world of Wana people and obtain a basic knowledge that will make it possible to engage with the rituals and to make a deeper reflection on them. This process will be similar to my second period of fieldwork, where I no longer had the shock of being immersed in an unknown environment, with little or no information at my disposal. In that second experience, I was more prepared for the rituals I was going to observe, and I had the maturity and the serenity to start focusing on the deeper level of Wana rituality and to see the significant value of the details.

In this and in the next chapter, I will describe and analyse the two most common Wana rituals: the *momago* (shamanic ritual) and the *kayori* (funeral). These two chapters add further information to the data given so far, leading towards the final chapter, which will dig deeper into the data collected and reach a new level of understanding that will expose the links between Wana values and rituals.

At this stage, I will initially explore the role and the duties of the *tau walia* and the indigenous conception of illness and what might be termed 'inner illness'. Then, I will describe the *momago*, detailing its complex structure and examining its music. I will also explore the meanings and aims of this ritual, which go well beyond the straightforward healing of the patient. In doing so, I aim to reveal the dichotomy intrinsic to the ritual: the counterpoint between the negative energies derived from illness and the playfulness that characterizes the occasion.

Encountering the *momago*

The *momago* is the most common shamanic ritual among the Wana people. It is a night-long ritual during which a group of *tau walia* enter into trance and travel between the human and the spiritual world to take care of the souls of their patients. The trance is made possible because of the ritual music, produced by two gongs[1] and a drum, which call the spirits and act as a bridge between the human and the spiritual/mythical world. The counterpoint between human and spiritual, conceived and expressed in opposing term between visible and non-visible, holds a special position in the Wana way of interpreting reality. The atmosphere of the *momago* is itself characterized by another duality, the continuous alternation of centrifugal and centripetal forces produced by the many shamanic journeys during which 'the centrifugality of the patient's vital elements is matched and conquered by the centrifugal path of the shaman and his familiar' (Atkinson 1989: 123).

These journeys are incorporated into a larger performance, during which the bystanders (both as observers and as actors) enjoy the opportunity to stay, drink and joke, contributing to the playful and chaotic atmosphere of the ritual. This dynamic, which is actually more organized that the 'chaos' I had initially seen it as, is marked by a counterpoint of opposite elements (dreadfulness vs. playfulness, centrifugal vs. centripetal, visible vs. non-visible and individual vs. community) and the role of this ritual in the survival of the entire community is a central topic that permeates this work.

The first record of the *momago* comes from the Dutch missionary Kruyt (1930). After a long period of academic neglect, almost half a century, this culture was studied in depth by the US anthropologist Jane Monnig Atkinson in the 1970s. Atkinson channelled her efforts into analysing the words of the shamanic chant of the *momago* ritual and its political role within the Wana community (1989). Reading her book, *The Art and Politics of Wana Shamanship*, convinced me to undertake my first fieldwork among Wana people, looking at the relationship between shamanism and music. While reading her publications I was also surprised to notice a lack of interest in one important element that, I think, makes the *momago* ritual so important in the lives of Wana people: ritual music. The desire to fill this gap is one of the reasons behind this research. The present chapter examines how the *momago*, supported by ritual music and religious beliefs, helps the collective in directing its emotions towards the regeneration of the emotionally wounded community.

I had spent less than three weeks inside the Morowali forest when, in February 2011, I witnessed my first *momago*. Although I did not request it, the event was organized expressly for me with the supposed intention of helping me with my research. In truth, the Taronggo villagers saw an opportunity to have a party offered by the *buleh* (rich white Westerner). At the beginning, I was quite dubious about this ritual being organized, worried about the ethical implications of the 'authenticity' of a ritual set up just for me, the researcher. Later, I understood that my moral dilemmas were products of this idea of 'authenticity', one based on the dichotomy between the original (a ritual made for the community) and the copy (a ritual made for the researcher/tourist) (Adams 1997; Hashimoto 2003). For the people I lived among, that dichotomy did not exist. They considered me only as the person who was to pay for the ritual and not as its focal point; that first ritual was an authentic *momago*. I later discovered that if there is somebody eager or able to pay for the rite, any reason is a good one to throw a *momago*; the healing of a single member is just a pretext, an incentive to encourage somebody to spend the money on the ritual. On the contrary, the real aim is for there to be a playful event that will emotionally heal the entire community, truly a moment of re-creation. Atkinson had a similar experience before discovering that 'Illness is only one excuse for a mabolong. Anticipation of misfortune, successful recoveries from previous illnesses, marriages, farming festivals, visits by prominent shamans, and a general desire to party, are all reasons to hold a mabolong' (1989: 6).

A few months later, another opportunity would present itself. I fell sick, I couldn't move my left leg, I had a high fever and I was so weak that when I tried to stand up, I fainted. Wana asked me if I wanted to organize a *momago* to be treated by a *tau walia*. At the time, inexperienced and worried about the little funding at my disposal (I was using my personal fundings), I refused the offer, but even now, after a decade, it is my biggest regret as a researcher. As we all know, the only way to become good at doing fieldwork is doing it. Mistakes are normal and common among scholars, a lesson that too often we forget to teach our students.

That first ritual quickly organized 'for me' (in their words), proved very useful for my research and my fieldwork, allowing me to start to have a first experience of a Wana shamanic ritual, and showing me how a negative event like the sickness of a person could be transformed into a positive one. Throughout the night, people joked, danced and ate in an apparently chaotic manner, although gradually an order started to become discernible. Before this first experience in the field, due to my readings on the Siberian shamanism (Balzer 1997; Müller 2001), I had always imagined shamanic rituals to be extremely serious and solemn events in which an error could anger the spirits and cause the ritual to fail. Seeing and, even more important, feeling the atmosphere that really characterizes a *momago* turned out to be an intense emotional revelation for me. That experience and dynamic deeply fascinated me and opened my eyes to a new world. Moreover, the absence of a main patient started to cast a light on the marginal or sometimes even unnecessary role of a main patient in the *momago*, giving the first hints of the real protagonist of the ritual: the community. Already in the 1970s, Atkinson underlined how 'The role of the patient at a mabolong is passive and usually minor. In fact, the patient need not even be conscious or present for treatment to occur' (1989: 124). Due to the absence of a main patient on that first occasion, the *tau walia* treated a series of adults and children for various minor issues. When there is a main patient, this individual is someone urgently in need of treatment and the most powerful *tau walia* takes care of him or her.

The Wana people's isolated rural circumstances mean that options for enjoying celebrations are limited, and the *momago* is perhaps their main form of festivity. Being an expensive event, however, it is usually held during wedding celebrations, or when there is the real need to cure somebody from 'inner illness'. This necessity forces the sick person to become a patron, the person paying for the ritual not only for their sake but also for the sake of the entire community. We start to see how *kasintuwu* (the sense of community) is at the base of the *momago*, showing how the community is more important than the single member and how life has a meaning and a direction only inside the community; this idea is already present in the *momago*, but it is pivotal in the *kayori* (funeral).

Last but not least, that ritual, almost forced on me, helped me greatly in learning how to approach the ritual and what to do or where to focus to make the best recordings and observations of it. When we go to the field the first time, everything is new and only with the experience we learn the best way to study a ritual or an event, where to put our camera and what to observe. Thus, in the end, I am still grateful for that first *momago* the Wana organized for me.

Shamans and medicine

'Inner illness' is something that cannot be cured by doctors or by using indigenous medical knowledge, because it is an illness of the soul, not of the body. Desjarlais (1992) calls the illness caused by the absence of the soul the 'loss of presence'. Shamans are often called medicine-men by many authors (Demetrio 1978; Eliade 1972; Lewis 1971; Miyazaki 2000; Winkelman 1990) but this term is inappropriate when discussing Wana shamanship. *Tau walia* do not have any more medical skills or knowledge than other members of the community, who ordinarily share a wide understanding of the medical plants growing inside the reserve and routinely use them to treat diarrhoea (*andolia*, *guampanha* and *gampu*), wounds (*koto*), colds (*umbu*), and lice and fleas (*kasiu* and *tambaole*). For more severe injuries, they resort to Western medicine, especially pills bought in small pharmacies outside the jungle,[2] and go to the local hospital in Kolonodale. The 'inner illness' that *tau walia* take care of refers to non-visible problems that affect a patient's soul; these problems include when the patient's soul gets lost, escapes as a result of strong emotion or is attacked by a *setan*. Nowadays, the term *setan* is used to refer to a wide range of different demons,[3] and is one of the many products of the influence of Christianity on Wana religion, which has provoked a simplification of their terminology.

In his monumental work on shamanism, *Le chamanisme et les techniques archaïques de l'extase*, Eliade notes that 'the Shaman is the great specialist in the human soul; he alone "sees" it, for he knows its "form" and its destiny' (Eliade 1972: 8). He continues: 'And wherever the immediate fate of the soul is not at issue, wherever there is no question of sickness (= loss of the soul) or death, or of misfortune, or of a great sacrificial rite involving some ecstatic experience (mystical journey to the sky or the underworld), the shaman is not indispensable' (Eliade 1972: 8). This description is consistent with the behaviour of Wana people, for whom shamanic services and presence are needed only to treat problems related to the soul. Rex L. Jones adds, 'One might conclude that, wherever illness has nothing to do with the "soul", shamans and shamanism will be conspicuously absent' (Jones 1968: 332–3). Wikan arrives to write 'when fright strikes, it is the spirit which is afflicted. For this reason, no medical doctor can effect a cure. Medical personnel can only aggravate the illness, perhaps beyond recall' (1989b: 33).

In my experience, even *tau walia* themselves use pills and other medicines to treat illnesses not related to the soul; once, Apa Tobi came to me asking for medicine for a toothache, while Apa Main asked me to buy some medicines from the pharmacy. Atkinson clarifies that 'medicines, in contrast to names and spells, are not a requisite for shamanhood, nor is their use a part of shamanic performance, whereas without verbal magic a shaman is not a shaman' (Atkinson 1989: 74), considering the fact that 'they treat not overt symptoms, but unseen causes' (Atkinson 1989: 75). All these affirmations are convincing, and I strongly support the idea that Wana shamanhood is strictly related to issues of the soul and not those of the body, in other words with the non-visible and not the visible. However, I must point out that I did also witness one incident suggesting that spells, in the present time at least, can be used to treat small ailments not related to the soul, such as fevers and headaches. Once, the grandson of Indo Pino, a powerful female *tau walia*, got a fever which I personally recorded as 37.8 °C/100.04 °F. He was clearly feeling terrible, shaking and complaining about the headache, until Indo Pino recited a *do'a* (spell) on the head of the child. He quickly felt better and went outside of the hut to play in the rain, without showing any adverse signs.

Nowadays, Wana culture is an agricultural one, and this already places their religious practices outside of the definition of pure shamanism given by Winkelman (1990), that requires a hunting and gathering environment. Moreover, while perfectly demonstrating all elements of a shaman/healer, agricultural and hunting magic is not performed anymore, and nor are animal spirits used. I prefer not to use the term 'healer' or 'medicine-man' because *tau walia* do not possess any special expertise in Wana medical culture beyond that which is shown by almost every member of the community. What characterizes the Wana phenomenon is a complete absence of specific medical knowledge, but an extreme specialization in matters of the spiritual/non-visible world.

The illnesses related to the soul are non-visible to common people. They are part of the spiritual reality, a world that in the past formed part of one single entity with the human realm, but which nowadays is not accessible by most humans. Only the shaman, sharing his or her status with the spirits, is able to shift from their human (visible) being to become a spiritual (non-visible) being through the control of their soul. Like in many other shamanic cultures (Eliade 1972; Roseman 1993), Wana people commonly believe human beings possess three souls: *lengke* (the shadow), *koro uli* (the blood) and *tanuana* (the 'agent of dreams'). While the *lengke* is always with his or her owner, and the *koro uli* is the soul that goes to heaven once the person dies, the *tanuana* leaves its owner every night during sleep to wander around the worlds. Wana people believe that what we see in our dreams is what the *tanuana* sees and experiences in its night wanderings. 'The tanuana is a tiny image of its owner, residing in the crown of the head at the fontanel. [...] When recounting a dream, a wana speaks of the dreamed self as "my tanuana"' (Atkinson 1989: 106). In these excursions, it is possible for the *tanuana* to be abducted or wounded by *setan*, or to get lost in the spirit realm. An intense negative emotion, such as anger or jealousy, can make the soul escape or get sick; for this reason, Wana people tend to have a resigned reaction to the negative events in their lives, often coping with pain through humour. When the soul is wounded or separated from its vessel for a long period, the person falls sick and the shaman must venture into the spirit realm, accompanied by their spirits, to find out the cause of the illness and to facilitate the eventual recovery of the soul. Marina Roseman describes the effect of the prolonged absence of the soul among the Temiar of Malaysia, a cultural community that shares many common traits with the Wana: 'Soul loss is marked by weariness, excessive sleeping, and weeping, and may lead to coma, delirium, and death' (Roseman 1990: 232). The Wana, like the Temiar and the Sakai (Porath 2013b: 8), also consider the head (specifically the area of the occipital bone)[4] to be the house of the soul, and they show similar symptoms when they have 'inner illness'. Like for the Temiar, the *tanuana* moves in the jungle with the other spirits, but the Wana conception of jungle goes well beyond the material manifestation. For Wana people, the jungle is a special place belonging to the spirits; in fact, almost all that is outside of the human realm of the village falls within the realm of the spirits, including the forest, dreams, the afterlife and even in the place of *Pue*. The human–spirit duality and its geographical representation through the centre–periphery duality lie at the heart of Wana people's understanding of the world, and it will be analysed in depth in the following chapters.

Liminality and overlapping

To succeed in their task, it is crucial for shamans to possess a wide knowledge of the non-visible world of the spirits, since travelling in the non-visible realm is dangerous and they could get lost and die. 'We should always keep in mind that shamanizing is not a spiritual nicety but an adventurous and, at times, arduous necessity fraught with dangers. At any time relations with spirits can go wrong' (Porath 2013b: 26).

In Wana culture, dreams, the afterlife and the spirit world are strongly related to each other, they even overlap sometimes. While dreaming, a Wana person becomes able to travel among the different worlds and into the afterlife. During this time as a pure soul separated from the body, they can do almost anything that was possible during mythical time; they return to that time when humans and spirits lived together. Wana people conceptualize dream space-time as something concrete in which the soul can become trapped forever. It is useful to note that 'Shamans' songs are likened to lullabies. (As one mother explained the difference, the former require magical spells and the latter do not) (Atkinson 1989: 284). It is not the right place and time to successfully explore the relationship between trance, healing rituals, movement and sleep but I would like to offer a short but, I hope, fruitful reflection. Plato, in his work *Laws*, discusses the role of music, exercise and dance in education offering an interesting testimony that stimulated my mind:

> [W]hen mothers want their restless children to go to sleep they do not employ rest, but, on the contrary, motion-rocking them in their arms; nor do they

give them silence, but they sing to them and lap them in sweet strains; and the Bacchic women are cured of their frenzy in the same manner but the use of the dance and of music.

(Plato 2004: 75)

While Plato's intentions did not include discussing music and trance in shamanic rituals, I see a useful connection between Atkinson's suggestions regarding lullabies and magic and Plato's reasoning, especially considering the similarity between the male shamanic dance and the movement of Wana cots (Figure 1). We will soon see how the *motaro*, the male shamanic dance, is composed of up and down movements, with *motaro* literally meaning 'jumping up and down'. In the same way, Wana cots (a *sarong* on a hook placed on a horizontal wooden stick) are not swung (←→) like Western cribs but rebounded (↑↓). Sometimes the hook is attached to a spring to increase the movement.

Moreover, the following testimony about a female *tau walia* from the north highlights relationships between trance and dreaming:

Indo Pino: 'There's a woman in Posangke called Mime. When she hears the music, she starts trembling. People cannot see them but there are spirits with her. And when she sings, *she is dreaming,* and the spirits speak for her.'[5]

Moreover, Atkinson affirms that 'Shamans see in waking states what others can see only in dreams. [...] People liken the experience of a performing shaman to "the state of a person dreaming" (*ewa kare'e tau mangipi*)' (Atkinson 1989: 92, emphasis in the original). Therefore, the trance of the *tau walia* and the state of dreaming are similar experiences for Wana people. 'Dreams – perceived through the agent of one's tanuana – are most people's only direct access to spirits and hidden realms of existence' (Atkinson 1989: 91). Like music, dreams act as a

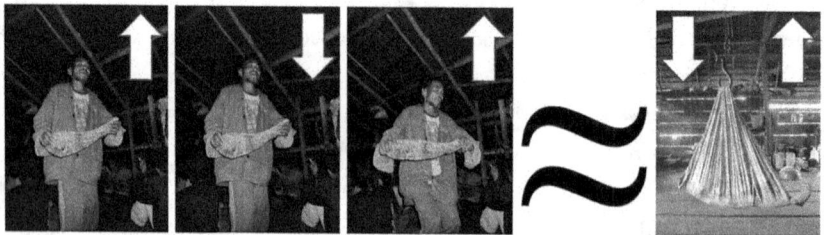

Figure 1 The vertical movement of the *motaro* has some similarity (≈) with the movement of Wana cribs. Source: Giorgio Scalici, photographer.

bridge between the visible and non-visible realms. I am aware that drawing connections between the *motaro* and the movement of cots is based only on an intuition, but it does seem more than plausible considering the similarity between trance and dreaming states in Wana culture. As de Martino explains, the exploitation of the lability of the oneiric consciousness as a preparation to trance, or as a direct means of communicating with 'spirits', has a clear psychological motivation. He stresses how 'oneiric events can have, for the magical consciousness and under given conditions, an equal (and sometimes greater) value in comparison with the events experienced by the waking consciousness' (de Martino 1967: 90).[6] More importantly, among Wana people, dreams are a gate on to mythical space-time, function as a liminal space-time where all wonders converge, and are the place where humans can embrace again the totality of the soul and the power of myth.

Being the living connection between the non-visible and the visible world is the key characteristic of a *tau walia*; they are the living proof of the existence of mythical space-time when humans and spirits lived together. They are a living *liminality*. The term used by Wana people to refer to a shaman is *tau walia*, which literally means 'human spirit', stressing their identity as both beings. Since the end of mythical space-time, the *tau walia* have been the only people able to abandon their humanity to access the spiritual realm. They are the point of conjunction between the visible (human world) and the non-visible (spirit and emotional world), a conjunction available to everybody before the end of mythical space-time, while today is the exclusive prerogative of the *tau walia*. During the *momago*, which with the aid of music transforms ordinary space-time into ritual-mythical space-time, *tau walia* can intentionally separate their soul from their body and become able to perform amazing wonders that are inaccessible to other members of the community, sharing their new status with the spirits.

Tau walia: A life for the community

Almost every Wana village hosts one or more *tau walia*, although they do not operate in only one village or area but instead are a resource for all the Wana people of Morowali. As shown in one of the documentaries made by the French filmmakers Journet and Nougarol (2007), *tau walia* are ready to help everybody, even those from far away; in the film, the *tau walia* Indo Pino tries to cure a friend of the couple from France. Moreover, it is not rare for a *tau walia*, while travelling between villages, to stop to help or cure somebody in need. These services, the *walia mangepe* described by Kruyt, are not free but their cost, circa 10,000 Indonesian rupiah (IDR), is a trivial amount even by local standards (in 2016, in the area, the cost of one litre of petrol was 7,000 IDR). People do not become *tau walia* for money or power, but to preserve the tradition and to benefit the community. Shamanism is not considered a job but a calling, and *tau walia* still have to work in mainstream jobs to sustain themselves and their families. In fact, the strongest *tau walia* I met (Apa Ingus, Indo Pino and Apa Main) were all less well-off than the average Wana person.

Obviously, shamanic treatments would not be possible without the trust and approval of the community, and this trust is based on a history of good outcomes from past rituals and on the religious and mythical systems that frame and give authority to the *tau walia*'s actions. According to myth, the first *tau walia* was *Dungola*, son of the first human couple *Santoto* and *Delemontu*. He was so powerful that his rituals lasted three days and three nights. *Dungola* was also the first musician, revealing the relationship between music and the world of spirits, and he was the first entertainer, underlining the important role of playfulness in shamanic rituals. Therefore, the three main characteristics of Wana shamanism are ritual, music and entertainment. Among the *tau walia* I met, Apa Ingus seemed the perfect incarnation of this 'shamanism-music-playfulness' triad. He is a powerful *tau walia*, respected by everyone; he is also a *geso* player and an extremely skilled *popondo* player, plus, to my great surprise, a harmonica player. Moreover, Apa Ingus is a remarkably funny person and he likes to make pranks and to joke with other people. He used to deliberately sing badly while I was recording him, laughing aloud at the humour of the situation. Apa Ingus's comic verve is also clear in his teknonymy. *Ingus* means 'mucus' in the Wana language, and he gave this name to his first daughter knowing that from that moment on he would be called 'Father of Mucus' (Apa Ingus). Indeed, when Ajeran, my guide, explained to me the meaning of the name, others present did not try to hide their fun or perplexity regarding the choice.

Just as in many other cultures, *tau walia* choose to undertake this path following a shamanic call. These calls usually happen in dreams, a space-time that, as has already been indicated, shares many characteristics with the non-visible world. Unlike in many other cultures around the world, however, a call is not mandatory in Wana culture. Studies of Japanese, Siberian and North American shamanism testify that refusing the call can bring illness and death to the individual; for these people, not to engage in shamanic practice is to refuse to externalize a powerful energy that they have inside them and that, if not used, could hurt, or even kill the owner. This phenomenon is commonly called 'shamanic illness' and it ends only when the shaman accepts his or her call (Balzer 1997; Eliade 1972; Kho 1987; Müller 2001). Among the Wana, there are three ways in which the shamanic call can be received: in dreams, by eating a stone that gives powers, or by meeting a spirit. Om Suma, a Wana of royal blood and the son of a *tau walia* himself, has eaten a power stone and is considered to have the potential to become a powerful *tau walia*. However, he does not want to begin his shamanic training, not wanting to deal with the responsibilities that this role involves.

> G. S.: 'Is it true that Om Suma could become a powerful *tau walia*?'
> Ajeran: 'Yes, but he does not want to.'
> G. S.: 'Why?'
> Ajeran: 'He is afraid.'
> G. S.: 'Afraid of what? His job [felling trees without protective equipment] is very dangerous.'
> Ajeran: 'Om Suma is not afraid to hurt himself, he is afraid of the responsibilities.'[7]

To understand this choice, we must consider that the work of a *tau walia* is dangerous, even more so than working without any protection in a palm oil plantation or felling trees with a chainsaw. The *tau walia* travels in worlds populated by demons and spirits, and he or she must always be ready to help the community: 'the desire to enter into contact with the sacred is counteracted by the fear of being obliged to renounce the simple human condition and become a more or less pliant instrument for some manifestation of the sacred (gods, spirits, ancestors, etc.)' (Eliade 1972: 23).

Therefore, theoretically, both men and women can be *tau walia*, but of all the *tau walia* I encountered during fieldwork just one was a woman. There are no rules that directly stop women from becoming *tau walia* but Wana culture implicitly encourages males to pursue the role more than females. As Atkinson insightfully noted:

> 'Anyone' could become a shaman, a rice specialist, or a legal expert. That those 'anyones' are predominantly male is treated as a fluke of fortune, rather than a categorical process of inclusion and exclusion. In this sense, Wana women represent the 'everyman,' the majority, who because of lack of bravery, fortune, good memory, or inclination never come to excel at what it takes to be a political leader in a Wana community.
>
> (Atkinson 1990: 88)

This gender differentiation is linked to the Wana conception of space and the cultural division between male and female space that will be discussed in the following chapters.

Here, though, I will briefly explain the link between space and power to give a general idea of why there are so few female *tau walia*. *Tau walia* work with spirits and the spirits dwell in the forest, a place where men travel daily while women rarely visit alone. The women's space is the village, or more precisely, the house. For a woman to travel alone in the jungle usually means that she is unmarried, a widow or that she does not display the same shyness (*mea*) that characterizes Wana women. Indo Pino, a powerful female *tau walia* and the only one in the Marisa and Taronggo area, was the personification of all these three characteristics. Until her death in 2016, she regularly travelled alone in the jungle, and she had a charisma that I did not find in any other Wana woman. She was respected and considered a powerful *tau walia* and a wise woman by the entire Wana community, although this did not exempt her from sometimes being the subject of jokes. Being a *tau walia* means being the centre of attention during rituals and under constant examination from the community, something that seems to clash with the shyness I noted among many Wana women.

After accepting the call, the future *tau walia* goes into the jungle to meditate for seven days and seven nights. Many Wana people, including *tau walia* Apa Oki, told me that, in fact, apprentice *tau walia* rarely spend so many days in the jungle because the mosquitos there are unbearable.[8] It seems that this stage in the shamanic training is more a theme than a reality, and Atkinson attests that it is usually enough just to study with a master. However, considering the symbolic value the jungle (the place of the spirits) has for the Wana, it still seems necessary to maintain at least a formal link to the extra-village reality (Atkinson 1989: 282). However, even if it is a dangerous place of the spirits and it is outside the domain of humans, men have more familiarity with the jungle than women do; men travel alone more to work and hunt in the jungle, while women stay in the village or usually travel escorted by men. This is one of the reasons that a great majority of *tau walia* are male.

Another way to become a *tau walia* is to have a master and train with him or her. In this case, the family of the apprentice pays the master with money and gifts, such as food, *sarongs*, dishes and machetes. The identity of the master must remain secret and none of the *tau walia* I interviewed revealed the name of their master. Likewise, the names of spirits must also remain secret, since if a name becomes public another *tau walia* could take control of that spirit and kidnap it. The duration of the training can vary, with the fee being different for each master and regulated by the relationship between master and pupil. The power of a *tau walia* depends on the number of spirits they possess, the larger the number the more powerful. One of the most powerful *tau walia* I met, Apa Main, affirmed to have twelve spirits. Sometimes the master donates some of his or her spirits to pupils to help them in their careers. Occasionally the shamanic tradition is passed from a parent to their offspring; in this case, the parent becomes the child's master or at least offers extra teaching to the son or daughter in addition to the teaching of the master. An example is Apa Rau, who learnt the *molawo* from his father. Beyond the teaching of a master, due to their link with the non-visible world, dreams have an important role in the life of the *tau walia*, being, alongside meditation, one of the most common ways to learn about shamanhood.

Shamanic powers and links to the spiritual realm

The ability to travel between the world of spirits and the human world, and their familiarity with both, places *tau walia* almost on the same level as that of *walia* (spirits). This liminal status, between humans and spirits, is the key to their powers. The following is a list of the powers that a *tau walia* can possess:

(1) Finding stolen objects. By casting a *do'a* (spell) and looking inside a glass of *pongas* (rice wine), they can see the object's thief. To accomplish this, it is necessary to know when the object was stolen.

(2) Healing people remotely. The *tau walia* requires an image of the patient, their name, and their location. The *tau walia* looks at the image and casts the *do'a*. This ritual is well documented in *Indo Pino*, a film by Journet and Nougarol (2007), in which the *tau walia* that gives the name to the film, Indo Pino, tries to cure a friend of the French filmmakers but she fails.

(3) Walking in the sky. This occurs when a powerful *tau walia* hears the music of the *momago* ritual and wishes to transport themselves to the ritual location quickly. If the music ends while the *tau walia* is walking in the sky, they fall back down to earth. Many people told me that Apa nTongi, the brother of Indo Pino, was so powerful that he had this ability. Atkinson stresses the important overlaps and the divergences in the abilities displayed by *tau walia* and *setan*, noting that while both can travel through the air, the former does so by walking while the latter flies (Atkinson 1989: 97).

(4) During the *momago*, the *tau walia* can make objects appear in his or her hand, usually food requested by the *walia*. The *tau walia* can also materialize the internal organs of a bystander in their hands, killing them on the spot.

(5) Hypnotizing (*doti*) people and forcing them to do what the *tau walia* wants. The details of this process vary from *tau walia* to *tau walia*, but in each case, the name of the person being hypnotized is needed.

(6) Communicating with the dead. The *tau walia* can evoke an 'angin-merokok' (wind-smoke) that assumes the shape of the deceased and speaks in the person's voice.

(7) Chiromancy. Wana people believe that *tau walia* can find *urat* (nerves that push people to do evil actions, show someone's predisposition to become a *tau walia*, or reveal other information) in the palm of the hand. Om Doti told me that a *tau walia* found in him an evil *urat* and extirpated it, telling him that doing so would save him from ending up fighting with his friends.[9]

(8) Invisibility (*jampu*). Thanks to a *doa*, the *tau walia* can become non-visible to normal people but not to powerful *tau walia*.

(9) Mastering fire. During a *momago*, I saw a *tau walia* put a red-hot coal in his mouth and eat it.[10]

The majority of these powers are available during the *momago*, especially in the presence of ritual music. At these moments, ritual music transforms ordinary space-time into ritual space-time, a space-time that shares its power with the myth. On these occasions, *tau walia* that occupy a liminal space between the visible world and the non-visible world of the spirits, between the everyday and the mythical, are able to perform wonders, to share their status with the spirits. Music acts as a bridge between the two worlds, a connection that the *tau walia* can use to tap from the power of the mythical era. When *momago* is celebrated, the ritual music brings back into existence mythical space-time. It is not by chance that *tau walia* can walk in the sky only in the presence of ritual music.

Among the shamanic powers mentioned above, invisibility seems to be the one that links the *tau walia* most strongly to mythical space-time and their spiritual being. Atkinson describes the *bolag*, spirits of the forest, as also possessing the *jampu* (Atkinson 1989: 37); this similarity would place the *tau walia* on the same plane of the existence of spirits while using that power. Moreover, among Wana people, invisibility is a necessary condition to express great power. One Wana myth tells of how the trickster *Langesong*[11] affirmed that the flight of the *tau Baraka* was impossible, and due to his words, some of them had fallen (Atkinson 1989: 45), because 'to report on an extraordinary fact (in Wana terms, to *magagang*) is to cause it to fail [...]. Miracles can still happen, but only in secret' (Atkinson 1989: 45). Atkinson clearly states that 'A mabolong performer [the shaman] rejects those divisions [between humans and spirits] and re-establishes direct connections with Pue' (Atkinson 1989: 205–6). In the same way, a *tau walia* would fall from the sky if another *tau walia* saw him or her. The relationship between invisibility and the hidden world of emotions and spirits will be discussed in depth in Chapter 5 and it plays a pivotal role in Wana culture.

Eliade tells us: '[in] Sumatra the *dukun* complete their shamanic instruction in solitude, on a mountain; there they learn to become non-visible and, at night, see the souls of the dead – which means that they *become* spirits, that they *are* dead' (Eliade 1972: 86, emphasis in the original). I believe that the same is true regarding the Wana; during the *momago*, the *tau walia* lose their human (*tau*) status to embrace their spirit (*walia*) status and use this new identity to perform wonders, to travel among realms and to serve the community. They do not act as if they were spirits; rather, they *are* spirits and, furthermore, they have the control of their soul during the *momago* – something that is impossible for the other members of the community. Atkinson again stresses the deep connection between shamanic trance and dreaming: 'In contrast to a dreamer, however, the shaman is conscious, and instead of relying on a "dream agent," or tanuana – a faculty possessed by everyone – he employs the agency of his sprit familiars' (1989: 92). *Tau walia*, then, are not just vessels for souls, but they have control over them; the *tau walia* can interact with them and be them, just as in mythical space-time. Of course, it is essential for a powerful and successful *tau walia* to possess a deep knowledge of the non-visible world, since venturing into the world of demons and spirits is a dangerous task and dying is a real threat. Usually these journeys are called 'shamanic flights', and sometimes the shaman even uses the drum as a mount (Balzer 1997; Desjarlais 1992; Eliade 1972; Kendal 2011). However, in the Wana context, it would be more correct to talk about the 'shamanic walk' since *tau walia* here walk in the sky, while flying is a *setan*'s prerogative.

The organization of the ritual

Tau walia take care of 'inner illness', the sickness of the *tanuana* (dream agent). While we sleep, the soul leaves the body to explore the visible and non-visible world. If during its journeys, the *tanuana* gets attacked by a *setan* or becomes lost, the vessel gets sick and there will be no choice but to organize a *momago*. Organizing a ritual is not a complicated process and it can be achieved in one day.

Unlike the *molawo* (the other Wana healing ritual), the *momago* is held inside the village, in the house of the organizer. To hold a successful ritual, the family must procure a large quantity of rice, alcohol and tobacco for the guests, some cloths and money as offering for the *tau walia*, and toothpaste, an egg, *wunga* (a plant that has a strong odour) and lemon leaves for the spirits. An essential element in a *momago* is the ensemble of ritual instruments: two gongs, one big and one small, and a wooden drum. A similar situation has been observed for the rituals of the Taman of Borneo, where the ritual music is played with drums, gongs and bowls (Bernstein 1997: 89). These instruments are kept in the house of the village chief or in that of a *tau walia*. The keeper is not the owner of the instruments because they, like the *tau walia*, are considered assets of the entire community. It caused a sensation when Indo Pino declared that she wished to be buried with the gongs and the drum on the day of her death. In 2016, when she died, she was buried without the instruments, and instead they were moved from the village of Kilo Sembilan to Marisa, to the house of the village chief Apa Rau. The last element needed for a *momago* is the *tau walia*. In fact, at least two *tau walia* are required, so they can help each other in moments of need. Usually, however, the number is much higher, and in all the rituals I attended there were six or more *tau walia* present.

There is no formal invitation calling people to a ritual; as it is a small community, word of mouth is usually enough. Funerals, weddings and the *momago* are the only three occasions for enjoying[12] a get-together and so the *momago* are highly anticipated, also drawing people from other villages. Nevertheless, in the rare case of there being someone who does not know about the ritual, the sound of the gongs means that they cannot avoid becoming aware as soon as it begins. As people can easily imagine, the jungle does not offer many ways to spend the nights, thus *momago* can be easily compared to a night out at the local disco or pub.

Moreover, to understand the centrality of the *momago* in the world of Wana entertainment, it is worth noting that a ritual is actually part of any major joyful community moment. The *momago* is considered an indispensable part of wedding and harvest festival celebrations, as well as itself being one of the main events of Wana life when it stands alone as a ritual. This connection between the healing ritual *momago* and festive events is also clear in the term *malae*, which is used both to say, 'going to the *momago*' and to refer to participation in any festive gathering. Funerals are the only major events that do not include the *momago*, and this is also because music is prohibited at funerals. For this reason, the *momago* does not carry any negative connotation but rather is strongly connected with the celebration of life and with playfulness. Atkinson writes, 'Apart from a mabolong, weddings, funerals, and four annual farming festivals, it is rare for co-residents of a swidden settlement to congregate as a group' (Atkinson 1989: 7) and the situation has not changed in the last forty years. The ritual is still perceived more as a party, a reason to congregate and to heal the entire community, than simply as about the healing of the main patient. Of course, the latter is still an important element, to the extent that it offers an excuse to organize the ritual. In fact, the healing is not limited to the individual; rather, the *tau walia* treats all the sick people presented to him or her. The ritual itself works as an emotional relief valve that allows the community to relax, express frustration and regenerate itself – to have a re-creational time.

However, during the period of the ritual itself, the main patient is put to one side, both physically and metaphorically, with just one *tau walia*, the main one, paying attention to him or her, and the attention of the many other people present lying elsewhere. The situation of the main patient during the *momago* exemplifies a main value of the Wana people, the aforementioned *kasintuwu*, where the individual is subordinate to the whole community. As expressed by their rituals, Wana people find meaning and purpose only when together. Similar phenomena can be found in Morocco, where 'the patient is not necessarily the center of attention during ceremonies, although he is the manifest cause for the ceremony. Indeed, he is often almost completely ignored' (Crapanzano 1973: 217).

Atkinson, again, recognizes the meaning of the ritual for Wana people: 'A mabolong is a social event, [...] adults, they don new clothes, apply makeup, and affect new hairstyles before a performance' (Atkinson 1989: 284). She underlines these ideas further: 'People go to mabolong to enjoy themselves, to receive treatment, and to demonstrate *kasintuwu*, "mutual support," an important social value [...] Although the mabolong is the most popular of healing events, its popularity comes from the fact that it involves much more than healing' (Atkinson 1989: 26).

The ritual

At the beginning of the *momago* ritual, dozens of people wait in the darkness of the hut where it will take place.[13] Darkness is one of the key elements of the *momago*, and we will see later that while music attracts the spirits, light keeps them away. For this reason, the *momago* must end before dawn and any strong light in the hut must be shaded or turned off. Once, during a ritual I witnessed in the Taronggo village, the only available light was considered too strong, and the patient had to be protected from it by a curtain.

During this part of the procedure, people start to come, and they take up places wherever they can find space; the ritual room becomes incredibly crowded. During one ritual, my only way to film was to place the camera outside the house and film through the window. The positions of the people usually follow a pattern based on their different role. On one side, next to an entrance, there are the music players with the drum positioned between the two gongs; on the other side there is the patient who organized the ritual; the bystanders are spread all around the room, and the only prescription for them seems to be to leave some space in front of the instruments to allow the *tau walia* to kneel and dance.

Of course, the positioning of the participants depends on the size and shape of the room, but it is common to find the musical instruments and the main patient/organizer at the edges of the room. The *tau walia* are not positioned in front of an audience, as in a traditional staged performance. Rather, they are surrounded by the participants, who do not form a passive crowd but play an active part in the ritual. They help the *tau walia* if they are in difficulty, are treated for minor ailments, influence the *tau walia*'s behaviour with jokes or simply contribute to the playful atmosphere of the *momago*. Like Atkinson, I also do not agree with Roy Rappaport's claim that 'dramas have audiences, rituals have congregations. An audience watches a drama, a congregation participates in a ritual' (1974: 8). First of all, Rappaport seems to forget how Western theatre, especially after the happenings in the 1950s,[14] aimed to transform the audience into actors. More importantly, I refuse a clear division between theatre and drama, especially knowing how the shamanic rituals and funerals are two of the few occasions the Wana have to organize a party. For these reasons, I will use the term 'audience' to underline the performative elements of the *momago*, where 'Wana shamans are performers who must attract – and can never presume – the interest, attention, and commitment of others in what they are doing' (Atkinson 1989: 219)

While the main patient has the attention of the one *tau walia*, usually the most powerful, for the entire night, all those in the village suffering from ailments have the opportunity to be visited, and ideally cured, by the other *tau walia*. It is not unusual for mothers to bring their children to the rituals, and many of them need treatment. Indeed, children are always present at Wana celebrations, be they weddings, funerals or the *momago*. The entire adult population of the village comes to a ritual and hence there is no one left at home to look after children; so, the children come too, and they become one of the most important elements of the ritual.

The infant mortality rate is quite high in Wana society. Almost every family I met had lost at least one child at a very young age. As a result, people are so accustomed to infant mortality that until the first months of life have passed, they do not give children names but simply refer to them as *ponka* (for males) or *vea* (for females). If a child dies during the first week of life, no ritual is officiated for them, and the precariousness of young children's health makes them some of the most common patients for *tau walia*. At the same time, children are a pure expression of life and vitality, balancing the negativity of sickness and contributing to the playfulness of the occasion. Moreover, they symbolize the continuity of the Wana community. Lastly, going to a ritual is the best way to learn about customs, beliefs and ritual music. Wana children do not learn in formalized teaching contexts, but instead, through imitation, a learning method very common among non-Western cultures (Baily 2001; Sanga 2009). Thus, rituals are valuable occasions to learn about Wana core values: religion, *tau walia*, *kasintuwu* and especially ritual music.

Indeed, ritual music should never be played away from the ritual itself,[15] because it would attract the spirits outside of the controlled situation of the *momago*. The only way to learn how to play the ritual music is to listen to it and gain experience playing it during downtimes in a ritual, when the *tau walia* are present and ready to intervene in case of need. In this context, playing means both 'playing a game' and 'playing a musical instrument'. Through the former kind of playing, children learn the latter, becoming accustomed to dealing with the instruments through incorporating them into their games. This playful learning process also contributes to the atmosphere that characterizes the ritual and that contributes to the healing of the entire community. The presence of children is a reminder of life's energy and of the community's future. In the end, it is also important to note the possibility that assiduous participation in the rituals from a young age makes listening to the ritual music in later life trigger various memories and emotions linked to those times: 'Music has become one with the ritual and is not a separate aesthetic category' (Kartomi 1973a: 166).

On one side, those memories reinforce the trust in *tau walia* and their healing power, while on the other they can help the *tau walia* to enter into trance (Becker 1994; Sturm 2000). The relationships between memory, music and emotions will be explored in Chapter 5, where we will see the role that MEAMs (music-evoked autobiographical memories) play during the *momago* and the *kayori* in enhancing the healing of the community and the playfulness of the rituals.

People's presence at rituals from a young age also ensures that they become deeply sensitized to ritual stimuli, so that the music unfailingly triggers an emotional response, bringing them to healing, playfulness or into trance. Wana people grow up experiencing a *momago* almost every two months from their first weeks of life, when their hearing is more developed than their vision and so is the main tool they use to understand their environment. It seems clear that a strong connection is created in the minds of infants between ritual music and playfulness (the sounds of people chatting and laughing). Other important elements, such as healing, rituality and trance, will be subsequently linked to the ritual music when other senses (especially sight) and conceptual understandings (the ideas of community, religion, ritual and so on) develop.

The children present at the ritual, like the adults, are also entertained by the unfolding of the ritual itself, which might be thought of as a dramatized description of the non-visible world. Rituals that function as teaching and leisure occasions are not unusual; it has been noted, for instance, that in African Pentecostal communities 'the church service has two unambiguous aims: to evangelize the gospel of salvation and to serve as a form of entertainment' (Manning 1976: 144). This should not be a surprise since play and religion are overlapping entities in pre-industrial cultures and the pre-television world (Norbeck 1976: 39). Moreover, playing means leaving the ordinary world to enter an extraordinary one with different rules. In this way, it helps people to enter mythical worlds where the rules of their daily life are transcended. Indeed, 'play soars beyond ordinary boundaries and creates a world in which extraordinary things are possible, where the unthinkable is *thought* and the forbidden is performed as a commonplace' (Salamone 2009: 88).

Ultimately, the *momago* provides the children with learning and playing opportunities. Moreover, enabling the expression of *kasintuwu*, it reinforces existing relationships and creates new bonds among people. Overall, this atmosphere of playfulness, joyousness and communality is also a resource for the patients; they are influenced by the positive energies around them and feel part of something that transcends their own existence. It is worth noting here more details about the nature of the 'inner illness'. It can be a symptom related to a physical illness such as cancer, or an issue of mental health, such as depression. 'Inner illness' can also be caused by a strong emotion that is not tamed, such as an extreme sadness, anger or jealousy; all of these emotions are potentially threatening for the stability of the community. We find a similar situation in Bali, where 'Fright, for instance, throws the spirit easily off balance and results in "soul loss" (*kesamber /rurutan*)' and '"bad emotions" weaken the spirit and cause it to shiver and be frail' (Wikan 1988: 457, also 1989b). Wana people often told me that the main cause of inner illness is 'speaking badly', meaning gossiping or swearing – in other words, being upset or undermining the stability of the community. Atkinson contributes a very useful example. She tells of a boy that fell onto the rocks while playing near the river. The *tau walia* that treated this child concluded that the real cause of the accident was the ghost of the mother, who had died a few days before, and who pushed the child onto the rocks, driven by the desire to stay together (Atkinson 1989: 173–4). A more psychological interpretation could be that the child, still depressed from the mother's departure, tried on a subconscious level to follow her destiny; desiring death is common after the death of a loved one. Young people require special support as they are not yet integrated and trained in the coping methods of the community, and this story highlights the role of *tau walia* in finding resolutions to emotional problems by giving people ways to understand what is happening to them.

The final aim of the *momago* is not just to eliminate illness but also to restore a healthy emotional state to the individual and, in doing so, to the entire community. The *tau walia* not only moves between the visible and the non-visible world, but their mediation and narration makes visible (comprehensible) the non-visible (incomprehensible), giving a shape and a materiality to the 'inner illness'. As Crapanzano notes regarding the Moroccan Hamadsha, '[Saints, jnun, and Baraka] are elements in which I would call the participational mode of explanation of illness and therapy. They may be considered *signs* of psychic states and *symbols* of socio-cultural processes' (1973: 213, emphasis in original). Moreover, Peters notes among the Tamang of Nepal that 'the curing activities involved in shamanic healing are not exercise in the treatment of organic disease but attempts to treat disturbing emotional states and interpersonal relations' (Peters 1978: 65).

In a society like that of the Wana, where people tend to support each other and where the community is more important than the individual, a conflict between two people can escalate and bring sickness to the community. The *momago* is an opportunity to dispel frustration and emotional stress. The ritual is an example of organized chaos that allows people a greater emotional freedom and, through alcohol, courtship and joking, to relax and resolve tensions inside the community. Like a carnival, social rules are looser; people can let themselves go by drinking, flirting, joking and dancing, even if extreme behaviour is still prohibited. Drinking is also now becoming a common behaviour outside of rituals, partially diminishing the uniqueness of the event. It is, however, not considered a good habit by many people, especially by women.

The structure

Having now analysed the main elements that make the *momago* so important to the Wana in a communal sense, we can examine the sequence of events that make up the ritual's structure. One of the most perplexing aspects of this ritual is ascertaining when it truly begins and ends. Wana people say that the ritual starts when the ritual music starts. This is understood as when the piece of music called *topo* (slapping) is played, and the ritual is said to end when the same piece is played again much later. It might equally be said that the real start comes earlier, when the first guest arrives, or later, when people start to dance. The building of atmosphere and bonding that occurs before the music begins is certainly worthy of study too. Indeed, hours before the beginning of the music, people have already gathered to chat, eat and drink together, generating the playful energy that will make the ritual successful, and preparing the field and the mood for the healing part of the *momago*. We could ask to ourselves, when does a party start? This is not to imply that the music is unimportant. On the contrary, the recognition of the music as the marker of the beginning and the end of the ritual is the confirmation of the important role and of the power the Wana people attribute to it. Music has many roles in the *momago*; not only does it mark ritual time, but it also attracts the spirits, helps the *tau walia* enter and maintain trance, triggers emotions and memories for the participants that support the healing of the patients and of the community and, ultimately, it influences the playfulness of the ritual. The happiness of the bystanders also contributes to the ritual; the entire community, and not just a single person, has to be healed from all the emotional frustration that can threaten the soundness of the community. Sharing playfulness in the community makes the ritual more powerful.

While people are relaxing and waiting for the beginning of the music, the *tau walia* and some other people gather to prepare the offerings that will be presented to the *walia* (spirits). Several objects are placed onto the *langu* (ritual tray): a plate of rice (this rice will be cooked and offered to the *tau walia* in the morning), toothpaste,[16] betel nuts, tobacco, alcohol, pieces of cloth, eggs, *wunga* (a plant with the strong odour), lemon leaves, a machete and some money (the latter is hidden from view). During the ritual, *tau walia* are free to take anything that they want from the *langu* as it is understood that when they do so, it is the *walia* acting through their bodies. Similar offerings are presented among the Tamang of Nepal where 'for the offering to the gods (Ta: sagun), Bhirendra procured one egg, rice beer (Ta: chang), *raksi* (a strong liquor made of grains and sometimes fruit), and cigarettes. [...] the drinks and smokes were for the shaman and audience to consume during the ritual' (Peters 1978: 67). Of course, away from this tray of offerings there is also a separate supply of tobacco, food and drink for the ordinary participants. Atkinson explains that, in her area, *tau walia* used to request food for the spirit familiae (*baku walia*) to the audience through riddles (1989: 176). I never saw anything similar during the rituals I observed, where the audience was ready to support and help the *tau walia* but never gave any food.

The music

Once the room is full and people have eaten, the atmosphere is set and the fall of darkness allows the *momago* to start calling the spirits. While the ritual structure is quite complicated – Atkinson describes it as 'a circus with more than one ring' (Atkinson 1989: 246) – the musical structure is quite simple.

A pair of gongs and a drum are the main instruments. The drum, called the *ganda*, is a double-skinned hourglass-shaped instrument of around 50 cm in length. On one side there is reptile (lizard or snake) skin, and on the other, there is mammal (cuscus, wild cat or deer) skin. During the *momago*, the *ganda* is suspended from the ceiling between the two gongs and played by two people positioned on either side of it. Atkinson affirms that 'Typically, young men and boys play the drums, and young women and girls the gongs' (1989: 27), although I never noticed any particular division of roles between the genders (Figure 2).

The reptile skin is struck with a rattan strip knotted at the end, while the mammal skin is hit with two wooden sticks. In the area studied by Atkinson, the *momago* ritual is called *mabolong*, literally meaning 'drumming'. She explains: 'The ritual takes its name from the two-skinned *bolong* drum, which, along with a pair of bronze gongs, produces the insistent rhythms that summon both humans and spirits to the ritual and accompany shamans as they dance' (Atkinson 1989: 1). The ritual can be also called *walia moganda* (Atkinson 1989: 207), literally meaning 'drumming the spirits' or 'the spirits of the drum'. The fact

Figure 2 The position of the ritual instruments: small gong on the left, *ganda* in the middle and large gong on the right. Source: Giorgio Scalici, photographer.

that the ritual is named after the main musical instrument stresses the important role of music in the ritual.

The drum plays a very important role in the ritual: keeping the *tau walia* safe. Any mistake made while playing the drum can hurt the *tau walia*. A wrong beat or unexpectedly stopping can cause a traumatic breaking of the bridge that links humans to the spirits and that allows the *tau walia* to go into trance. These problems are called *ganda masala* (problems of/with the drum) and can cause *tau walia* to convulse and become rigid in the limbs; when this happens, the audience has to be ready to help the *tau walia* and to calm them or to stretch the affected limb.

The ring at the centre of the drum's body is decorated and there is a hole of less than a centimetre in diameter for resonance. Inside the instrument there is also a grain of dry corn, which is believed to add to the volume of sound the drum produces; it may also be considered as serving the function of warding off harm. As Combarieu observes, instruments can bring together 'particles of the whole natural kingdom: cane or bamboo, shell of some fruits, metal, hard wood, stone, animal skins, carapace, bones, hollow horns, silk, braided raffia, horsehair, guts;

the instruments constitute a synthesis of the cosmos'[17] (Combarieu 1982: 325). I believe it is reasonable to say that the animal skins represent animals in general, with the reptiles being associated with fish and water life through their skin and their laying of eggs, while the mammals are connected with the ground. Wood represents the plants of the forest, and corn is the cultural world of the village. Dried grains of corn are used as a unit of measurement indicating the amount a Wana person has to pay as compensation if a marriage is not lawful and, in the past, it was also put into a coconut shell and shaken as a musical instrument at a *kayori* (traditional funeral). Likewise, in other contexts of Wana life, a grain of corn used to be placed inside a small rattle called a *diodio*, which was tied to the machete of a warrior to attract women.

The smaller of the two gongs used during the ritual has an average diameter of 26 cm, while the larger has a diameter of around 41 cm. The instruments are not made locally; Apa Rau and other people told me that the large gong of Marisa village was brought into the village of Kayu Poli around thirty years ago by a man called Nyole. The small gong in Taronggo was brought in 2010 by Grumblies, who had purchased the gong in Bali. The large gong in Taronggo village seems to have been present in the jungle for at least forty years. Apa Main, one of the most powerful *tau walia* in the Taronggo area, told me that the gong was already around when he was a child and that he does not have any idea of what could have been played during the *momago* before it arrived.

The introduction of these instruments into Wana ritual life seems to be a fairly recent event, perhaps occurring less than 100 years ago. With local Wana people not being able to build the instruments themselves, they told me that they had existed *dari pertama* (literally 'from the first time'). After an investigation in which I interviewed people from more remote areas of Morowali, I arrived at the conclusion that the first gong was brought into the area by Javanese or Balinese settlers during one of the waves of the *transmigrasi* programme.[18] It seems that Wana people were fascinated by their sound, shape (the circle is a great symbol of life and regeneration) and their mythical status (because of the fact they come from the largely unknown realm of outside the jungle), and they slowly replaced the old ritual instrument (a bamboo zither called the *tetebua*) with gongs.[19] As mentioned in the previous chapter, similar instruments are common all-around Southeast Asia and, as attested to by Marina Roseman regarding the Temiar of Malaysia (1990), some of them are used in shamanic rituals.

Every *momago* opens with a rhythm called *topo*, which is played by only one person on the drum, and this is followed by a fast rhythm called *pakoba manoto* or *majoli kojo* (240 bpm, 4/4), played three times.[20] This rhythm also has a quaternary rhythm, though the tempo is 100 bpm faster than *malenyilenyi*. The left hand strikes the mammal skin twice in each rhythmic cycle, both of these coming in very quick succession between the third and fourth beats.

This leads into the rhythmic pattern that will be played all night long, called *tumba* or *malenyilenyi* (140 bpm, 4/4). The ritual is eventually closed by the *pakoba manoto* being played again three times and, finally, with the *topo* being heard again. While the male *tau walia* dance the *motaro*, literally 'to jump up and down', the women dance the *salonde* 'something beautiful' (Atkinson 1989: 94). For this courtship and shamanic dance, there is a specific rhythm called *ngaya* or *tumba balanghe*.

> The salonde has aesthetic appeal and can be done without implying that the dancer is embarked on a shamanic career. For a man to motaro suggests that he is attempting to engage spirit familiars; for a woman to salonde may suggest either that she has shaman aspirations or that she is simply showing off her skills as a graceful dancer. The equivocality of the interpretation placed on a woman's dancing reveals a tacit but powerful assumption that Wana shamanship is largely a male game.
>
> (Atkinson 1989: 94)

The *ngaya*, which is played at roughly 185 bpm.[21] While the other rhythms are characterized by extreme synchronization and precision, this rhythm is more fluid, with interlocking[22] an even more prominent feature than in the other rhythms. When played at about 185 bpm, a sense of fluidity results. The rhythm of the music evokes the fluid motion of the woman's arms when dancing the *salonde*, which contrasts with the simple 'jumping up and down' of the *motaro*. The flowing movements of the arms and body – for its seductive purpose – require more flexible music, giving more freedom of expression and space for inventiveness to the performer. This courtship dance, however, seems to be gradually disappearing. Wana women, in my experience, appear shy and the younger generation prefer not to be the centre of attention, instead staying on the sides of the room chatting, joking or playing the ritual music. They do not shun dancing altogether, however; women dance the *modero*, or *dero*, in groups at weddings. It is a circle dance that is spread widely around Sulawesi and is accompanied by Indonesian pop music. After the death of Indo Pino in 2016, though, I was not able to see the *salonde* again. I was told that many women could dance the *salonde* in the Uewaju village, but this could be explained as wishful thinking related to the fact that Uewaju is located on the mythical mountain of *Tunda n'Tana* and therefore has a mythical aura.

The sound of the gongs resonates well beyond the duration of the beat, amalgamating with the sound produced by the preceding beat, exacerbating the tension, and encouraging trance. The ritual music is played for more than six hours, becoming a sound like a mantra that infiltrates into the listeners' minds and helps the *tau walia* to dissociate themselves from the surrounding environment. After a ritual, the sound of the gongs and drum remained in my head for days. It is also possible that this kind of sonic wall influences the way of thinking of the audience, symbolically separating them from the human time, but also distracting their mind from the human way of thinking, increasing the pure sensation of the moment. I invite the reader to listen to the *momago* music for few minutes and imagining the effect of the music after hours of listening.

During one of the rituals I observed, I noted a woman who danced the *motaro* in a very particular way. She was an old woman, and she had a *sarong* rolled around her chest that passed under her armpits and was tied at her back (Figure 3). Another person held the excess material at her back like a leash. It was explained to me that this woman was a rare kind of *tau walia*, called a *walia muansang*, who breathe from their armpits while dancing the *motaro*, because 'they are like fish that breathe from their gills'.[23]

Thus, if this woman's armpits had not been covered with the *sarong*, the air would have leaked from her lungs, and she would have died. Moreover, this kind of *tau walia* tends to have problems stretching their legs (because they have fins instead?), and bystanders often have to step in to help. It is possible that the *walia muansang* are remnants of an ancient belief in different kinds of *tau walia* being related to particular animals. The need to cover their armpits (as if they were gills) and the inability to stretch their legs could link these *tau walia* to fishes. I do not have enough data on this kind of shamanism, but it could open the door to a shamanic shape-shifting rituality among the Wana people that has never been discussed before. In her in-depth work, Atkinson never mentions anything similar or cases in which female *tau walia* perform the *motaro*.

Music is always present when Wana people face moments of crisis, such as illness or death. As Walter Friedrich Otto writes: 'what is essential and great requires to be sung'[24] (1996: 125). During the rituals, the music transforms everyday space-time into mythical space-time and brings the power of the non-visible world into the visible one. The music is the link to the non-visible world, to myth, and it becomes a testimony of the presence of spirits.

Beyond helping the *tau walia* to get into trance, ritual music has many functions and roles within the *momago*. First, it functions as a ritual and emotional marker. In a ritual with a complex structure like the *momago*, music

Figure 3 The sarong rolled around the chest of the *walia muansang,* covering her armpits. Source: Giorgio Scalici, photographer.

is the only way to mark the official start and end and to distinguish ritual space-time from ordinary space-time. *Momago* is a very common event, but it always brings the exceptionality associated with rituals and celebrations. The music also stresses the playfulness of the situation. It is the only Wana traditional music that people here dance to outside of funerals, and it is crucial in creating the sense that the *momago* is a party, and in defining its role as a moment of social re-creation.

Tau walia sing to invoke their spirits and to describe their journeys in the realm of the spirits.

Here is a small extract.[25]

> Apa Main: *Oode dago, oh!*
> *Tulungi makutu lo'ongi go bamago.*
> *Tulungi le maku.*

> Apa Main: Oh mercy oh!
> Please play the gong for the ritual treatment
> Please have mercy on me.

In this short extract, there is an exhortation for the player not to stop playing the gong. If the ritual music were to end, it would inhibit the *tau walia* in using their powers.

Although somewhat masked by the loud music and the chatting of the bystanders, the shamanic song is comprehensible to the people present,[26] and they often intervene with comments about what the *tau walia* says or sees during their journey. Indeed, I was told that it is essential for the song to be heard and understood by the patient, who has to remain vigilant throughout the night. Although the music is very loud and often obscures the words, people listening are still able to take advantage of any errors to make jokes. I also witnessed girls trying to join in with the dancing for fun, and their clumsiness causing much laughter among the bystanders. In all of these shamanic flights, there is a continuous coming and going to and from the hidden world, and the different actions of the various *tau walia*, combined with the alcohol, joking, chatting and music, allow the event to proceed until the morning without people getting bored. The repeating of the *momago* also implies a renewal of its creative and generative force, thanks to the unique improvisations and interaction between *tau walia*, musicians and participants on each occasion. It is ironic to note that in the midst of this organized chaos the sufferer almost disappears. They are downgraded to a mere pretext once the ritual's engine gives way to people's entertainment.

Singing, with its exceptionality and its lyrics, is one of the key elements in restoring mythical space-time. As Eliade states, by listening to the shamanic song 'symbolically, the sick "goes backwards", he or she is made contemporary of Creation; he experiences again the initial state of fullness. The injured organism is not healed, it *is made anew*' (Eliade 1971: 47, emphasis in the original). In this way the patient revives the myth and becomes one with it.

This internal process is reinforced by the memories and emotions triggered by the song that he or she has listened to since childhood. Without trust and this multi-layered emotion–memory connection, it would seem impossible for the patient to be cured by the *tau walia*'s powers.

It is important to keep in mind that the *momago* is not just a healing ritual for the single person but a cathartic moment for all the community. Like the *kayori*, the *momago* is an occasion to have a party, to spend time together drinking, joking and eating while the music and the *tau walia* entertain the bystanders, who themselves take active roles in the ritual.

The circus

The presence and participation of the public is always a very important factor in shamanic rituals, as we find documented in many sources. Sergei Mikhailovich Shirokogoroff writes: 'several shamans told [...] that they were unable to perform without an audience. "All people present," one of them told him, "helped me go to the lower world"" (Shirokogoroff 1935: 363), while Pietro Scarduelli states: 'even though it was just one person to fall into a trance, the session was, indeed, a collective psychodrama'[27] (Scarduelli 2007a: 154). The role of the community, the audience, is crucial in the correct and successful development of the shamanic ritual. Without an audience, the *tau walia* would only partially fulfil his duty. Among the Wana, *tau walia* need the community for many reasons: creating a playful atmosphere, recreating the primordial density when all the Wana were just on the top of a wooden spinning top and, most importantly, not only healing the single patient but re-creating the entire community. Nobody is passive or useless, but everybody has a role and the power, and duty, to help the other. There is a constant interplay between all the members of the community, everybody is important, but only because part of the community, especially *tau walia*.

I never saw as few as two *tau walia* participating in a ritual, and often there were over five. The presence of numerous religious actors makes the ritual structure, at first glance, seem unclear and chaotic, particularly as they do not seem to be working directly together. There can be a *tau walia* curing a patient while others are dancing and yet another is calling the spirits. Each follows an individual path during the ritual, but at the same time, an interaction between them is maintained. At any one moment, three *tau walia* might be dancing together, while one could be lending their power to another, and so on. Indeed, the presence of so many actors makes downtimes in the ritual rare and causes the event to be quite unpredictable. However, some structural pattern is recognizable. In fact, the *momago* does not have a linear structure, since it is '"performed-centered": governed less by liturgy and more by the action and inclinations of individual practitioners' (Atkinson 1989: 14). However, it is still worth attempting to outline the basic structure of the ritual and to describe all of the various alternatives. Atkinson divided the ritual into four steps: 'summoning spirit familiars, treating patients, traveling up to the sky to negotiate with the Owner on behalf of the patient, and requesting foods for spirit familiars' (1989: 15). I partially agree with her interpretation of the ritual's structure. However, I did not observe the final request of food during my time in the field, and therefore I consider the final part of the ritual to be the cure of the patient, with the lost soul placed back into the body. We must be aware that even considering this practical organization, all of these parts are performed at different times by different *tau walia*, except the dance, which is sometimes engaged in by more than one *tau walia* at a time. It is worth noting that I never saw any of the *tau walia* considered to be particularly powerful by the community dance with other *tau walia*. These individuals always had 'solo' performances, while less powerful *tau walia* danced in groups. Each part, except for the initial kneeling, is repeated many times during the night (Figure 4).

Following this basic structure, then, I now describe the unfolding of a typical *momago*. As mentioned already, the event is understood to start when the introductory music, called *topo*, is played. At this point, the *tau walia* are usually still seated, although occasionally they can start to sing while still sitting down. At a certain point, the main *tau walia* stands up and kneels in front of the drum, having already covered his or her face with the *pompolonzu*[28] (ritual piece of cloth) to aid concentration. This cloth should be white to symbolize the *tau walia*'s pureness, but this rule is not always followed. It seems more important, though, to avoid red cloth because that colour represents the evil in the heart of people. Sometimes *tau walia* can use the *pompolonzu* as a link

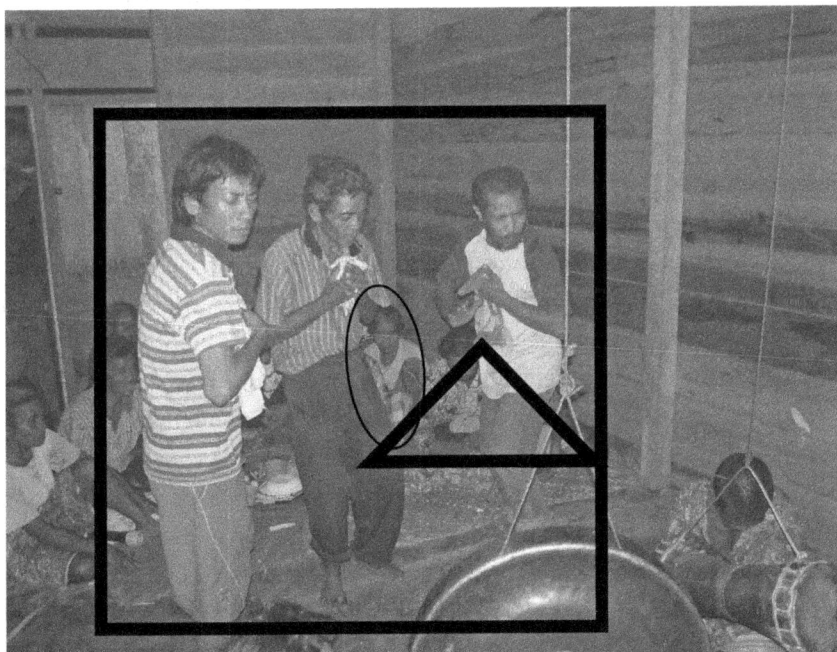

Figure 4 Three *tau walia* performing the *motaro* together. In the background is the *tau walia* Apa Main (in the blue triangle) treating a patient laying on the floor, while the female *tau walia* Indo Pino prays near the ritual tray (the arm of her blue top is just visible in the red circle). Source: Giorgio Scalici, photographer.

between them and the musical instruments, placing one end of the cloth on his or her forehead and the other end on the instrument, creating a connection first with the drum, then with the small and big gong. Once in this position, the *tau walia* starts singing to evoke the spirits.

After the invocation song, the *tau walia* stands up and passes the cloth all over his or her body, to purify him or herself, before starting to dance the *motaro*. Again, the purpose of the shamanic dance is mostly to aid concentration:

'The *motaro* helps one to see more clearly.'[29]

As I have noted before, the ability to see the non-visible world is one of the main characteristics of *tau walia*, so the *pompolonzu* covering the physical eyes of the *tau walia* helps him or her to enter a dream-like state and to 'see' the non-visible world. In some cases, the trance achieved is so deep that the *tau walia* are not able to stand or to stop dancing. In these cases, people are always on hand to support the *tau walia* or to stop the *motaro* by physically blocking them. When the dance has ended, *tau walia* concentrate on the patient. The shamanic cure, whether in a *momago* or in a different context, consists of attempting to suck the inner illness out of the body, often from the head or the back, and to cast it away. These actions are performed with the hands and the mouth, or with the help of the *pompolonzu*. The cloth is also used to 'clean' the sickness, with the *tau walia* spitting on the cloth and passing it over the patient's body. This part of the ritual is accompanied by shamanic chanting. The dramatization of the healing process through the sucking and spitting out of evil is not a factor seen only in Wana rituals but is, in fact, quite common in such diverse locations as California (Whiting 1950: 40) and Nepal. In the latter, 'this process is known as jharnu, or to blow the illness away' (Peters 1978: 66).

Particularly fascinating is an idea from Peters that 'the underlying effect of all these exercises in Tamang healing puja is to transmute the patient's symptoms and behavior into socially useful channels. In accomplishing this purpose, the symbol serves, I believe, as a guide or vehicle for the reorganization of the emotions released during the traumatic cathartic experience' (1978: 85–86). As we will see in the next chapter, the Wana wear a bracelet since the first day of mourning and it will be replaced twice during the key moments of the *kayori*. At the end, the last bracelet will eventually fall out symbolizing the end of the mourning period and all the emotional pain that wears off with time.

We should note that while the individual *tau walia* are busy with their trance, all around them are *tau walia* who are intent on dancing or treating people and bystanders who are chatting, joking and drinking. With myth, drama and performance, the *tau walia* create a frame that brings sense to the pain of the patient. For a community with almost no access to the healthcare system, it is much more difficult to explain things like asthma or psychological problems than explaining a broken bone or a skin wound, without reference to the hidden world. During the *momago* the illness is presented as a material object within the patient that the *tau walia* has to suck up and dispose of. This materialization of the non-visible makes sense of what otherwise could not be understood:

> The care consists in making acceptable to the mind that pain that the body refuses to tolerate. That the shaman mythology does not correspond to an objective reality is a trivial fact: the sick believes, and s/he is a member of a society that believes in it. The guardian spirits and evil spirits, the supernatural monsters and magical animals, are part of a coherent system that bases the indigenous conception of the universe. The patient accepts them, or, more exactly, no one has ever questioned. What he does not accept is the pain, inconsistent and arbitrary, which, however, constitute a foreign element to his system, but that, by resorting to myth, are replaced by the shaman in a set in which everything has a reason for being.
>
> (Levi-Strauss 1958: 221–2)

So, the shaman's role has two sides. One is to entertain bystanders and facilitate social interaction; the other is to cure the patient by giving them a way of understanding their pain. Through the interplay of pain and pleasure, illness and playfulness, Wana rituality is developed and valorized.

Conclusions

In this chapter came the first encounter with the *momago*, a shamanic ritual that is, above all, one of the main occasions for a party among Wana people. The ritual not only brings together the community, but it clearly expresses several of the key values of Wana culture. First of all, it articulates the *kasintuwu*. This comes through not only from just one family paying for the entire ritual and giving all participants the opportunity to be healed by the *tau walia*, but also through the presence of the community itself being necessary to cure the main patient. Having dozens of people together in a small hut or room recreates the primordial density that brought mythical power to Wana people, a power that was lost when the land of the Wana was scattered around the world. Secondly, the visible and non-visible have a central part in the organization of the ritual.

Light keeps away the spirits, they cannot and should not be seen, while the music (non-visible) calls them, creating a bridge between the human and the spirit worlds. The life of *tau walia* is based on this liminal status; they are humans who share a few traits with the spirits and can act as a mediator between the two worlds thanks to their position.

The final important element is the playfulness that characterizes Wana rituality. This positive energy is used to transform any negative situation, such as illness, into a positive event. It helps the community re-create itself – both enjoying the 'recreation' of entertainment and undergoing regeneration. All these elements will also be present in the next chapter about the *kayori*, a ritual that in some ways is a larger-scale *momago*, and they will be analysed further in Chapter 5.

The *kayori*

This chapter will explore how Wana people transform pain from the loss of a loved one into playful moments, through the *kayori* (funerary ritual). After passing through several explosions of controlled violence and an alternation of centripetal and centrifugal emotional forces, *kasintuwu* (sense of community) is reinforced and the emotional equilibrium of the family of the deceased and of the whole community is restored.

Rituality as a guide

To succeed in safely overcoming the dangers related to the death of a community member, Wana people put in motion a series of small and large rituals that help to establish a rhythm and pace for the healing process. The rituals escort the deceased individual, together with the entire community, through all the emotions roused by death – a process that starts with the physical death, then continues with the transformation of the body into a corpse, the cultural death and the arrival of the soul into *suruga* (heaven). These processes last between sixteen and eighteen days in total. During this mourning period, the deceased is not actually considered dead; although the corpse is already in its grave and the *koro uli*, one of the three Wana souls,[1] is separated from its body-vessel, the soul is still present amongst the living. For this reason, it is forbidden for the living to cry, except in the form of a ritualized expression of pain called *mandeke*, which occurs during certain moments of the ritual, especially in the two last days. Anyone who fails to respect the prohibition of crying becomes a victim of mockery from the whole community.[2] This behaviour flows from the belief that a human is made up of a body and souls, and that both of these elements must receive a ritual send-off from the community before the person can be considered completely dead. For this reason, crying before the end of the ritual is considered a pointless action; it would be like mourning somebody still alive. Of course, controlling emotions is not always easy and I will show later in this work how pain and tears are hidden and disguised.

Avoiding the expression of strong feelings is a common trait in many Southeast Asian cultures. Wana people believe that strong emotions can be dangerous for a person; it can lead to illness of the soul and the need for shamanic treatment. A similar attitude is found among the Toraja people of Sulawesi, who 'believe that emotional upset has an adverse effect upon one's health' (Wellenkamp 1988: 492).

Considering that the period being described lasts almost three weeks, I will offer a basic timeline of the Wana mourning for basic orientation:

> Day One: A person dies. The body is washed, the corpse is buried and the *uba* (a bag with offerings that is also the representation of the deceased and a passport for the afterlife) is prepared.
>
> Day Three: After collecting all the necessary materials (bamboo, wood, leaves for the roof, etc.), the family and friends start to build the *dumbaru* (ritual hut).
>
> Day Nine for a dead man (henceforth M), and Day 10 for a dead woman (W): In the middle of the mourning period, the community gathers and renews the *uba*.
>
> Day Fourteen (M)/Day 16 (W): *Wuri moapu* (cooking night), the first night of the ritual takes place.
>
> Day Fifteen (M)/Day 17 (W): *Wuri mankoni* (eating night), the second night of the ritual.
>
> Day Sixteen (M)/Day 18 (w): *Mantabu uba njotanoa* (bringing the *uba* to the grave), the last day of *kayori*.
>
> Day Seventeen (M)/Day 19 (W): The last lunch and the disassembly of the *dumbaru*.

Wana people consider the end of the *kayori* to fall on either day sixteen or eighteen; at this point, two sets of either eight or nine days have passed, the significance of which will be detailed below. However, even though I was told that the ritual was finished after the *mantabu uba njotanoa* and it was clear that many people headed back home even before the end of that day, after many months of research I discovered that there is actually another final ritual day immediately following. This day is not considered part of the *kayori* since it does not involve the wider community, but it is nevertheless important for the family.

The following discussion will chart the *kayori's* progress through these various stages.

The origin myth

As is often the case in oral cultures, the reasons behind many Wana practices can be explained through reference to mythical tales. Often when I asked people to explain why they did things in a certain way, their answer would begin with the words '*dari pertama*' (from the first time), and (when lucky) they would go on to recount a mythical story. Indeed, the reasons for conducting the *kayori* over this particular period of time – two sets of eight days for men and two sets of nine days for women – can be traced back to myth. I collected two tales about death. The first explains that in the golden era, humans did not know they could die; it is only when a *tau baraka* (a person from mythical space-time) sees that a fallen tree does not stand again that he discovers what it means to die:

> In those time, humans did not know anything about death. They did not know they could die. When struck by illness, age, or a lethal wound, they would lie down and get up again shortly afterwards, without evidence of their wound or their health issues.[3] On one occasion, one of the people of mythical time saw a tree fall down and not get up again. In that moment, he understood that humans could die, and he started crying. From then on, people that lay down dead did not get up again.

While this story tells us *why* people must die, the following story tells us *how* Wana people die in a cultural sense:

> At that time, when death did not exist, there was a man and a woman. They were walking while playing music. The man played the popondo (flatbar zither) while the woman played the tulali (three-holed flute). They were so immersed in their music, as if in a trance, that they accidentally entered two separate holes in the ground, and there they each continued playing without food or water. After two sets of eight days, another man went to look for them. The man called out to the couple but the melody of the tulali was the only reply; it was in this moment that he realised the popondo-playing man must have already died. He returned the next day and listened to the tulali music again, and this was repeated the following day, two sets of nine days after the couple had gone missing. This time he did not hear the tulali, and the man understood that both had now died.[4] From that day, the kayori has lasted two sets of eight days for men[5] and two sets of nine days for women[6] (Figures 5 and 6).

The number of days is also equal to the number of ribs Wana people think each gender possesses, since they believe that men have two fewer ribs less than women, and hence are lacking.[7] 'Eight and nine are inauspicious numbers that

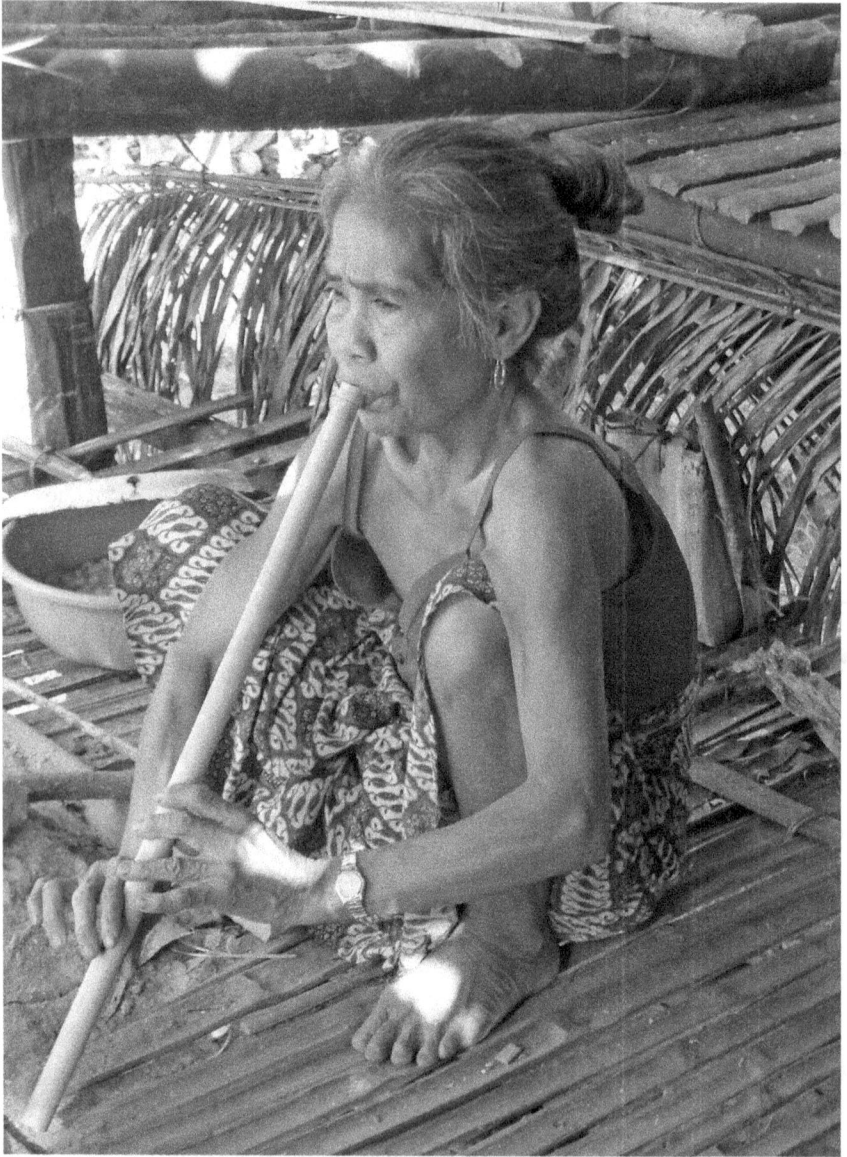

Figure 5 Indo n'Tibe playing the *tuali*. Source: Giorgio Scalici, photographer.

follow the auspicious count from one to seven that spells out a full life' (Atkinson 1990: 81–2). These beliefs establish the Wana custom of waiting a certain period of time between the burial of the corpse and the end of the mourning period. In addition, the role of music in this story could be the motivation behind the prohibition of playing music during the two days of the main ritual. The

Figure 6 Apa Jupi playing the *popondo*. Source: Giorgio Scalici, photographer.

presence of these two specific instruments in this foundation myth is also very important. These instruments have a special connection with sex and *eros* that none of the other Wana traditional instruments have. *Popondo* and *tulali* clearly have a strong connection with the hidden world of emotions and spirits – a connection that actually pervades the Wana understanding of all instruments and music in general. Atkinson explains that 'it is not uncommon for one who is skilled at playing a musical instrument such as flute or stringed chest resonator [*popondo*] to play haunting and plaintive songs to attract hidden beings' (Atkinson 1989: 54). These testimonies reveal the strong connection that exists between Wana music and the non-visible world; ritual instruments recall spirits, the *balo pombongo* (war trumpet) recalls war, and the *popondo* and *tulali* control sexual attraction. In a similar way, ritual mourning song calls up and guides the emotions of people involved, marking the different moments of the soul's journey to heaven and its slow transformation from being a live member of the community to taking the status of an ancestor.

This link between erotic music and death stresses the juxtaposition between the negativity of death and the excess of life that Wana people actively explore during the *kayori*. Death casts a shadow threatening to undermine people's faith in the meaning of their lives and of the community's rules and conventions. To protect against the disintegration of the community at these moments of crisis, Wana people try to fill the hole created by death with an excess of life that reinforces the bond between community members, creates new bonds among people from different villages, makes the community's physical and emotional presence felt, and guarantees that individuals and the Wana people as a whole will continue their journey. Similar rituals have been excellently explored in *Death and the Regeneration of Life*, a book edited by Bloch and Parry (1982). According to them, many cultures consider life a limited good, and the rituals surrounding death are a source of life, an occasion to create new life (Bloch and Parry 1982: 9). Any loss must be balanced by a gaining; the social structure must be constantly balanced to avoid the extinction of the community. In this way, the awareness of the limits of life is contrasted by the idea that the life of the community is 'timeless'. Even if few members die, the community is able to replace them, through an excess of life, the community will always exist and death, and its negative energies and consequences, will be controlled and defeated. 'It is evident, then, that individuality and unrepeatable time are problems which must be overcome if the social order is to be represented as eternal' (Bloch and Parry 1982: 15).

Day 1: Dying

When a death occurs in a village, the deceased is washed to purify the corpse of the pollution that is thought to arise from the process of dying. This belief is extraordinarily widespread across cultures, including in Tibet, where the corpse is washed with scented water (Sangay and Kilty 2011: 52), in Egypt, where soap is used in conjunction with water (el-Aswad 1987: 217), in Japan, where the *yukan* process is performed (Clark 1994: 129–31), in Ghana (Abasi 1995: 454), and among the communities of Lombok (Telle 2000: 785). Among the Wana people, special care is reserved for the head and the face of the deceased to make sure that they are presented as well as possible for their arrival into the afterlife.[8] Then, the corpse is wiped and dressed; the individual's best clothes are used and a machete is placed on the side of the corpse, on the left if the deceased is male and on the right if female. Machetes are objects that all Wana people possess from a young age; they are used for a great many actions, from peeling fruit to making canoes. Moreover, machetes are indispensable equipment for travelling in the jungle, both to open new paths and to protect oneself; it is almost unthinkable to travel in the jungle without one. I was unlucky enough to have a guide that did not bring a machete with him and when I told the story to my Wana friends they were all shocked by the irresponsibility of his actions. For this reason, it is realistic to believe that the machete is placed in the coffin to make sure that the deceased is able to safely undertake their journey to *suruga* (heaven).

The body, both when being prepared at home and when buried in the grave, is placed with the feet pointing to the east, where *suruga* is thought to be located, and the head pointing to the west, towards the land of the spirits. The rationale is that, from this position, the dead person can easily stand up and start walking in the right direction, leaving the world of spirits behind them.

While seated on *lemu*, *pokae* and *arat* leaves, the village chief, or somebody else who knows the tradition, dips a comb in a mixture of water and coconut water and passes it three times (a number we already met many times), from the top to the bottom of the forehead of the dead person to keep positive memories and emotions inside the soul. At the midpoint of the mourning period, a similar action is performed on the living relatives and friends, although in the opposite direction and performing the opposite function – dispelling negative emotions and thoughts. The leaves on which the chief sits prevent the propagation of illness. An illness, that how we already saw, is being considered by Wana people a concrete object like a stone or fishing hooks.

At the end of this process, the corpse is placed inside a *sarong*[9] and put into a wooden coffin. *Sarongs* are used in everyday life as blankets and people tend to cover their whole bodies with them while sleeping. It could be that covering the corpse with a *sarong* is a way to represent the deceased as a sleeping person who will wake up again to start their journey in the afterlife. A *pokae* twig is passed over the corpse, starting from the feet and working up to the head, and is then thrown away. Another twig is then passed from the head to the feet and thrown away too. The same action is performed upon the grave itself once the coffin is buried. This action, very similar to that seen in the *molawo* ritual where plants and chickens are passed over the body of the patient to dispel illness, serves to indicate to the soul the path it must take to reach heaven (the movement from the head to the feet) and also to dispel the spirits, sending them away to their realm (the movement from the feet to the head).

The burial can happen only during daylight. If somebody dies during the night (the time that belongs to the spirits), the coffin is kept closed inside the house. The dead are buried in their *banua mate* (house of the dead), a tomb dug outside the village, on which a roof made of palm leaves is built, and a place for the fire is allocated on one side. The tomb is a literal representation of a traditional Wana hut, with no walls and a place for the fire. Indeed, this will be the house of the deceased's soul until the end of the *kayori*.

After the burial, everyone who has touched the corpse washes themselves to purify themselves from the pollution; this action, like the duty to wash the corpse, is also related to the understanding of death as an infectious event. Nowadays, Wana people have an almost sedentary culture but, in the past, after a funeral they used to move entire villages to new uncontaminated places. Again, since Wana people believe that illness is a concrete object that can pass from person to person by contact, by washing they are making sure that the illness does not infect themselves or anyone else.

Once at home, the family prepares the deceased person's *uba*, the traditional Wana travelling purse. In this case, the *uba* maintains the function of serving as a travelling bag, but it is changed in its material composition and shape. In fact, the funeral *uba* is not made of rattan and palm but is a sack made of fabric.

Within it is placed a change of clothes for the dead, some betel nuts, *siri* (a plant usually eaten with betel) and *tiula* (a white powder derived from the tylomelania snail shell),[10] and a small case containing the *mata* (rattan thread with knots tied in it). The *mata* has sixteen knots tied in it for a man and eighteen for a woman. Each knot represents one mourning day and every day a knot is cut off and placed in the case. This daily action helps regulate the family's progression through the ritual period, giving a pace to their pain. Every day, the family members are obliged to conduct such actions, and these offer a constant behavioural guide that safely escorts them through the mourning period (Figure 7).

I also theorize, but I didn't get any confirmation from the Wana, that the *mata* also represents the rib cage, and each knot is a rib that is used to count the days the soul needs to get to the afterlife. I base this theory, not only on the shape

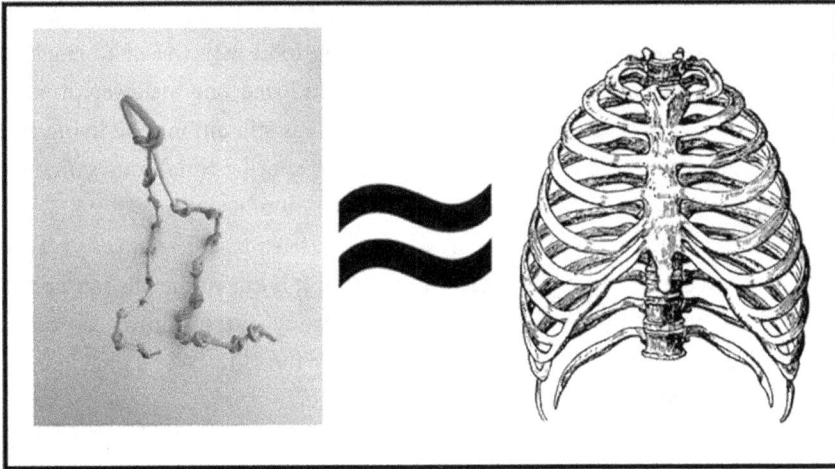

Figure 7 It is possible that the *mata* (left) is made to recall the rib cage, and that it is symbolically linked to the days needed to organize a *kayori*. Source: Giorgio Scalici, photographer.

of the mata, with the central knot representing the head of the deceased, but also on the clear link the Wana draw between the number of ribs each gender possesses, according to them, and the number of days each gender needs to reach the afterlife.

The same cloth that the *uba* is made from also provides the *yoku*, ritual arm bands for the close relatives and friends. Similarly, if the dead person is a man, his widow wears a band of this cloth around her chest from shoulder to shoulder, or if the dead person is a woman, her widower wears it around his head.

According to Atkinson 'at death, the betel bag of the deceased represents its owner's continued social presence through the funeral observance until finally it is carried to the gravesite, thus signaling the departure of the dead from the community' (1989: 183). At the time of my fieldwork the traditional betel bag had been replaced with a bag made of cloth and its role was more than signalling the social presence of the deceased. The *uba* has a threefold role: it is a travel bag for the dead, a passport[11] that allows the soul to enter heaven and, most importantly, it represents the dead during the *kayori*. Without the *uba*, the soul would not be able to enter heaven and it would become a ghost. This fact clearly states how much the community is important in the life and in the afterlife of a Wana. Without a community preparing your *uba*, reaching the heaven is simply impossible. Once again, we have the affirmation that the life outside the community is simply not possible. Moreover, portions of food and alcohol are served daily to the *uba* both to make sure that the soul is happy and to ensure that it does not become a ghost. Sharing food with the *uba* brings an air of normality and makes separation from the loved one a slower process. The physical body is dead but the *koro uli* (soul) is still among the living and it dwells there until the end of the *kayori*, when a specific ritual song sanctions both its entrance into *suruga* and the transformation of its status.[12] The first day of the *kayori* is the only day during which close friends and relatives visit the family of the deceased to offer their condolences. It is one of the few safe spaces for the grieving Wana to express their pain through explosion of controlled violence, called *mandeke*. Sometimes, people even hurt themselves during these expressions of pain.

During this time, they also discuss the organization of the ritual, which is one of the largest events that ever takes place in this context and requires the work of dozens of people.

Day 3: The *dumbaru*

The building of the *dumbaru* (the funerary hut) begins on the morning of the third day of the *kayori*. Beyond the symbolic and mythological power of the number three, there is also a practical reason to start the building of the *dumbaru* on the third day. While the first day is dedicated to the dead, undertaking burial rituals, and making other arrangements, the second day is the first available time to gather enough wood and bamboo for the building process, and so it is not possible to start the actual construction until the third day. Traditionally, the hut is built outside the village and isolated from other structures, but I also saw ritual huts built as an extension of the family's house. The walls of the hut consist of trunks and branches bound together, the floor is traditionally made of bark or bamboo (although nowadays the use of wooden boards is spreading), and the roof is made of palm leaves (although the use of tarpaulins is also becoming quite common). Four poles are planted in the hut, and the ritual song is later sung around the one nearest the *uba*.

Building a hut big enough to host hundreds of people is a task that requires a substantial workforce. The materials needed are collected in many different places; for example, the banana leaves required for the final ceremony are collected in the forest near Kolonodale, outside the reserve. There are similarities in Madagascar, where 'some men chop wood, [and] others prepare the temporary house which will receive the guest' (Bloch 1971: 152).

This community effort clearly expresses a key Wana value: *kasintuwu* (sense of community). Like many other Indonesian and Malaysian groups, such as the Toraja (Hollan 1988: 55), Wana people place a high value on affiliation within the community and emphasize the importance of social harmony.

The *kayori* is one of the most expensive and time-consuming events that a Wana family ever experiences. Without the help of the community, both economically and as a work force, it would be impossible for a family to organize a *kayori*, stressing again the need for, and importance attached to, the individual existing as a member of the community.

Although death inflicts a deep wound upon the community, which must respond by reiterating the triumph of life, it also provides an opportunity to emphasize community values and internal cohesion. So, it is no coincidence that the *kayori*, like the *momago*, is one of the occasions where *kasintuwu* permeates much of the activity. As in the *momago*, it is just one family that takes care of the ritual's costs, but friends and extended relations are there to help with the construction of the ritual hut, the preparation of food, and also with their physical presence and playfulness. They are there for themselves, not only to enjoy the feast and to say goodbye to a friend or family member, but also to communicate that they, and the community with them, are alive.

In larger and more fragmented or scattered communities, like those present in Western society, the death of a single member can pass unnoticed by people living even close by. In smaller communities, like those of Wana people, every single person is considered crucial for the survival of the group, and the group is crucial for the survival of the single member. In this case, if a single person were to become lost in the pain caused by the death of a loved one, this negativity – the pollution of death – could become contagious and spread throughout the entire village. To avoid this ruinous occurrence, the presence of behavioural and emotional guides such as the *kayori* can be viewed as the key to the persistence of Wana culture.

Building the *dumbaru* takes some time but tradition decrees that the construction must be completed on the day before *wuri moapu* (the cooking night, day 14/16). The building process sees many people working together and the family visiting the grave daily. People spend a great amount of time cooperating during the day and then eating, joking and having fun after sunset. The period between day 3 and day 15–17 is characterized by particularly pronounced playfulness and *kasintuwu* and, in fact, it constitutes the only period of time during which Wana people gamble, playing dominos and a version of poker.[13] People here are aware that gambling is illegal in Indonesia, and for this reason they stake only small amounts of money (typically 1,000 IDR, corresponding to *c.* £0.05), or they use a system of forfeits, in which the loser of a bet might have to sit on pebbles or pin clothes pegs to their ears. During these days, split between daytime preparations and evening games and drinking, the mourning family is constantly surrounded by friends and family in an atmosphere of playfulness and vitality that drives away any sensation of loneliness.

Day 9–10: The midpoint

On the ninth day for men, and the tenth day for women, the family focuses on a series of rituals that marks the midpoint of the mourning period and reaffirms the status of the deceased. The first ritual to be officiated is the passing of the comb. Close friends and relatives travel to a water source near the house, taking the *uba* with them. The village headman, or somebody else who knows the *adat*[14] (tradition), prepares a bowl with a mix of normal and coconut water. Into this mix he dips a comb (*siu*), while uttering some magic words. Then he passes the comb three times over the heads of the close relatives and friends, just above the forehead, with a movement from the bottom to the top. This action both expels bad thoughts and feelings and protects people from them. These actions are similar (apart from being in the opposite direction) to those carried out on the deceased during the first day of the *kayori*.

After a short break, people gather again inside the house to put raw rice inside four pieces of bamboo. The rice is placed on a tray – the same kind of tray used during the *momago* and also to sift rice in everyday life. In one of the rituals I saw, the widow then gave a signal for everyone present to start pounding the rice and to cry. This episode, which is repeated at the end of the *kayori*, is one of many spreads across the ritual period in which people give themselves licence to express and vent controlled violence against life, a kind of revenge against the loss of a loved one. Here, we must consider that rice is the principal, and sometimes the only, source of sustenance for Wana people, and that a failed harvest can mean death. Moreover, the harvest of the rice corresponds to its death (Friedberg 2011: 50); rice has a strong symbolic connection to both life and to death, and to the sacrifice of the individual for the survival of the community. Rappoport, in her studies on rice songs of the Lamaholot of Eastern Flores, Indonesia (2011, 2013, 2014, 2016, 2017), explains the widespread presence of death-related themes in these songs, and how the death of the plant could be related to the death of a person and provoke similar feelings: 'When

Lamaholot sing collectively about the rice maiden's transformation, they are genuinely sad to have lost a sister; they connect this mythical loss with real human losses' (Rappoport 2016: 176). She goes on to suggest that the rice songs describe 'how a human body is transformed into an edible plant, vital to the renewal of society. In the process of the cultivation of a crop, death is connected to fecundity' (Rappoport 2016: 174), stressing the relationship between death and life and the necessary sacrifice of the individual to allow the entire society to thrive and continue as an endless being.[15]

After this short episode of violence has passed, people put the rice inside four pieces of bamboo called *balo baili*, which have previously been cleaned and dried. Once filled with rice, a dried peel cob is put inside each of them to act as a stopper. Meanwhile, eight pieces of cloth (two larger and six smaller) are taken from inside the *uba*. The same cloth is then cut eight or nine times, depending upon the gender of the deceased. Then, two of the pieces of bamboo are closed with another peel cob tied with two *nilo* bark wires, and two more pieces of bamboo are closed with some pieces of cloth taken from the *uba* and tied with three wires made from *nilo* bark and a fourth made from the *uba* cloth.

Once the *balo baili* have been completed, people start making bracelets called *yoku* or *kamawu*. These bracelets, which are also made from the *uba* cloth, are to replace the *yoku* made on the first day of the *kayori*. On the last day of the ritual, they are replaced with a third and last set of *yoku*, which are either cut off during the week following the *kayori* and brought to the grave or kept on until they wear out. It is clear that the *yoku* is a material representation of grief; once again the Wana manage to transform the non-visible pain into a visible object. Wearing it from the day somebody dies and changing it throughout the mourning period waiting for it to fall off clearly represent the grieving process and the pain which progressively fades away with time.

After the preparation of the new *yoku*, the crowd prepares the *kadompe*. This is a bamboo holder to contain handmade cigarettes that are arranged in an alternating fashion – two groups of sixteen for men, and two groups of eighteen for women. The cigarettes are of the traditional Wana variety, made of tobacco and peel cob. Tobacco is widely present in Wana life, and almost all Wana people smoke since an extremely young age.[16]

Locks of hair are cut from the heads of friends and relatives by the village chief and tied to the *kadompe* with bark string. To ensure that the hair will grow back again, the village chief then blows on the spot that he has cut and says a *doa*. According to Edmund Leach, in a speculative essay (1958), the symbolism behind the hair locks is manifold. For example, he sees a phallic symbolism in them, suggesting that the male head is a phallus, and thus male hair represent the semen, while the female head represents the vagina and the hair of the vaginal extrusions. I do not think that Wana people make this strong connection between hair and sexuality, and consider their cut a form of castration, but it is plausible that hair represents life and vitality, and that the cutting of hair therefore constitutes another expression of organized violence and self-harm. Moreover, Christopher Hallpike lists a series of characteristics that make hair so unique and important: (1) it grows constantly; (2) it can be cut painlessly; (3) it grows in great quantity; (4) head hair is apparent on infants of both sexes at birth; (5) genital-anal hair appears at puberty in both sexes; (6) males develop facial hair after puberty; (7) hair on different parts of the body is of different texture; (8) in old age, hair often turns white and/or falls out; (9) hair is a prominent feature of animals (1969: 257). Personally, more than a connection with the human sexuality, I would like to focus on the ability of hair to regrow, in an almost unlimited way. Like the construction, wearing and cutting up of the *yoku*, the act of cutting a lock of hair and putting it in the *uba* can be regarded as a dramatization of loss; although something (the hair) is no longer part of us, that will not stop the rest of us (our remaining hair) from growing.[17] I believe the cut of locks of hair symbolizes the loss of the loved one, or a member of the community – a hole that we will feel but that with time will be refilled by new members and new hair. In the end, this and the other small rituals that form the *kayori* help the Wana in understanding and making concrete something that it can be extremely difficult to understand with words: that death is unavoidable and the pain we feel is the prelude of a new life, and everything will just follow its natural and cultural path. Like the *tau walia* extracting the 'inner illness' during the *momago*, the non-visible and untouchable pain caused by death is made it concrete and, in doing so, bearable.

Wuri moapu: The cooking night

With the approach of the *wuri moapu* (day 14 for men, day 16 for women), it is not only the mourners who come to the place of ritual but also sellers of various goods. The playful atmosphere of the *kayori* makes this event more similar to a fair than to a Western funeral and, being one of the largest meeting opportunities for Wana people, it becomes a major business opportunity for these sellers. The most common are those who sell sweets, alcohol and tobacco; usually they are Wana themselves and have spent the last few days preparing food and alcohol to sell. When the ritual is held in a place easy to reach by cars and scooters, sellers from other cultural groups (Bugis, Mori or Indonesians) often come to sell clothes, watches and other items.

In this way, people that usually do not have the opportunity to buy certain kinds of goods because they live far away from towns can do some shopping during the ritual. I clearly remember the daughters of Apa Reilin asking for money to do some shopping. Moreover, the ritual is usually held outside the village, which can isolate the participants and force them to stay under the roof of the ritual hut for two days and two nights, especially if the weather is bad. During the long nights in these conditions, people relish the opportunity to buy sweets for the children and cigarettes or alcohol for themselves. In this way, the dreadful occurrence of a death engenders a positive occasion for many others, yielding money for the sellers, leisure and sweets for the children, and new clothes for youngsters – none of which are plentiful in the jungle.

For children and teenagers, the *kayori* also provides an opportunity to stay up until late playing with friends and meeting new people from other villages, maybe even a future husband or wife. The *kayori* is also a positive event for the adults. Apa Reilin told me that his father, Apa Rau, liked to go to as many *kayori* as possible, to spend time eating and drinking with old friends and new acquaintances. For Apa Rau, and indeed all Wana people, the *kayori* is only a partially negative event if the deceased was a close friend or relative; otherwise, it is a two-night opportunity for socializing and having a good time with their friends.

A gift to themselves

The *kayori* is one of the two most expensive events in the life of Wana people, the other being weddings. The great difference between the two ceremonies is that, while the expenses of a wedding are provided entirely by the two families, the entire community contributes economically towards the *kayori*'s organization. When arriving at the ritual hut, all the participants go to the organizer of the *kayori* and hand over their gifts (rice, *pongas* or *chaptikus*,[18] or chickens) while saying '*aku punya*', which literally means 'I have', although it can be translated in this context as 'from me'.

The offering has many functions; first of all, it is a gift to the mourning family and a gesture of economic help that also expresses *kasintuwu*. Second, it stresses the necessity of living inside the community because, without these gifts, it would be impossible to organize the *kayori*. Third, it creates a bond and a debt; once one community member has helped another with a funeral, they expect that help to be repaid at the appropriate time. Ultimately, it makes sure that the participants enjoy themselves for several nights, and in so doing, this helps in the healing of the community. In this sense, one might even claim that the guests' gifts are, in the long term, gifts to themselves. Christopher Gregory makes a similar observation: 'A gift is like a tennis ball with an elastic band attached to it. The owner of the ball may lose possession of it for a time, but the ball will spring back to the owner if the elastic band is given a jerk' (1980: 640). It is very similar to when we bring our favourite dessert or beverage to a dinner party, so we are sure there will be something we will like to drink or eat.

One of the most important elements of the *kayori* is the banquet and, in the following paragraphs, I will show how this event is pivotal for the success of the *kayori*. Bringing food to the ritual is an act of generosity that reinforces a bond between community members and expresses *kasintuwu* but, at the same time, the guests are making sure that there is enough food, and especially alcohol to support a pleasant time for themselves. Again, we can see that the line between personal and communal gain is blurred in Wana culture, where the individual has meaning only as part of the community.

Playfulness and violence

While there is usually more than enough food to satisfy the whole community, and what is left is often distributed among the participants after the *kayori*, there is never enough alcohol, and more and more is bought over the course of the ritual. Wana people often asked me for money to buy alcohol, and, knowing my interest in ritual music, the village chief of Taronggo, Apa Ede, once told me:

> Alcohol makes people sing better. It will be better for you.[19]

What at first might seem like a mischievous ploy to convince me to buy alcohol for everybody conceals a deeper meaning. It is true that without a playful atmosphere the ritual would not be successful, so people rely upon a copious amount of drink. It is no coincidence that some of the bystanders pour out wine for the singers all night long. The wine, either made from rice or palm, is especially intended for the singers, to help keep them awake and strong all night. Apart from the closest relatives, throughout the rituals I never perceived sadness. Rather, all the activity is pervaded with enthusiasm – drunk people chatting and hugging, boys and girls flirting, playing, and listening to music, and friends meeting again after a long time.

Whole families, with children in tow, continue to arrive until late evening, completely filling the interior of the hut. Only one area of the hut is left free, providing space for the *mokayori*, the dance of the *kayori*. On this side of the hut there is a mat with the *uba* upon it. The latter is treated like the living representation of the dead, so people stay close to it, bring food and drink to it and chat nearby, so the spirit never feels alone. Near the *uba* there is also a torch, *soga*, which is lit at night. This torch is made of leaves and resin, *damar babi*, and it enables the soul to observe what it is happening at its funeral (Figures 8 and 9).

At the *kayori* that I attended, at one point as people were still coming from all over the reserve to participate, something notable occurred. Although it is difficult to explain precisely, I (and presumably other participants) began to feel a sense that something was about to happen. Sure enough, near the ritual hut, some recent arrivals were experiencing a *mandeke*.[20] They approached the *uba* and seemed to enter a trance state, articulating a violent explosion of pain with loud crying, and screaming. There is evidently gender differentiation in the way people perform a *mandeke*, men swinging their machetes, stamping their feet, and getting on their knees to cry, and women directly getting on their knees and starting to cry and scream. This episode is reminiscent of 'running amok syndrome', a phenomenon of Indonesian and Malaysian culture in which a person (often male) suddenly assaults people or objects with a weapon, usually a *kriss* or machete. This episode of controlled explosion gives the community members an opportunity to express their emotions in a safe time and place without having to suppress them during their daily life or express them in dangerous ways.

Moreover, the *mandeke* offers men an opportunity to show their own strength – that they are able to do destroy a hut with their feet or with their machetes. Again, there is a strong correlation between life and death, with funerals being an opportunity to foster new relationships, especially sexual relationships. For the women present, meanwhile, pain is more internalized, and its expression is subtler. They tend to contract their bodies inwards in front of the *uba* and to express a centripetal movement of their pain, turning the violence inwards upon themselves. The men, on the other hand, tend to expand their bodies into the available space, evoking a centrifugal movement. This way of representing behaviour seems to apply more widely to everyday life too; women are linked to the village and the house, while men go out to travel between villages.

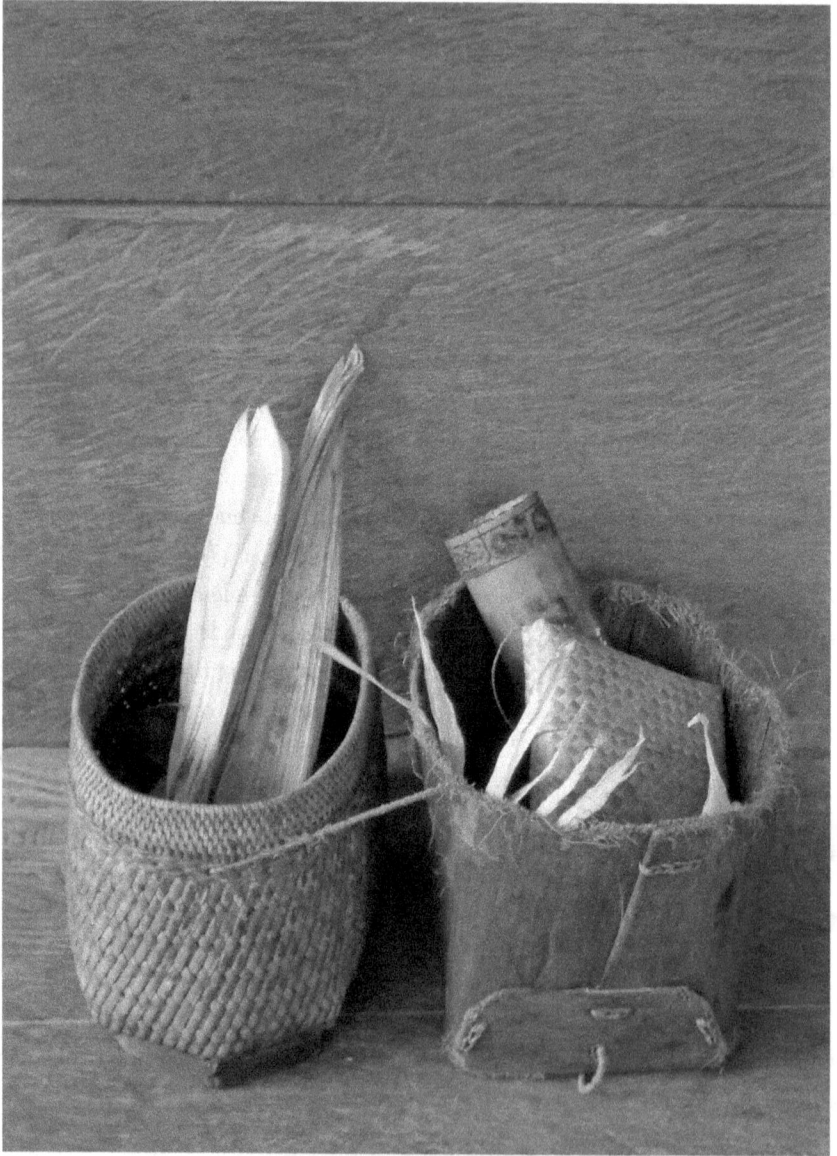

Figure 8 A traditional not death-related *uba*. Source: Giorgio Scalici, photographer.

In many cultures, women have a special relationship with emotion. Parry, for example, observes that in Banaras it is women who cry and men who express their sexuality: 'while the women wail, the young men dance in a burlesque of female sexuality – gyrating hips, upturned thumbs held in front of the chest to

Figure 9 An *uba* with a rice offering. Source: Giorgio Scalici, photographer.

suggest breasts, and sometimes a woman's shawl draped over the head and with mock allurement half across the face' (Parry 1994: 155). Bloch also alludes to the special connection between women and emotion: 'The reason why it is important that women should touch them [the dead] is that women are the recognised vessels of kinship emotions' (Bloch 1971: 156). Ultimately, as Agneta Fischer and

Antony Manstead conclude from a cross-cultural survey, 'women in all countries reported more intense emotions, and of a longer duration, and that they also expressed their emotions more overtly' (Fischer and Manstead 2000: 88).

After the initial *mandeke* is concluded and the majority of the participants have arrived, the preparations for the ritual feast can begin. Here, again, there is clear gender differentiation regarding duties. While inside the hut the women prepare the *siri* leaves and clean vegetables and the banana leaves that will be needed to cook the rice, the men, both inside and outside the hut, cut long stretches of bamboo into pieces, within which the rice will later be cooked. This dish – rice wrapped in leaves and cooked in bamboo – is called *iranueki* and it is only ever cooked for the *kayori*. It is considered delicious due to the particular flavour the rice gains having been cooked inside the bamboo. Throughout all these proceedings, the hut clearly represents the wider village as a safe cultural space connected with women. In contrast, the space outside the hut represents the jungle as the dangerous realm of men and spirits. Meanwhile, those who are not busy preparing food spend the time talking and joking.

When night falls, somebody who knows the tradition approaches the sacks of rice that are placed around the pole closest to the *uba*, the same pole around which the *mokayori* will later be sung. This person places some *tiula*, *siri* and betel nut on a leaf that functions as a tray, lifts and puts his head under the sheet covering the sacks and gives this offering to the rice spirits. They utter a few words beseeching the spirits to allow the participants to eat the rice without falling sick or having stomach-ache. The person then opens the sacks and, using a plastic bowl, puts three portions of rice on two trays that have been placed nearby. A few women then use these portions of rice to make twenty-seven *iranueki*, which are placed in three pieces of bamboo, nine (three sets of three) in each. Once these three bamboo pieces have been prepared, the other women join in and, all together, they prepare enough *iranueki* for the whole throng – nine banana-leaf packages of rice in each piece of bamboo. While the women are occupied with this task, a group of men makes a circle around the pole and, holding each other's hands, starts singing and dancing the *dendelo*.

Many reasons to sing

The *dendelo* is performed three times over the two days: at the opening of the first night, and both at the beginning and end of the second night. Thus, the *dendelo* performances serve to open and close the ritual. Holding each other by the wrists, the men begin to move around the pole. They sway left and right, then perform a heavy and noisy step to the right.

At first, both the movement and the singing are tentative, as though the men do not want to disturb the bystanders. As other people join the group, however, the singing grows louder, and movements become more determined. This is the start of the *dendelo*, the opening and closing song of the *mokayori*. They are sung by men only, and are always composed of the same stanza, which is repeated seven times because 'seven is associated with a full life span' (Atkinson 1989: 160).

When the *dendelo* ends, there is a short break and then another singing group is formed. This is a group of women, and it tends to be smaller than those of men. Possibly due to the shyness we discuss previously. There are no rules that prescribe who can join at this point; anyone is allowed to, even if they do not know the words. There are now two groups, one of men and one of women, and they form two semicircles around one of the poles of the *dumbaru*. These two groups, without touching each other, continue singing the *kayori* until dawn. The men place their right elbows on the shoulders of the men on their right and lay their heads on their own right hands. The women have their arms entwined. During the night, many people alternate in the singing, and there is much joking, helped by the alcohol poured by surrounding friends. As can be seen from the photos, although the *kayori* is a funeral and the singers have a pivotal role in escorting the soul to the afterlife, the atmosphere among them is relaxed and playful.

For a total of twelve hours or more during the two nights, the funeral song guides the soul in its difficult and dangerous journey from the land of the living to *suruga*; without the indications provided by the song, the soul would get lost and become a ghost. Again, the destiny of the single Wana person is controlled by the community, in the afterlife as in life.

The funeral song describes a journey to paradise on board a large canoe. At the end of the first ritual night, this canoe is replaced by a smaller canoe that takes the soul to its destination, and perhaps this can be connected to the custom prevalent in Southeast Asia of the second burial, in which the journey to the afterlife is divided into more parts.

It is highly possible that in the past, also the Wana practised a form of second burial that with time and the influence of Christians and Muslim has gradually changed in the rituals I observed. We saw how the *kayori* is clearly divided into two parts, indeed the days of the kayori are twice eight days or twice nine days and not sixteen and eighteen days. Moreover, the clear-cut separation from the day of the physical death and the one of the arrival of the soul in the afterlife is possibly another remnant of a previous second burial. Furthermore, the change of the size of the canoe, beyond the possibly allegory of the passage from a larger to a smaller coffin or burial, it reminds me of the passage from the large canoe used to cross the sea to the small canoe used to navigate the rivers in the jungle, as if dying were considered a return home after a long journey. In fact, the afterlife is also partially the space-time of the myth; therefore, it is to all intents and purposes a return to the origin.

Additionally, the song also aims to reinforce *kasintuwu* and to reaffirm the cultural laws.

Lagu mogombo serita
Sesinjuyu linga-linga
Atora rapasawiya
Naka siwaju pey kit[21]

It is much better to tell stories (myths)
Singing in the same direction
The rule is confirmed.
We are together.

In these lines, there is clear affirmation of the values of unity and of belonging to the community. The first and the third lines focus on myth and law respectively as the basis of cultural behaviour, while the second and the last lines focus more on the Wana sense of community. The singing is performed through the alternation of a solo voice and a chorus, the collective unison singing serving to stress the importance of staying and acting together. Nicholas Cook's observations about the singing of the national anthem in South Africa rings true for Wana group singing too: 'Like all choral performance, from singing a hymn to chanting at a football match, it involves communal participation and interaction. Everybody has to listen to everyone else and move forward together. It doesn't just symbolize unity, it enacts it' (Cook 2000: 79–80). Collective song in the *kayori* may result from the need for the community to re-energize, both through physical contact between the singers and by the union of voices into a single entity, symbolizing unity of the community. Wana people gather and sing together to face death together, and to act together as a single endless being. The relationship between the single member and the community will be fully explored in the next chapter.

Moreover, the circular movement around the pole can be interpreted as a call to life. Not only does it represent the movement of the sun, and thus life itself, but it also recalls an Indonesian dance often performed at weddings: the *modero* (Figure 10).

This dance is playful and has strong courtship traits. Like the *dendelo*, it consists of people circling a pole, but this time it sees men and women holding hands with each other. Circular dance as a symbol of life is not uncommon; for example, the Nevada Shoshoni perform a round dance that has the extra purpose of rainmaking and promoting crop fertility (Steward 1941: 265). Furthermore, in a culture where people do not hug or kiss in public, the presence of physical contact between males and females in controlled public contexts creates an opportunity for new relations. As Jack Harris notes, 'beyond courtship, the Round Dance helped produce social cohesion as it "wove a loose net of linkages"' (Harris 1940: 55). As Durkheim notes in the context of religious ceremonies, such behaviour serves to bring 'individuals together, multiplying

Figure 10 This round dance around a pole was observed at a Mori wedding (it is possible to see the traditional cloths). Round dances related to weedings or fertility festivals are very common in Sulawesi. Source: Giorgio Scalici, photographer.

contacts between them, and making these contacts more intimate' (Durkheim 1915: 586).

I agree with Wolf when he says that 'music and dance [...] provide conventionalized categories through which sometimes subtle emotional modalities are given concrete representation; they act as "signposts" for what I will call the emotional texture or contour of a ceremony' (Wolf 2001: 380). In this context, the music and dance stress the importance of the community and contribute to the festive atmosphere: 'In effect, at least three layers of musical meaning are engaged in dynamic interaction: 1) music as an announcement, or label, for, in this case, an emotional state; 2) music as an active constituent of the emotional texture of a ceremony as it unfolds; 3) music as directly affecting the feelings of the ritual participants (whether or not the effect can be adequately described)' (Wolf 2001: 382).

In addition, children are present in great numbers at the *momago*. This fact serves as another affirmation that it is an event orientated to life as much as to death. At the same time, having participated in the rituals from their earliest years, children internalize the Wana values proclaimed by the ritual and learn by observation how to express their emotions in similar situations. In other words, the *kayori* becomes a school of social, religious and emotional behaviour. Lonnie Yoder also recognizes this essential characteristic of funerals: 'As social ceremonies that bring together a relatively large group of family members and friends, funerals are important socialization experiences that help transmit the values of the culture from generation to generation' (Yoder 1986: 152). Moreover, there are many similarities with the Kota people's funeral culture, as suggested by Wolf again: 'in my estimation, about five people die in each Kota village every year. In such intimate surroundings, children become accustomed to viewing corpses virtually from the moment they are old enough to use their eyes. This process of socialization to death is also musical, for Kota experiences of death are mediated through sound' (Wolf 2001: 400–401).

Day 15/17: *Wuri mankoni*, the eating night

The second day of communal activity begins with the preparation of food. Again, there is a gender-based differentiation of roles. Inside the hut, the women prepare the grated dry coconut used to flavour the meat and the vegetables that will be served in the *wuri mankoni*. Meanwhile, the men cut and cook the chicken, while also preparing the bamboo that will contain the *iranueki*. The *iranueki* are roasted outside the hut and the chicken pieces are boiled with the coconut and the vegetables to make a stew-like dish. Chicken is not common in Wana meals; although they breed chickens in their villages, the meat is only eaten during funerals. This saving of chicken for funerals happens for two reasons: firstly, Wana people do not feel the need to use something if it is not strictly necessary, and they save the few chickens in their possession for special occasions. Secondly, chickens have a strong connection with Wana mythology; a hen is the pet of their god *Pue* and many stories within Wana mythology are about the seven mythological chickens that eat people. A chicken is also used for the dangerous healing ritual called *molawo* (briefly discussed in the first chapter), in which a patient's illness is passed into the bird. Until a few years ago, the chicken was the only animal to live inside Wana villages, attesting to its importance within their culture.

On another fire, the widower or widow cooks three smaller bamboos that are destined for the deceased. Meanwhile, in another spot, some women cut large banana leaves into squares. These squares are then roughly shaped into bowls and used to serve the food. Nowadays it is possible to see some industrial plates, but there are never enough of them to serve the food to the hundreds of people present. In the meantime, the same person that earlier said the prayer to the rice spirits makes two small trays and places portions of food, alcohol, *tiula*, *siri*, tobacco and betel nut upon them. Once ready, this individual places the trays, covered with banana leaves, near the *uba*. These trays are offerings to the spirits of the jungle, recognizing that, for Wana people, it is not only people who need to eat but also spirits. The trays are hung from two poles situated at opposite entrances of the camp. An invocation is recited to make sure that the spirits are happy and that they will make sure to guard the ritual and the people participating in it. It is possible that this action recalls the mythical past when humans and non-humans are believed to have eaten together as peers. During all of these preparations, the atmosphere is joyful and relaxed; some people socialize while others make preparations, and there is no sense of soberness.

Once ready, the food is delivered to everyone attending the ritual, with each person receiving one or two *iranueki*. The most prestigious figures within the community are served their food first on bamboo trays; typically, these figures include powerful *tau walia*, skilled village leaders and wise elders. Although they receive the same food as others, they are treated to some extra items – *siri*, *tiula* and betel nuts – which are also placed on their trays. Feeding these respected figures in a different manner demarcates and reaffirms existing hierarchies within the community, although it should be noted that these hierarchies are of very little significance in everyday life anymore; in almost all respects, *tau walia* and village leaders are treated just like other people and, in fact, I noted that *tau walia* tend to have relatively poor economic standing, even by Wana standards. Maybe these special trays are a way to thank these figures for the work they do for the community.

Before the beginning of the banquet, two of the elders approach the *uba* and pass each other an *iranueki* with their right hands and take another with their left. This ritual exchange between the two elders happens twice before the *iranueki* are placed on the roof of the ritual hut – a symbolic offering to those who were not able to attend the *wuri mankoni*. Louis-Vincent Thomas explains the function and importance of the ritual feast, noting that it 'is celebrated for him [the dead person, as] a farewell banquet, to allow the ancestors to accept him in their society [...] [T]his generalization of the phenomenon of death contributes effectively to making it less unusual and intolerable, and to show those who are grieving that what is happening is just a trivial fact'[22] (Thomas 1976: 474). Wana people believe that another banquet awaits the soul in heaven – another celebration to make this painful transition more 'normal', festive and acceptable. Funeral meals are an important feature in a great many cultures. Yoder, for example, points to traditions in Sri Lanka, Iran, Ethiopia, Nigeria, Sweden, Poland, Hungary, Romania, England and the United States, and incisively articulates one of the meal's main functions: 'its purpose [is] to reunite all the surviving members of the group with each other, and sometimes also with the deceased, in the same way that a chain which has been broken by the disappearance of one of its links must be rejoined' (Yoder 1986: 149). He notes how the meal, as a common everyday experience, is a symbol that life will continue for the bereaved. The meal enables the bereaved to experience a new social role in a public setting. Although the bereaved has had some preliminary experience without the deceased in the events surrounding the wake, the service and the burial or cremation, now the deceased's body is no longer present. The bereaved is, thereby, given a new kind of opportunity to experience life without the deceased. The bereaved person has an opportunity to experiment, role-play as it were, in the context of the familiar, structured setting of a meal (Yoder 1986: 155). And again, Yoder explains:

> The meal can also serve to soften the abruptness of the change from much defined ritual surrounding the funeral to the emptiness and loneliness that are likely to occur in the days and weeks following the funeral. Often the funeral meal will involve a smaller group of persons than that which attended the funeral. These persons are often significant others in the life of the bereaved. If support can be provided at the time of the meal and/or planned for the future, it will serve an

invaluable function in helping the bereaved deal with grief. Studies have shown that resolution of grief is helped by the presence of support systems in the period following the death, for example, a widow-to-widow group.

(Yoder 1986: 156)

Mandeke

Beyond the ritual banquet, this night (*wuri mankoni*) at the end of the ritual is full of significance. The end of the funeral song that coincides with the moment of separation from the soul leads to an extraordinary explosion of pain among family members. This moment marks the soul's arrival into heaven and the complete cultural and social death of the person, and the close relatives begin to scream and cry. Again, there is a gender division that can be characterized by the opposite forces, centrifugal for men and centripetal for women. If the deceased person is a man, the women grieve by pulling out their hair, scratching their skin and beating down upon the earth, trashing the ritual hut in an intense self-destructive expression of pain. On the other hand, if the deceased person is a woman, the men wreck part of the hut with their machetes and feet, externalizing their pain. This wild violence is all the more striking on account of the calm that immediately precedes it and the abruptness of the behavioural transformation. Those present accept these manifestations of pain, but with a degree of fear and disapproval. While some people try to prevent the afflicted from doing too much damage, others lose no opportunity to make fun of their behaviour.

Humour is present here not only because these violent explosions are considered to be almost a form of play, but also because humour is a part of wider Wana life. It is another essential tool to control the behaviour of the community and, in this specific case, to prevent the afflicted from losing control of their emotions. Wana people abhor negative emotions just as do those in many other Indonesian and Malaysian cultures (Hollan 1988: 4), believing that they lead to sickness. Humour helps them express their disapproval in a safe way, giving them a harmless means to control other members of the community and the excessive emotions that they show. Wana people tend to laugh at pain, be it emotional or physical. As in Bali, 'to express "good" *(buik)* emotions is a moral obligation. Add to this a presumption that expression nurtures feeling, and it should be clear why laughter and cheerfulness emerge as the sensible response to any kind of distress' (Wikan 1988: 457). Wana might laugh or smile as if to express that it is useless to become upset if one cannot control the situation.

Social relationships are also controlled by jokes and laughter, with all unaccepted behaviours, small or large, being met with humour rather than punitive action. In this way, Wana people can control each other and express their resentment towards others in a safe and peaceful way.

Day 16/18: *Mantabu uba njotanoa*

By the time calm has fallen over the night's activities, it is already morning, and the singers close the *kayori* with a last *dendelo*. While the ritual participants relax after the long night, other non-participants are just waking up, and a peaceful calm prevails. Everything remains calm until a group of close relatives gather near the *uba* and start to pound the rice in much the same violent manner as occurred during the midpoint rituals. After the pounding and some further damage is done to the hut, the group goes to the tomb, reverting to calmness in a strikingly abrupt fashion as they make the journey – only to suddenly switch back into violent *mandeke* behaviour on arrival at the grave. All this tightly prescribed rituality is required because funerals are not only a way to guarantee a good afterlife for the dead but also a primary means to heal the wounded community. Although it is commonly assumed that funerals are designed to honour the deceased, it is primarily the living that they target – to negotiate the meaning of death, to overcome it and to put it at the service of life and of the people left behind. Although it may seem contrived to an outside observer, this firm organization of emotions helps Wana people deal with the destabilizing event of death. Within the close-knit community, comprising hundreds of people all packed together under the same roof, different people perform different emotional roles. Music marks emotional time, and the sequence of actions guides the suffering individuals through the period of crisis and brings the whole community along with them.

Day 17/19: The last meal

Only at the very end of my six months of fieldwork, I discover that the *kayori* is followed by another day of mourning dedicated to the closest relatives and friends. However, this extra day is not considered part of the *kayori*. At this point, the majority of people – counted in the hundreds, including all the sellers – have already gone home and it is only the inner circle of loved ones who meet to eat together and dismantle the hut. The atmosphere is suddenly quieter and more relaxed. While the men take apart the hut piece by piece, the women cook pieces of coconut trunk and chicken. In one corner, some people weep, but this time it is different – calm, soft and less ritualized. In the privacy of this day, the family can finally cry in a less demonstrative and performance-orientated fashion.

As Yoder points out, this type of post-funeral meal brings different values and emotions, serving as both a ritual expression of bereavement and as a means to soften the shift from the grieving period back into the everyday life of the village: 'it often serves as a time where the immediate bereaved begins an emotional re-integration process. After the experience of intense emotions in the public settings of the wake, the service, and the burial, the meal provides an opportunity for the bereaved to establish some emotional bearing in a public setting. This can be reassuring for both the bereaved and the larger community as they begin to adjust to the loss. The meal can also serve to soften the abruptness of the change from much defined ritual surrounding the funeral to the emptiness and loneliness that are likely to occur in the days and weeks following the funeral' (Yoder 1986: 155–6). Eating together has an important role in the rituality of the *kayori* and the

Figure 11 A family chat and smile on the grave of a loved one after the last visit. Source: Giorgio Scalici, photographer.

re-creation of the community after a loss. As Mark Mosko points out regarding the North Mekeo, 'one of the stated purposes of mortuary feasts is to end the deceased's clan's mourning ordeals so they can return to ordinary village life. But this involves a reorganization of their relations and affiliations to the other clans of the endogamous tribe' (1985: 108). The chaos caused by the death of a member of the community first managed and then transformed in order through a specific rituality is marked by important events like eating together. The division of roles for the organization of the meal and the presence of the community gives its members a new reinforced order to follow, and in which they can feel safe. After lunch, the group goes to the grave for the last time, to weep, share stories about the dead and thereby mark the end of the grieving period (Figure 11).

Celebrating life

As I mentioned previously, the first day of the *kayori* is characterized by the arrival of the guests and the preparations for the feast. In all the rituals I witnessed, the influx of people was always copious, with some even travelling from quite distant villages. The ritual is as much representative of a fraternal feeling among them as it is also a trade opportunity. As I noted above, a large number of people selling various goods take the opportunity to find good business here. It is important to note that the ritual is long and tiring; people have to spend two whole nights in a hut in close contact with other people, often unable to return home because of the distance or weather. The traders are, therefore, meeting a genuine need, especially that of the alcohol that flows copiously at the ritual, just as it does in all kinds of Wana meetings and celebrations.

The gathering of people, the party and the singing all contribute to making death easier to comprehend and to affirm the continuity of life. The response to the death of an individual must be considered a parenthesis in time that should not destabilize the normal course of events. What characterizes the ritual is the fact that it is a public and collective action that has the power to bring about the adjustment of social relations and to induce individuals to conform to socially prescribed behaviours. This ultimately 'reinforces the participants' sense of belonging to the social body'[23] (Fabietti 1991: 23). That the *kayori* requires the active participation of a large community of people – from the construction of the hut to the preparation of the banquet – links it to *kasintuwu*. The group singing and the physical proximity with which people spend two nights together create both a physical and an emotional communion in which each Wana person might feel part of a group that is perpetuated through the generations, despite the death of the single individual.

The reaffirmation of life is linked to the circular dance that accompanies the singing throughout the nights. The circularity can be connected to the movement of the sun and the stars and may symbolize the continuity of life; as Apa Rau said, 'Re eo, re Wana',[24] literally translated as 'If there is sun, there are Wana.'

This directly relates to Thomas's observations regarding the underlying functions of funeral rituals: 'The funeral rites, in fact, celebrate life [...] This is not to deny death, but to accept it as a condition of regeneration'[25] (Thomas 1976: 473–4).

It is important to underline the fact that I found Wana people generally to be pessimistic about their own lives, considering themselves to be living through an era of terrible hardship in comparison with the situation in mythical space-time, although they do acknowledge that their circumstances are better than those of their grandparents' generation.[26] They face the challenges of their lives through looking ahead to the end of time as they know it and to the return of mythical space-time. Death and the afterlife in heaven have much in common for this yearning for mythical space-time; both bring the promise of better things and the fulfilment of all wishes. Heaven is also a reward for dealing with the difficulties of the current life: 'Heaven is thus taken to be compensation for life on earth. For the Wana, who suffer so much in their mundane mortal existence, the afterlife offers deserved leisure and comfort' (Atkinson 1988: 55).

Conclusions

Death is one of the greatest dangers a community can face. Not only does it produce great pain in the single members and the entire community, but it spreads a contagious and polluting sense of meaninglessness. The negative energies unleashed by death must be tamed and culturally controlled to avoid the risk of a disintegration of the community. To avoid that fate, communities around the world tend to respond to the negativity of death with an excess of life, balancing the two forces and allowing the community to become 'timeless'. Wana people employ a long funerary ritual, the *kayori*, that offers all members a guide for not getting lost in their pain, thanks to the smaller rituals that compose it. Each Wana person knows their role, that they are not alone, and that the community is there to help and support them.

This support is both non-visible (spiritual and emotional) and visible (economic). Small actions, such as cutting off a lock of hair or counting the days with the *mata*, offer to the single members an emotional guide that makes them feel safe and tells them what, when, where and how to feel their pain. The *kayori* would be impossible to organize without the practical and economic help of community members, and this transmits the message that it is possible to die properly only when a person is part of a community taking care of them in life and after death. I have shown how Wana people make a clear distinction between natural death and cultural death. They forbid the non-ritualized expression of pain because this is meaningless considering that before the ritual is complete a person is not fully dead. In fact, cultural death arrives at the end of the *mokayori*, the ritual song that guides the soul into the afterlife, and only at the end of this do Wana people express their pain, in an extremely ritualized way. The *mandeke* allows the community to safely express their pain while also expressing sexual messages of physical strength. Indeed, the *kayori*, like the *momago*, is an occasion to reinforce the *kasintuwu* and create new bonds. In this way, the negativity of death can be transformed into a positive event that re-creates the community and guarantees its continuity.

6

The expression of cultural values in rituals

In the previous chapters, I explored the cultural world of the Wana people, invoking a gradual immersion in Wana culture and rituality. In the third and fourth chapters, I presented and described the two major rituals, the *momago* and the *kayori*. It is now time to discuss the Wana values expressed in these rituals and to making more explicit the cultural connections between all of the elements introduced. My intention is now to present the bigger picture of the religious life of the Wana people.

Thus, this chapter analyses and explores the cultural values underlying that bigger picture of Wana people's worldviews. To discuss these values, I focus on the juxtaposition of elements on which they are founded. Several dualities are at the foundations of everyday life and, at the same time, are reinforced and expressed during rituals, in a continuing interplay between life and ritual. Dyads such as 'Wana and non-Wana', 'centre and periphery' and 'visible and non-visible' are just a few of the juxtapositions I will discuss in this chapter. I have already introduced all of these paired ideas during the introduction to Wana culture, and now the task is to show connections between them that may not yet be obvious (see Table 2).

Table 2 Major dichotomies in Wana culture

Male	Female
Jungle	Village
West	Tana Wana
Periphery	Centre
Nomadic	Settlers
Spirit	Human
Nature	Culture
Centrifugal	Centripetal
Brave	Shy
Outside	Inside

Wana and non-Wana

As I noted in the second chapter, Wana people define themselves in relation to not only their own mythology (they consider themselves the offspring of mythical people) but also their history and their power relationships with colonial empires (Indian, Arab and Dutch) and their neighbours (especially Mori and Bugis). The Wana people consider themselves inferior to other cultural groups, and a poor and cowardly community (Atkinson 1990). Moreover, they are often looked down upon by other groups in the area and by the Indonesian government. Perhaps for these reasons, the Wana people appear very united and supportive of each other, valuing peacefulness and serenity above everything else. It is also possible that their vision of themselves may be bound up with the fact that 'in the regional game of headhunting, the Wana were quite often the heads' (Atkinson 1990: 65). I consider Anthony Cohen's idea that community is a symbolic and contrastive construct and that it is shaped by the perception of boundaries marking off one social group from another (1985). It is reasonable to suggest that a sense of cultural inferiority and vulnerability in battle could have played an important role in creating the profound sense of community I have observed in the expression of *kasintuwu* permeating daily life. Together Wana people are stronger and can face the perceived difficulties and sufferings of their lives more successfully.

Wana people's idea of community goes well beyond the concept of 'community as the structure of relationships through which a localised population meets its daily requirements' (Matarrita-Cascante and Brennan 2012: 294). It is also more than 'the common life of beings who are guided essentially from within, actively, spontaneously, and freely [...] relating themselves to one another, weaving for themselves a complex web of social unity' (MacIver 1917: 34). Instead, it becomes a form of kinship that ties together all Wana people. Very often, people told me:

Kami satu keluarga (we are one family).

This assertion expresses a kind of nurtured kinship (Schneider 1984), where the sense of affiliation is looser and includes relationships not exclusively based on blood and marriage. As far back as in 1889, William Smith in his *Lectures on the Religion of the Semites* discussed an idea of kinship not based on blood, but on social relationships. What tied people together in bonds of mutual obligation often involved food and drink (Smith 1889: 265), and this seems to ring true in the Wana context too. Beyond the fact that Wana people believe themselves all to be descended from common mythical ancestors, there is a more concrete sense in which they all share some kind of direct kinship, linked to the fact that the community has only around 5,000 members. I constantly heard people telling me 'I have relatives in that [other] village' and then listing all of the distant relatives living there to emphasize to me their connection to that place. I interpret this as expressing a deep sense of *kasintuwu*, a bond that goes beyond direct blood ties. Part of this, too, is surely connected to their precarious life in the jungle, where selfish acts or orientations could have dangerous consequences. Almost everything is shared with others, and there is a moral imperative to pay back generosity whenever possible, rather than taking advantage of it. In any village, it is possible for people to ask for food or help from other members. While, of course, there are richer and poorer people, and society is certainly not organized on the basis that everything is in common ownership, the basic needs of housing and food are guaranteed by the community and by a sense of friendship and kinship that pushes people to support each other. When a hunter comes back with a wild pig, the meat is shared around the community; some people might decide to sell part of their share of the meat in another village, while others simply consume it by themselves. It is clear, though, how the efforts of a single member can benefit the entire community.

Being that Wana people are quick to share their goods with others, taking advantage of this generosity is not well received. I discussed in the second chapter how the behaviour of Wana Christians, in expecting to use canoes from the Marisa village without payment, has created many social issues. They have been known to commandeer the vessels as part of their business trading with the town of Kolonodale without compensating the owners in any way. In fact, it is very common for canoe owners to offer to take people from Marisa to Kolonodale. However, in this case there is a clear sense of exploitation and that their efforts and expenses are not taken into proper consideration; it is extremely heavy work to transport the Christians' large quantities of wood, rattan and resin, plus there is the need to buy fuel and make repairs to propellers broken in low tide. It is not a coincidence that the Wana Christians wish to become independent and to cut relations with the core community; they simply do not want to be involved in *kasintuwu* and wish to avoid supporting others in daily and ritual life. Wana Christians do not take part in Wana funerals or healing rituals.

This example involving Wana Christians illustrates an 'us and them' mentality. Wana people take the passive 'them' role in this separation, rather than themselves actively rejecting other groups. While Wana culture is very inclusive,[1] it is other groups of people that they come into contact with (Christians, the Indonesian government, Bugis, Mori and so on) who seem minded to isolate them, being influenced by a negative representation of indigenous cultures and religion deeply rooted in Indonesian culture. Wana people have experienced an unfavourable history of relations with the other inhabitants of Sulawesi, as described in Chapter 2.

Individual and community

This representation of Wana community as a large family has an impact on how the single members of the community relate to each other and the community itself. The desire to help and support each other is expressed in both daily lives, through the sharing of resources and support, and in ritual life. An example regarding mundane life happened during the time of my first fieldwork in 2011; a single person in the village of Marisa regularly paid for the petrol needed to power the electricity generator giving all inhabitants of the village the opportunity to watch movies and to charge their phones. These social occasions were very similar in intent to the *momago*: an entire village, sharing the same space, a hut and time, the night, acting as a single unity. These viewings were way more than simple TV time, they were an opportunity to express and experience *kasintuwu*, to become something more than a single Wana. This is particularly remarkable in a culture that does not miss an opportunity to define itself as poor and wretched; despite this, single members can be relied upon to share their hard-earned possessions to benefit the entire community. Accordingly, the *momago* is a healing ritual for the entire community that is possible only thanks to the effort and money of a single family or family member, who offers the opportunity to be treated by the *tau walia* for free to all those in need. The emotional and spiritual health of the entire community is supported by the economic efforts of a single family that decides to organize the ritual. The single member or family sacrifices something personal (usually money) to benefit the entire community; he or she alone becomes the starting point for the re-creation of the entire community. It is not just a single person giving to the community but all the members of the community that gives and takes from each other, each one according to their own possibilities. The organizer of the ritual covers all the expenses of the shamanic services, services that benefit everyone present. The result is an increase in power, derived from the re-enactment of the primordial density, that will be used to heal the main patient and the entire community alike. The *tau walia* themselves put the community in front of their own lives, being always available to help others in exchange for very little economic rewards, safe in the knowledge that they contribute to the inestimable wellness of the community.

Kasintuwu is expressed during all parts of the rituals; both the *momago* and the *kayori*. This reinforces the message that the life of the individual only has meaning inside the community. I believe that the main aim of these rituals is not to take care of the sick or dead person, both almost completely ignored by the participants of the rituals, but that it is actually the reaffirmation of the primacy of the community over the individual, and of the power generated by this coming together. Chappie and Coon (1942) stepped beyond Van Gennep's theory of 'rites of passage' (1960) by beginning to use the term 'rites of intensification'. While rites of passage are focused on the single member, rites of intensification relate to crises of the entire community and intensify the power of the community. Both of these kinds of rite are useful when describing the *momago* and the *kayori*. Both act as rites of passage (from illness to wellness and from life to death) and of intensification (placing the community at their centre). However, I propose taking a further step in understanding them to take into consideration the specifics of Wana culture. I define the rituals as 'rites of densification'. Their major aim and justification lie in the reacquiring of lost plenitude (Traube 1989); this is both the aim of the rituals and their source of power. Through this re-creation of the primordial plenitude, or density, they can at the same time reaffirm the rules of the community (as in rites of intensification) and also allow for the change of status of a single member or of the entire community (as in rites of passage). Just as 'it is well known how every myth is a quest for the golden era' (Lévi-Strauss 1958: 229), so every rite is a representation of myth, and the primordial density occupies a crucial position in Wana culture.

When someone gets sick or dies, the individual, and with them the community, loses their plenitude, their density. These rituals have the aim of recalling the community into a common space to establish again and increase that endangered density. I use the word 'density' instead of 'plenitude' or other similar terms because this is the best term to describe the primordial state when, according to myth, the whole world was condensed in a single spot (the first land). Moreover, taking into consideration the important role of centrifugal and centripetal forces for Wana people that I have already discussed, there is a constant alternation of concentration (centripetal) and dissipation (centrifugal) states, coinciding with phases of wellness and weakness.

In the third chapter, I outlined the structure of the *momago* and suggested that the participation of the community is a core element, along with the presence of the *tau walia* and of the musical instruments which are, indeed, owned by the community and not by individuals. The *patudu* is a simpler and cheaper version of the *momago* in which the community does not take part to the same extent. As I noted in the third chapter, the *patudu* is considered a basic version of the *momago* for emergency situations in which a lack of money, ritual instruments or something else mean a full *momago* cannot be arranged. It involves just two *tau walia* and a single family for the treatment of a single patient. For people who consider themselves poor, it might seem advantageous to fulfil the aim of curing an ill person through expending the fewest resources possible in this way. Nevertheless, Wana people still prefer to invest time, money and energy organizing the *momago*. How, then, can this preference be explained? The answer needs to consider that the main aim of a shamanic ritual like the *momago* is not, in fact, to cure a single person. It is actually to renovate and heal the community and to bring about the dense concentration of people that evokes the mythical time when the community was one. In fact, the *momago* would be impossible without the presence of the community; it would be a different ritual. It seems that the community's presence brings something more than simply playfulness and participation.

A similar situation is also true regarding the *kayori*. The entire ritual seems to have as its main message that the right death, like the right life, is only possible inside the community. First, the construction of the *dumbaru* (ritual hut) is possible only thanks to the help of friends and relatives. Even if this preliminary work could be achieved with a small group of people, the main part of the ritual, the two final days, would be impossible to organize without the help of the entire community. In Chapter 4, I noted that the only way to feed the hundred people or more who come for the ritual is for each of them to bring and share something. Bringing food to a ritual secures the reciprocal support of others when the next family is bereaved; this is a clear manifestation of the mutual support, or *kasintuwu*, which creates indissoluble relations in both life and death. The community is necessary not only for the life of its members but also for their death.

Funerals are very expensive events, and it would be impossible for a single family to cover all the expenses; unlike in the case of the *momago*, there is no cheaper version. As a result, attending a funeral gives the sense that entering heaven would be impossible without the support of the community. The wider group not only pays for the funeral, and brings food and alcohol, but it actively helps with the organization of the event, with building the ritual hut, cooking, and serving food, and, most importantly, with singing. The singing is a communal activity, and the song is crucial in allowing the soul to reach the afterlife. That is, without the community's singing, the soul would get lost and become a ghost. In this way, being part of a community becomes a necessity that gives sense to life as a whole. Moreover, from a more physical point of view, during the night of the ritual, the individual member can physically feel the presence of the community and the density of the situation. Hundreds of people have to sleep in a big hut, leaving almost no space to walk around. For the ritual, Wana people come together in a single place from all parts of the jungle. This place becomes the centre of the world, symbolized by the pole around which the *kayori* will be sung. People return not only geographically but also temporally to the primordial status of powerfulness, when all Wana people shared the same space (the womb or the spinning top).

At the same time, the community is both the starting and the ending point of Wana life and rituality. The *momago* and the *kayori* would not be possible without the participation and presence of the community and, at the same time, they are needed to reinforce the community itself, in a circle of mutual reliance. The everyday life of Wana people is full of perils, pain and frustration, and mustering the energy needed to control constantly the negative emotions that could lead to sickness requires a great psychological effort. From the Wana point of view, a person's illness and related death is caused by the absence of the soul. This loss of density is due to a centrifugal force (a strong emotion) that pushes away the soul from its body (centre), leaving it wretched and destined to die if a centripetal force (the *tau walia*) will not restore the natural and cultural density. To restore the lost density and, more importantly, to avoid the spread of negative emotional states that are interpreted as caused by the escape of the soul, Wana people organize these rituals to heal the entire community and to offer a release valve for all of the frustration of life.

Among Wana people, the life of a single member is incomplete outside the community and the crucial moments in life are characterized by the community's role. While in other societies it might be possible (if a little unusual) for there to be only a very small group of guests at a wedding, funeral or a baptism, in Wana society this is not an option. Life is organized in such a way that the community becomes necessary to fulfil successfully all the key tasks of a life (weddings, healing rituals, harvest rituals and funeral). In general, Wana people are very independent, often working, hunting and building houses alone, and they are highly self-sufficient in demanding daily tasks that arise when living in the forest. This signifies that the tasks are considered straightforward and that they do not carry particularly strong social value. Moving to the key moments of life (illness, marriage and death), however, Wana people need the community to complete their tasks. An exception to this comes when a child is born, and it reveals that birth is not necessarily to be thought of as such an important event. Although usually there is the help of an older woman acting as midwife, giving birth is a private experience. Om Dobi and his wife were very proud to tell me she gave birth to her second child entirely alone. Beyond such neutral events (childbirth, building a house and other 'daily' tasks), the community has a role on all occasions.

Centre and periphery

I have shown that the rituals are aimed at restoring the primordial density that vanished with the dispersal of mythical people, land and power outwards from the centre of the world, *Tana Taa* (Wana land). Considering the important role that the juxtaposition of centre and periphery plays in Wana reality, I will now explore this relationship with the intention of understanding how Wana people categorize space and place themselves in it. The division of space in patterns of concentric circles has an impact not only on the way Wana people interact with the world, but also on how they understand themselves and their emotions. These concentric circles have different degrees of mythical power, and access to each space is limited to different categories of beings: *tau walia*, men, women, *tau Baraka* and so on.

Before beginning the main discussion, it is worth pointing out again that one scholar has already deeply explored the relationship between centre and periphery and the marginality of the Wana people. The German anthropologist Anna Grumblies wrote her PhD thesis on marginality and the relationship between Wana people and the wider world, most importantly the Indonesian government, palm oil companies and the Christian groups of the area. She explored not only how Wana people are marginal to the spheres dominated by the Indonesian government and other powers, but also how they deal with and react to this state of affairs. She explains that her thesis is 'about people who are described as marginal and who consider themselves marginal. But it is also about people who have developed their very own understanding of their marginality and who have recently started to use their marginal position as a powerful tool to counteract marginalization processes directed towards them' (2016: 6).

While this is necessary and valuable work, I must again point out a crucial difference in our two approaches. When Grumblies labels the centre and the peripheral, she does so from a point of view that is more etic than emic, accepting that the Indonesian government represents a natural 'centre'. In many ways, her reflections are quite justified, not least because even the Wana people themselves have internalized this sense of their own isolation and marginalization (meaning that they recognize having been forced into a position of powerlessness). I argue, however, that taking an emic point of view, the whole idea and the characteristics of the centre and the periphery are completely inverted.

Wana people, however, conceive of a world in which the centre is a place that used to have a high concentration of power but that is now powerless, while the periphery now has real power but only because it took it from the centre. Moreover, Grumblies affirms that 'Wana see their land as the navel of the world, *pusen tana*. This land is, furthermore, the source of *baraka* (power), *kasugi* (wealth) and *pagansani* (knowledge)' (2016: 103, emphasis in the original). Therefore, the very idea of being marginalized or peripheral is turned on its head; Wana people are aware that they are powerless due to mythological and historical reasons, but their powerlessness derives from their central position, not from their place on the periphery. After all, as scholars such as Anna Tsing (1993) and Tania Li (1999) have all explored, centre and periphery are social constructions and vary culture by culture.

Considering the important role that mythology has in traditional culture (Lévi-Strauss 1955), and that mythology is still one of the few sources of information about the world outside the jungle, to understand the cultural background of the Wana world it is important to start with mythological stories. According to the myths I heard and collected during fieldwork, at the beginning of time, the Wana land was the first that Pue placed on the water; it was a dense mass of land that formed the sacred mountain *Tunda n'tana*, and the mountain was the centre of the world. Once created, pigs started rooting around the mountain soil, spreading the land around the world and creating the continents. This event, along with various others, began the erosion of the power of the Wana land and the diffusion of its power around the word. The original land lost its density and became less powerful. After that event, the people of myth also left the Wana land, spreading to the West, especially the Netherlands, and the edge of the world (*Joe n'Tana*). This signalled the end of mythical time and the beginning of the Wana people's unprosperous life. Atkinson claims that 'over time, [...] Wana have grown smaller and weaker. Time, by the Wana equation, spells degeneration' (1989: 49). I agree with Atkinson, but I would say that space, and not time, spells degeneration. According to my observation of Wana culture and conception of time, it is not time that creates a degeneration, because time is something Wana do not consider, but it is the distance from the mythical space-time, something concrete that it is not temporally far away but spatially. The mythical West is not happening in the past, but it is happening now, along with Wana reality and time, almost parallel to it. The myth is in another space more than another time, and the power of the Wana is directly proportional to the proximity of the mythical reality.

This lack of 'density' and the dispersal of mythical power from the Wana land towards the West has a deep influence on how Wana people divide the world and interact with it. Looking at Wana people's division of the world, there is the village at the centre; this is the place of the human. The village is the place of culture, but no power from mythical space-time remains here. Outside there is the jungle, the place of the spirits. The jungle is where people go to look for knowledge and to become *tau walia*. It is generally considered a dangerous place, but Wana men travel and even sleep in the jungle without any fear. I have already clarified that the concept of the centre is subjective and locally constructed; each village is the centre for the people who live there, but at the same time, on a more universal level, the religious centre of the Wana land and the world in general is the *Tunda n'tana* mountain and the village located there, Uewaju. Therefore, on the one hand the real centre of the world is the sacred mountain, but on the other hand, in daily life it is one's own village. From each village, each inhabitant's life spreads into outside realms.

Following Rob Shields's (1991) idea that each space has a specific rank in relation with other spaces, I will now try to describe the ways in which Wana people rank their geography based on distance from the 'centre'. The world outside the villages and the jungle is divided into areas. The closest to the Wana land is Indonesia, a liminal place hovering between them and the mythical West. Apa Rau dreams of and talks about Jakarta as a 'heavenly city', but it is also a world that is known to Wana people, since they go there to trade goods and to buy objects such as TVs, movies, and t-shirts, all of which have an origin that is mysterious to them. Beyond Indonesia there is the West, or the Netherlands.[2] That Indonesia is a former Dutch colony means that these two concepts often overlap, and the term *Belanda*, the Indonesian world for the Netherlands, is used as a general one to refer to the West and to the world beyond Indonesia more widely.

It is important to clarify the understanding of the difference between East and West when explaining the Wana division of the world. Even considering that, in Wana culture, the West is thought of as the place of the spirits and of wealth, in opposition to the East, which is the place of the afterlife, this division is not something grounded in geographical reality. Instead, it is a categorization made on the basis of the perceived movement of the Sun; Wana people believe that the Earth is flat and that the Sun goes around it. The East is the place where the Sun rises, and it represents life and power; it is not a coincidence that the dead are buried with their feet aiming to the East to be ready to stand up and move in the right direction. At the same time, the West is not only the new dwelling of mythical power but, due to it being the place where the Sun disappears, it is also related to the dangerous world of the spirits. The dichotomy of East and West is based on categories of, for instance, light and dark, more than on directions. The West is a category and not a direction; everywhere outside of the Wana land, no matter in which compass direction it lies, is considered the West and a mythical place. Indeed, the mythical character of the West is manifest in the wealth of all of its inhabitants, that its streets are made of gold and that everything is full of power. During fieldwork, even I was considered almost a mythical person; people wanted to touch me and my belongings were considered extraordinary.

It is for these reasons that I represent how Wana people categorize the geographical world as a series of concentric circles (Figure 9). At the edge of the world there is the *Joe n'Tana* where mythical people dwell. Again, according to myth, mythical people that once moved from the Tana Wana to the edge of the world will one day come back to the Wana land, bringing back Wana people's lost power and prosperity, and re-establishing the integrity and density that was lost with their departure.

A criticism of this concentric circle model is that it only takes into consideration horizontal space and does not incorporate the vertical plain of Wana reality. This verticality is a feature of the world as it is in relation to the sky over the *Tunda'n tana*. In this world there is *Pue* and the afterlife, while the underground, even if in the past it was considered a separate realm with its own god, is nowadays almost ignored by Wana people. My reason for focusing on the horizontal is that, in the Wana case, there is no reason to consider vertical and horizontal as opposites. Instead, I imagine the Wana world as a series of concentric spheres, with the Wana land at the core and the *Jo n'Tana* at the outer border, and in between there is the West and the afterlife. In Wana culture the West and *Pue* have the same 'mythical grade'. Wana people move in horizontal plains, but *tau walia* can move both vertically, to visit the afterlife, and horizontally, to the West. Even the dead, who follow the pole in the *dumbaru* to reach the afterlife, are usually described as travelling eastwards. The key to this apparent contradiction is that Wana people do not give the same value and sense to cardinal directions when talking about power, and that these issues are more matters of distance than direction.

Gender, space and power

I see, then, all of Wana reality and rituality as constructed upon this juxtaposition between centre-powerless and periphery-powerful and the constant movement between spaces. Each day, Wana men move from their house to the jungle to work (collecting rattan or resin), to hunt (bats, monitor lizards, wild pigs) or, in the case of some from the villages closer to the borders of the jungle, to travel to the outside to trade. They then return to the village. On the other side, Wana women stay in their homes or villages, or go to their gardens, which are considered part of the village. Here it is evident that Wana culture divides space between genders.[3] In her essay 'Gender in Wana Society' Atkinson offers a fascinating discussion of the role and value that women and men have in this society, and she often underlines how 'Although men and women may be the same sort of beings going about their tasks in Wana communities, men gain something extra by travelling farther in the realms of both the wilderness and the state' (Atkinson 1990: 80).

Travelling far is what actually differentiates male and female among Wana people. While it might seem obvious to point out gender differentiation in sex and procreation, actually 'the participation of men and women in the process is conceptualized not as complementary, but as identical. Both sexes menstruate, both become pregnant, and both are the "source" of humanity' (Atkinson 1990: 77). Men and women are culturally considered equal, but space and labour are nonetheless clearly divided by gender. Men are linked to the space outside the village, where they hunt, work or simply travel. That space (the forest, Indonesia or even the West) is the place of spirits and knowledge; it is here that a *tau walia* goes to learn about the world. Women are tied to the village; they almost never travel alone, and their tasks almost always concern life in the home. The crucial point is that there is no rule that forbids women from behaving in the same ways as men, but women simply do not do so. Often humour and jokes are used to control people's behaviour, but I never saw a woman patently blocked from covering a task usually performed by men. On the contrary, it seems that through education and cultural training Wana culture creates unconscious blocks that prevent women from reaching positions of power, such as *tau walia* or village chief. As we saw in Chapter 2, in her analysis of gender relationships among Wana people, Atkinson states:

> 'Anyone' could become a shaman, a rice specialist, or a legal expert. That those 'anyones' are predominantly male is treated as a fluke of fortune, rather than a categorical process of inclusion and exclusion. In this sense, Wana women

represent the 'everyman', the majority, who because of lack of bravery, fortune, good memory, or inclination never come to excel at what it takes to be a political leader in a Wana community.

(Atkinson 1990: 88)

I think that 'inclination' is the key word; without specific rules blocking women from power, why are women not inclined to become *tau walia* or a village chief? A simple answer might be that they are shy. Culture undoubtedly plays a crucial role in shaping the desires of people and how individuals interact with the world around them. For this reason, it is strongly possible that the shyness that characterizes Wana women is a cultural tool that has been used by Wana society to control access to power. It effectively bars women from positions of power without the need for any form of physical strength to be used. Violence goes against one of the most important cultural values of Wana people that strong emotions are dangerous and must be avoided.

It has been suggested by Sherry Ortner (1974) that females are viewed as closer to nature and males as closer to culture. I take issue with this formulation in the Wana context. For Wana people, the village is a safe place of culture, while the jungle is a dangerous place of spirits and nature. If women are confined to their villages, it is because 'nature' is considered too dangerous or, even more importantly, too powerful for them to be allowed to get close. Rather than there being an opposition between nature and culture, among Wana people, the real opposition is between visible (human/powerless) and non-visible (*walia/* powerful). In this binary, men are closer to spirits than women. It is perhaps not a coincidence that nowadays the closest people to the spirits are *tau walia*, and the great majority of them are male.

Standing still

Finally, it is also important to note that the central position, characterized by living in the jungle and remaining poor, is also a choice for Wana people. Grumblies explains how 'if the millennial promise shall fulfil one day, bringing them a new Golden Era, Wana need to remain *masi yasi*, pitiful, poor, dumb, in other words: marginal' (2016: 123). The Wana transformed an imposed social and economic subalternity into a position of power. They inverted the periphery-centre power relationship, self-positioning at the centre of the world. Even in their immobility, Wana manage to respond to the attacks from the world and to obtain, in the future, the power that will free them. Since space, time and power overlap in Wana culture, physical and economic immobility is crucial if Wana people are to be ready for the return of the *tau baraka* and the restoration of the golden era. In this section, I have tried to show, though, that the word 'marginal' in Grumblies' understanding here might be replaced with 'central'.

> [Wana] claim that Muslims live their heaven here on earth, as demonstrated by their comparative wealth and preoccupation with purity. In the Muslim section of heaven […] people live in filth (pointedly portrayed as pig excrement) and they are so hungry that their souls take the form of wild boar that root through Wana gardens in search of food. As for Christian souls, they have only scraps of clouds to eat (an apparent reference to Bible school pictures of Jesus and angels floating about on cumulus banquettes).
>
> (Atkinson 1992: 691)

This report from Atkinson shows how Wana believe that the return of the golden era will be the reward for everything they are presently suffering, while Christians and Muslims already live in paradise. Following this reasoning, only the Wana people who remain *miskin* (poor) and at the centre of the world will be in place for the restoration of the *tana Wana* (Wana Land) as the renewed power core of the world. In other words, 'Wana, in millennial fashion, foresee a time when their now-despised religion will be accorded proper honors. If history is to be a succession of eras, as the dominant culture asserts, then it is only right that […] history should end where it began – the first, who are now last, shall be first again' (Atkinson 1983: 692) or

> Breaking out of this current marginalized standing by becoming powerful, educated and rich due to their new empowerment will make them no longer suitable for their spiritual friends, the *tawᴬ baraka*. They would no longer fit the bill of the pitiful marginal people; a picture that they needed to attend. Thus, some of my interlocutors expressed fears that once they would experience empowerment they would no longer be proper candidates for the *taw baraka*.
>
> (Grumblies 2016: 280, emphasis in the original)

Centrifugal and centripetal

The movements between centre and periphery raise a constant juxtaposition between centrifugal and centripetal forces. I now explore this contrast and its impacts upon mundane and ritual life. Every day, Wana men travel from their village to the jungle or to other villages to trade or work, and then come back. At night, their souls leave their bodies to wander around the world before returning to their bodies, if, that is, they are not kidnapped by a *setan* first. This movement is constantly evident during rituals too. Atkinson has already noted that *momago* is a dramatization of these two forces; during the ritual, the *tau walia* leave their bodies to travel among the realms as spirits, looking for the lost soul so they can bring it back.

During the *kayori*, the soul of the deceased is sent away through the chanting. The movement of the singers itself gives a sensation of centrifugal energy; they swing three times before falling heavily on one side. In a more physical sense, the acts involved in organizing the *kayori* require constant movement from the village to the forest and back, as people look for and bring the materials needed. There is also movement from other villages to the place of the *kayori*, as people come to mourn and then return to their villages. The movement from the hut to the tomb also enacts a similar centrifugal phenomenon. Initially daily, and then during the moments of the ritual, close friends and relatives leave the *dumbaru* to visit the tomb, in an act that recalls leaving the place of humans (the hut) to venture into the place of spirits (the tomb).

When somebody gets inner illness, it is because their soul has got lost or wounded, this making the person less 'dense' and sick. To remedy this state of lower density, the *tau walia* must venture into the world of spirits, leaving the safe village to wander on the world's periphery, before coming back to the village once he or she has found the lost soul. Even more significant here than the village is the house in which the ritual is held. During the *momago*, this hut becomes the temporary centre of the world, the *Tunda n'tana* and the axis mundi that, thanks to the music, allows for the transition from the human world to the spiritual world. Moreover, the rituals and the music bring back to the land of Wana the power of the myth, dragging this power from the edge of space and time to the centre of the cultural world, the house of the ritual. This is a centripetal movement in opposition to the centrifugal movement of the *tau walia*. To reproduce mythical space-time and harness its power again requires the replication of the mythical condition, in which everything is dense and concentrated into one point. It is for this reason that hundreds of people gather together in the hut; they recreate, on a much smaller scale, the density of the beginning whose power allowed humans to achieve fantastic feats and to be complete. The *momago* ritual acts as a gravitational centre that attracts and concentrates everything around it. Thus, during the night, in a normal village house, the community, the spirits and mythical space-time all converge to regenerate the community, to make it anew and heal all of its sick people.

Of course, with only one sick person, the threat to the community is small, and so there is only a small reunion. However, the *momago* can be understood as a kind of pre-*kayori*; its role is to take care of the sick, equivalent to that of the *kayori* as taking care of the dead, which is a much greater danger to the collective and one requiring a much larger response to save the community and allow for its regeneration. In the end, the main aim of both rituals is the re-creation of the community through the densification of it. A bigger emotional wound, the death of a loved one, needs a bigger power to be healed. To obtain that power, a larger number of Wana people take part in a *kayori*, possibly ten times the number who take part in a *momago*, generating a stronger densification of the community and with it a stronger power.

Much more than the *momago*, though, the *kayori* is reliant upon recalling the density of mythical space-time. When a person dies, their soul leaves the body but is kept by the centripetal forces of the community inside the human world of the village. Friends and relatives bring a gift and interact with the soul to keep it happy and connected to the world of humans, before the journey begins that brings it to the edge of the spiritual world, the *suruga*. At the same time, the men go outside of the village to look for the material needed to build the hut and come back with it, as if it were mythical power itself, to build the hut. Once the preparations are over, hundreds of people gather from all over the jungle and even further afield to participate in the ritual, recalling the return of the mythical people from the edge of the world and their reuniting in a single point, the *dumabaru*. During the ritual, the *dumbaru* becomes the centre of the world; in this case it is not the musical instrument that plays the role of the axis mundi but rather the pole around which the people sing, indicating the path to heaven that the soul will climb to reach the afterlife. Death represents a greater danger for the community than illness, so a larger body of people has to gather. In a sense, the people who do gather represent the entire Wana community, since people come from all villages, and those who do not make the journey are stood in for by the exchange of the *iranueki* between elders. In this way, the whole community can be restored and regenerated through the density that is found again. Hundreds of people gather under the same roof, in a hut that is not big enough to host everybody, and this forces them to stay physically close to each other. In this way, the power of myth is recalled, and the original integrity is reaffirmed, in preparation for the explosion of the final violence and the end of the ritual. At this point, a small group of people go from the centre of the hut to the outside to visit the tomb, and finally come back. The significance of going outside is that this is the place of spirits. It is not a coincidence that an elder places the offerings to the spirits at the borders of the village; the territory beyond this border belongs to the spirits. At the end of the ritual, people go back to their villages, decreasing the density of the community but restabilising the 'normal' status that will prevail until the next *kayori* or until the final return of mythical people.

Similarly, men and women are trained to follow the duality between the centre and the periphery. During the organization of the ritual, men always take care of business outside, they go to the jungle to look for building material and they cook outside the hut. Women, on the other hand, never leave the hut and cook or prepare what is needed while remaining inside the hut. The inside is the world of women, while the outside is the world of men. Men and women also follow this dichotomy when expressing emotion. As we saw with the *mandeke*, men tend to expand physically in the space, destroying the hut with their machetes, externalizing both their virility and their freedom of movement. Women, on the contrary, even when expressing rage against life (pounding the rice), tend to become smaller, to close their body. This dichotomy between men's destruction of the hut and women's pounding of the rice, again, is consistent with the differences between the genders in Wana daily life. Men travel around the jungle almost daily with the machete that is a necessity while travelling, and they use it to cut down trees or clear paths. Women take care of paddy fields and gardens, which are located outside of the village but are still considered part of it. In life, then, as in death, they take care of rice, the main source of nutrition. The whole process involved in cultivating and preparing rice is taken care of by women, from the paddy field, to cooking and draining. Even if reflective of a position of less freedom, women have great power inside the home; controlling everything to do with rice means controlling the life of the family and its food. If, though, women usually do not tend to cover roles that are considered male domains, men on the other hand do sometimes 'invade' the sphere of women. Men cook, work in the paddy field, garden and do some work inside the hut of the *kayori*. It seems that men have a wider mobility than women do, moving not only outside the village but also within it. In *mandeke* of the morning, we can see how the women briefly try to wreck the hut but this is more a symbolic act than a real intention.[5]

Even if, in terms of status, Wana people are fixed in their position of powerless centrality, in an everyday sense, they do move from the centre (the village) to external parts of their geography and return to the centre. I understand this as a constant combination of centrifugal and centripetal forces (Figure 10). These movements are reproduced in Wana rituality and in the different expression of emotions for men and women.

Atkinson briefly discusses similar issues, when she identifies as a central idea in Wana culture the movement forwards and backwards from different realms: 'Wana associate the most valued forms of cultural knowledge with distance from their own settlements' (1990: 72).

The alternation of centrifugal and centripetal energies that characterizes Wana reality is found easily not only in the *momago*, but also in the *kayori* and in all of Wana mythology. Centrifugal movements usually accompany a loss of density (the soul leaving the body renders the owner sick), while centripetal energies signal a return of that density (the return of mythical people bringing new power to the Wana people). Taking Atkinson's intuition as my starting point, I will explore this relationship between movement, space and power. This takes me towards thinking of movement in space as related to the ways men and women express their emotions during the *kayori*, that these behaviours embody the Wana categorization of space.

Atkinson (1989) explains that the *momago* is built upon constant centrifugal and centripetal movements, with *tau walia* travelling with their souls among the different realms and then coming back, repeating this almost all night long. In her essay on gender among Wana people (1990), she notes that there is no rule prohibiting women from becoming *tau walia*, but instead that men make *tau walia* more easily because they are more commonly seen travelling outside of the village and into the dangerous place of the spirits. The same happens during the *momago*. It seems no coincidence that the ritual is held in a house and not in the jungle like the *molawo*. The *tau walia* travel from the safe place of the house to explore the space outside the village, and at the same time outside of the human world itself, into the realm of spirits. This dangerous task is considered a male one because women are enculturated to be more reticent and shyer. The conception of the world as divided into female and male spaces is important in the *momago*.

Similar processes and conceptions are evident in the *kayori*. Here, the number of days needed for a man's and a woman's funeral is different, because women are thought of as travelling more slowly than men, both in real life and during the journey to the afterlife. This is usually because they carry children, and so travel is more dangerous for them. In addition, there is a centripetal and centrifugal movement involved in people going from their villages to the house of the ritual and then back to their village. Likewise, the soul travels from the house of the dead to the afterlife. In particular, though, it seems useful to draw a connection between these centrifugal (male) and centripetal (female) movements and the expression of emotion.

It is not a coincidence that Wana women are characterized by their 'shyness', something that is recognized both by men and women. This shyness was noted by Atkinson in the 1970s and presented itself to me as a key feature of Wana culture and the gender differentiation in 2016 too. As Grumblies also notes, 'The "timidity" is still an important point of self-reference and is deeply connected to a self-marginalization process [...] in which Wana often portray themselves as "stupid," "poor" and "helpless"' (2016: 226). This shyness or timidity, therefore, affects the whole Wana community and its vision of itself, but is particularly strong among women. To reconnect this trait to the lack of female *tau walia*, it is worth mentioning that I never saw a woman under the age of sixty dance in a *momago*, and they explained this as being down to their shyness. This shyness among Wana women has the effect of keeping women outside of the spheres of power. It is interesting to notice how young Wana are not shy when dancing in other celebrations, such as weddings.

During the *momago*, the *tau walia* move backwards and forwards from the house to the place of the spirits and, at the same time, the spirits come to the human world and return to their spirit world. In everyday life, men move from the house, the place of women, to the forest, the place of spirits, or sometimes to the villages outside of the forest to trade and then back again. The funeral has a similar structure, with the soul moving from the land of humans to the afterlife, following the *Tunda'n tana*. On top of all this, emotional expression follows a similar pattern. While men tend to expand in the space while expressing themselves during funerals, women tend to simulate their daily space, the house. They are more introverted, just as their shyness means they rarely dance during shamanic rituals.

In 'Gender in Wana Society', Atkinson discusses some elements of gender division among Wana people and concludes that 'Wana underscore the fundamental likeness of the sexes and the complementary nature of their work' (1990: 63). She also clearly describes how their world is organized by gender:

> The world of a conjugal unit is divided into gendered tasks. Men clear brush, fell trees, and burn plots for planting; women are primarily responsible for planting, weeding, and harvesting, although the last of these three tasks is in fact one in which both sexes freely participate. In addition, men hunt and both sexes forage for riverine and forest food. Men build houses and granaries; women make items like mats, baskets, and clothing. And, importantly, men travel long

distances to coastal markets to trade Wana products like rice, resin, and in some
areas, rattan, for cloth, salt, and metal implements.

(1990: 69)

The complementarity of the two genders is reflected in their daily tasks
(cooking, working in the paddy, taking care of children and so on), some of
which are shared by both sexes. The most important difference between the two
genders is the relationship with the space around them: 'Whereas women tend
to be "settled" (rodo), men go off to distant places from which come both danger
and power' (1990: 71). More importantly, 'Wana identify both women and men
as life-givers. Asserting a fundamental likeness between the sexes, however,
Wana culture celebrates powers removed by space and time from human
settlements and defines access to these powers in a manner befitting men's, not
women's, activities' (1990: 79).

Pain as part of life

How it is possible to see in the videos, during the *mandeke*, the controlled
explosion of grief, women tend to become smaller. They become an embodiment
of the centripetal energies that control their lives, while men move more
expansively in the space before calming down and closing their bodies on
themselves like the women. Looking at Atkinson's research, it seems that similar
contrasting behaviours were present forty years ago: 'men appropriately express
their grief through displays of anger; women, by contrast, wail' (1990: 68). In
addition, male behaviour was heavily oriented towards the centrifugal forces
that pushed them away from the village to safely express their emotions and
pain: 'men's greater mobility and capacity for violence once offered them another
outlet for their grief. I was told that in the past a man could mantau kamawo
nraya, "carry out his grief," by killing someone. As an act of mourning, he would
don a white headscarf to wear until he had fulfilled his vow to take a life' (1990:
68). The headscarf described by Atkinson is still present nowadays and marks
another gender difference in grieving.

After the death of her partner, the widow produces a band from the *uba* to
place around her torso, from the shoulder to the opposite hip, like a sash worn
inside the clothes. On the other hand, the men, as noted by Atkinson, wear a
headscarf made from the *uba* as a mark of their grief. Of course, nowadays Wana

Figure 12 Indo Derhi asked for a photo of her with the *uba* of her husband. For her, this photograph is a kind of family portrait, because both she and her husband are present. It is possible to see a part of her mourning sash made with the same cloth of the *uba*, and the same material is also used for the *balo baili*. Source: Giorgio Scalici, photographer.

people do not go to the forest looking to take a life to balance their loss, but instead express their pain through the *mandeke*. In both cases, the expression of controlled violence not only 'safely' channels the pain out of the griever but also offers a safe environment for the community to express that pain. In a culture like this, where negative emotions are closely controlled and considered in a negative light, profound loss would be impossible just to ignore or laugh about. Like the *momago*, the *kayori* offers a safe space and time in which to express all of the frustration and pain, and an opportunity to regenerate the entire community through episodes of controlled violence and playfulness. Considering the role played by the two musical instruments linked to courtship, the *popondo* and the *tutali*, it is reasonable to think that the manhunt in the past and the *mandeke* now are also opportunities for men to show off their masculinity to the women present at the rituals and to look for new partners. In fact, large events like the *kayori* provide significant opportunities to create new bonds and to reinforce the community, where one relationship ends another one can be born. In Wana culture, life has a meaning only if shared with other members; the *kayori*, like the *momago*, comes about as a result of a traumatic event, but more than anything else, it is a celebration of life. The relationship between wretchedness and playfulness in Wana rituality will be addressed later (Figure 12).

Crying

Just like the rest of the *mandeke*, the crying is also extremely ritualized. Listening to Wana people crying during the *mandeke*, it is clear that the crying of each person is very similar and follows the same pattern. Indeed, the ritualization could be linked to the fact that 'Weeping appears to be involved in the reduction of stress, the relief of suffering, and the release of tension' (Christian 2004: 47) and the excessive emotions have already been tamed and what is left is just a less powerful and dangerous residue of the emotional turmoil of a few weeks before.

The four samples discussed here were recorded at three different moments. First (**1. Crying – arrival to the *dumbaru*)**[6] is the crying of Ingus from when she arrives at the place of the funeral and cries in front of the *uba*. Then (**2. Crying – end of the *mokayori*)**, there is a group of women crying at the end of the *kayori* song, and another group of women crying at the end of the *kayori* before going to visit the tomb during the last morning of the ritual (**3. Crying – before the visit to the grave**). Finally, there is a group of people crying once they have arrived at the tomb (**4. Crying-at-the-grave**).

There are differences in the sounds in each of these recordings, and they result from the different sound environments, and reflect the timbres produced by people of different number and gender in each case. Aside from these differences, it seems that each sample of crying follows a similar melodic and rhythmic pattern to all the others. There is an initial melisma on a vowel, usually *e* or *u*, and then a high note is reached that descends to become a mumble whose words are hard to understand. Usually these words are of desperation, expressing some kind of negation of death, and reflecting Davies (2017: 4) theories on words that rage against death.

There are few studies on crying songs (Magowan 2001; Tolbert 1990; Urban 1988), weeping as expression of cultural identity (Huang 2003), ritual crying (Kondi 2012), the psychological benefit of crying (Bylsma, Rottenberg and Vingerhoets 2008), and even if Gary Ebersole stated that 'our focus must be on "performative" tears (those shed in rituals proper or in ritualized social situations that perform cultural work), as well as on the discursive activity that takes place around tears-as-signs' (2004: 187), I am not aware of any existing studies that offer an acoustic analysis of crying.[7] What follows, though, is my own reflection on what it is happening among Wana people. While my informants reported that *mandeke* and the other expressions of ritualized pain were a kind of play, there is certainly true pain here and the crying is tightly controlled by cultural training, and it becomes a 'sign vehicle' for an emotion (Urban 1988: 387) that is expressed in front of the entire community.

It might be reasonable to expect that a random sample of people from the same cultural background would produce a lot of variety in the vowels, rhythm, melody and style of their crying. The Wana people involved in the funerals here, though, seem to show a very standardized way of expressing pain. Beyond that, once the *kayori* ends, and only the close friends and relatives remain to dismantle the ritual hut, I heard a very different form of crying. In 2011 I decided not to record the Wana during the *mandeke*. In 2016, I understood that the problem was only on my side and the Wana had no issue with being recorded while screaming, crying or destroying the hut because for them it was a play. Once I discovered the existence of a private day after the end of the *kayori* I had the occasion to observe a different kind of weeping, a weeping that once again placed an ethical dilemma. In the end, I have decided to respect the privacy of my informants because I understood the different quality of that weeping and its spontaneity and intimacy. I noted that on this day after the *kayori* there is no screaming and that the crying is softer, gentler and more private. Usually, people cry alone or when they are slightly isolated from the group. The public (visible) and private (almost non-visible) expressions are very different and exist almost at the two opposite ends of a spectrum of emotional externalization.

On one side we have the instinctual and spontaneous pain felt by the members of the community, on the other side there is the requested social behaviour. During the *kayori* the 'spontaneous' and private expression of emotions is forbidden, because cultural death has not occurred and also because this kind of behaviour should not be seen by other people. After the ritual has ended and the density has dissipated again, it is possible to express pain in a more spontaneous way. There are precisely five moments when people cry during the *kayori*: (1) at the first day of the *kayori*, when people get the news of the death of a friend or relative (something that I did not witness, but I heard many stories of people hurting themselves performing the *mandeke* having found out about a loss); (2) when arriving at the *dumbaru* on the first day of the final stage of the ritual, and the crying person takes the centre of the scene in an empty space in front the *uba*; (3) at the end of the song that escorts the soul to the afterlife, when the entire community knows what is going to happen; (4) before the visit to the tomb, on the last morning of the ritual; (5) once arrived at the tomb. All these moments are highly ritualized and controlled by the community. There is no surprise and they are the key emotional moments of the ritual, ones that attract the interest of a large part of the audience and that are influenced by the audience's gaze. On the other hand, the day after the *kayori* there is less control from the community. There are a few friends and relatives around, all sharing the same pain during the *kayori*, while the majority of people are there to enjoy the party and to get drunk with their friends. However, on the day after the *kayori*, relatives are left largely alone and the social expectation on them to maintain controlled expression of emotions is relaxed. Now there is space for a more intimate support and understanding befitting close family relationships, and finally they have an opportunity to break free from the ritualized expression of grief.

The ritual is over and ritual space-time has given way to profane space-time, one that is less powerful and less dangerous, and where the density is close to zero. This status gives the mourners the freedom to express their emotions as they prefer.

A more minor energy needs a lesser density to control it, and this gives people the opportunity to safely express their emotions again, this time not in front the entire community (high density) but just in front a close circle of people (low density) (Figure 13).

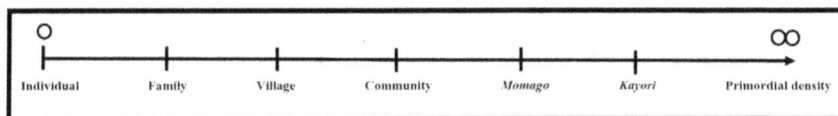

Figure 13 The power increases with the increasing of the density. The grade zero is the individual, which by himself has no power and no meaning. The final grade is the primordial density, the reward and aspiration of any Wana; the apex of the power. Source: Giorgio Scalici, photographer.

Smiling pain

If on one side we have this powerful expression of pain called *mandeke,* on the other *momago* and *kayori* are events characterized by the constant presence of smiles and laughs. Joking, at funerals, shouldn't come as a surprise to us, it is common, at least in the near past, in many cultures (De Martino 1958; Drucker-Brown 1982; Harlow 2003; Mosquera 2018), and it serves many purposes.

Linda Francis described the role of humour as 'generating positive sentiments among members of an interacting group by bonding them and/or reducing an external threat, often at the expense of some excluded person(s), event(s), or object(s)' (1994: 152). This description perfectly fits the situation among the Wana, where humour is used to literally reduce the external threat of death and illness, and to control the behaviour of the people who can't follow the social norms and, thus, represent a menace for the stability of the community. Contrary of what Mary Douglas (1999: 159) wrote, 'the joke consists in challenging a dominant structure and belittling it', among the Wana, humour is not used to belittling the norm but to reinforce it, but in a way that doesn't require physical violence. The norm, coming directly from the mythical time, must be respected because it is the only to assure the survival of the community. Sadly, in the last years, the Wana are experiencing an aggressive influence from Christians, modernity, new economic systems and the Indonesian government that is changing their lifestyle, creating cracks and issues inside the community. Beyond the friction with the Christians in the area that don't want to be part of any ritual, traditions are changing, and not always for the best. In my last fieldwork, I had the unhappy opportunity to observe a failing *kayori.* A ritual during which the community didn't have the opportunity to come together, create the playful atmosphere we will see in the following pages, heal the community and, especially, supporting the mourning family. Instead of a one dense group, the Wana scattered in many small groups, outside the ritual hut, and in so doing they failed to re-propose the primordial density which allows the regeneration of the community and the affirmation of the immortality of the Wana community.

Despite these changes and complications, certain rules are still respected. In fact, one of the major sources of humour in funerals, beyond the abundant alcohol, are the jokes made on the expenses of the people who cry, outside the dedicated moments, during them. As much as it can seem cruel and strange to many readers, Wana people believe a person isn't completely dead until the end of the long funeral, between seventeen and nineteen days, when the ritual song marks the exact moment the soul of the deceased arrives in heaven, and it is not any longer part of the community. For this reason, people who cry before that moment, and not in a ritualistic manner, are seen as infringing social norm and doing something, from their point of view, absurd, as crying for somebody who it is still considered alive and, actually, spiritually present at the funeral. All this seems to support Polimeni's idea that 'the primary evolutionary function of humour is to optimise social norms, while laughter serves to synchronise social attitudes around subjective social norms' (2016: 70). For the Wana, humour is indeed the main tool for social control. Anyone, from normal members to chiefs or shaman, can be a target, and it is normally used to point out some dangerous or abnormal behaviour both during and outside funerals. I recall the time when somebody made a joke on Indo Pino, a powerful and respected female shaman, when noticed she used an old laundry detergent bottle as a water bottle. The joker wanted to point out the dangers of doing that and being a powerful shaman didn't save Indo Pino for criticism. Indeed, 'Humor is such an essential ingredient in communication that it has been referred to as a lubricant for social life' (Zinker 2003) and this is especially true here.

Moreover, it is extremely on point what Hammond (1964: 264) wrote:

> As a means of communication, joking provides a permissive and flexible context which a grievance can be expressed, thus allowing for its rectification and the restoration of amity. As a means of control, the public nature of most joking serves to shame the object of the jocular offensive, to invoke social pressure for his conformity, and elicit support for the complainant. As a means of catharsis, the joking expression of aggressive feelings reduces frustration and thus serves indirectly to perpetuate the amicable aspect of the relationship in which it occurs.

This idea is also supported by Martineau (1972: 117) when he writes 'humor, therefore, acts as a safety valve for expressing grievance or controlled hostility against deviance. The result is that the normative system is reinforced and social cohesion prevails'.

Moreover, humour in healing rituals and in funerals not only is used to control the behaviour of the members of the community, but it is also a needed break from a negative and emotionally draining experience. 'It is a momentary humorous respite from the seriousness of lengthy concentration on a collective task, a respite that facilitates the completion of that task by refreshing the participants' (Stebbins 1979: 96–7). 'Other societies, however, encourage or even require humor in order to lighten such occasions. The Maori and the Maria Gond are examples of the latter pattern. At Lesu burial rites, interestingly, emotional weeping and laughter may alternate. Either is considered appropriate' (Alford and Alford 1981: 154). In the case of the Wana, the use of humour to make the emotional stress more bearable is more than a necessity due to the long duration of the *momago*, one night and the mourning period, almost three weeks. Joking and relaxing becomes a necessity to being able not only to slowly elaborate the emotions related to the loss, but also to being able to enjoy the presence of the other people we love and who are still with us.

Therefore, especially in a culture where violence is avoided at any cost, like the Wana one is, 'humor can also be used as a coping mechanism to avoid conflict, allowing people to remain until they are ready to deal with the painful events in life' (Dziegielewski et al. 2003: 79). During my entire time spent among the Wana I only saw the beginning of a fight, a fight that didn't continue because everybody there was ready to defuse that alarming situation. I don't think it is a coincidence, but it did happen at the end of a funeral – a moment when the Wana are exceptionally vulnerable to feel strong and dangerous emotion. Indeed,

> The conflict function of humor is expressed largely by means of irony, satire, sarcasm, caricature, parody, burlesque, and the like. The particular adaptability of humor as a conflict weapon lies in the fact that humor may conceal malice and allow expression of aggression without the consequences of other overt behavior. In this capacity, analysis of humor is particularly revealing of tensions and attitudes which may not be expressed in any other form.
> (Stephenson 1951: 569)

Moreover, 'As a means of social control, humor may function to express approval or disapproval of social form and action, express common group sentiments, develop and perpetuate stereotypes, relieve awkward or tense situations, and express collective, *sub rosa* approbation of action not explicitly approved' (Stephenson 1951: 570). In the end, it has been demonstrated how humour can influence and facilitate the grieving process (Bonanno 2004). In fact, Drucker-Brown wisely comments about the use of jokes in the funeral setting: 'Put in another way one might say that the joking behaviour comforts the grieving mourners by pointing out that other emotions accompany grief' (1982: 726).

Last but not least, humour has a deep relationship with our emotion, and it can shape them. As pointed out by Alford and Alford, 'we can even use humor to block emotions, as when we joke with people who are getting scared, angry, or sad. A number of psychiatric techniques, in fact, take advantage of the opposition between humor and emotions' (1981: 150). As indicated before, Wana tend to control strong emotion because they believe they can get sick from it. Emotions are strongly related to the soul, and a strong or negative emotion can make the soul leave the body, making the owner sick and in need of a shamanic treatment. It is clear how the death of a loved one, with the related emotional turmoil, can be extremely dangerous for the well-being of the Wana since they could experience an emotional domino effect which would deeply endanger the entire community. Having control, or the perception of it, over a terrible situation is often associated with better emotional well-being, better methods of coping with stress, better health and physiological outcomes (Martin and Lefcourt 1983; Solomon 1996). 'Extensive research has been done on the concept of perceived control and its relationship to physical and psychological conditions. The results of these studies indicate that people more often than not experience positive outcomes from perceiving that they have control over what affects them and they experience negative outcomes, such as depression, when they perceive a lack of control' (Dziegielewski et al. 2003: 80). Furthermore, humour allows people to gain control by redefining situations as less threatening (Solomon 1996).

Moreover, humour relieves anxiety and fear, breaches inhibitions and acts as a safety valve for difficult subjects and feelings (Palmer 1993: 62). Again 'most tension-relieving jokes express or at least imply a point of view. Nevertheless, tension management is an analytically distinct function of humor, and there are some sallies which seem primarily to serve this end' (Miller 1967: 269), but also 'the mutual ribbing among members of the council promotes the solidarity of the group by creating an atmosphere of good feeling' (Miller 1967: 266). In the end, 'humor helps to release tension and gives the participant a feeling of belonging' (Dziegielewski et al. 2003: 85).

In the end, 'when communicating about difficult issues like death and dying, people may use several coping strategies to manage their discomfort. In particular, they may use humor, which provides a means for relieving emotions and fostering positive interactions with others' (Lambert South, Elton and Lietzenmayer 2020: 1).

Visible and non-visible

Related to the dichotomies between centre and periphery, it is crucial to explore the important role that the sense of sight has in Wana culture, and also the relationship between the visible and the non-visible. This is especially pertinent considering that Indonesian traditional communities 'are not marked by a division between sacred and profane. Rather, the critical line is between the sphere of man and that of ancestors/spirits, the seen and unseen world' (McVey 1999: 6). Atkinson often uses the term 'hidden' when referring to the spiritual realm ('hidden realm'), the spirits ('hidden beings') and inner illness ('hidden illness'). This stresses that spirit-related realities are not visible to normal people, only to *tau walia* (1992, 1990). She elaborates, '"We should distinguish the "ordinary"' not from the '"extraordinary,"' but from the '"hidden"' (Atkinson 1989: 40).[8] Moreover, 'the Sakais conceptualize the world as either materially physical or materially non-physical. […] The physical dimension is called the human dimension (alap manusio) and the non-physical dimension is most commonly called the […] spirit dimension' (Porath 2008: 650). I prefer the term 'non-visible'[9] to 'hidden', because I interpret this realm as not being actively concealed but instead as being simply not possible to see (from the Latin *in-*'not'+*visibilis*) for those grounded in the human world and divorced from mythical space-time. Spirits and demons are not hiding – their world often overlaps with the human world – but non-*tau walia* cannot see them.

There are connections between, on the one hand, the near, visible and powerless, and, on the other, the far, non-visible and powerful. For Wana people, what is near is powerless and, of course, can easily be seen, so contains no mystery. What is far away, on the other hand, is not visible but is full of power and mystery. Atkinson goes on to mention that even since the end of the mythical era 'miracles can still happen, but only in secret' (1989: 46), meaning that they occur away from sight or are not spoken about. It is no coincidence that the place that *tau walia* go to looking for spirits and knowledge is a place where visibility is minimal, the jungle (Figure 14). For Wana people, 'forests were full of "people" (*tau*) who for some reason were not seen, people who lived

Figure 14 Indo n'Pino walking in the jungle. This photo shows the low visibility inside the jungle. Source: Giorgio Scalici, photographer.

and farmed like the people here but who kept themselves hidden from sight' (Atkinson 1989: 37).

Grumblies' work is particularly effective in describing these aspects of the Wana world: 'There is this world that everyone can see, and then there is this other [place] that only people can see like taw walia [shamans] during a momago, or when you are alone in the dark, in the forest, or sometimes when you do not expect anything' (2016: 96). The situations Grumblies talks about here as part of the *other place* have in common that there is low visibility. Even the last case, 'when you do not expect anything' can be interpreted as 'when you are not paying attention, when you are not really looking'. In the *momago*, like in the forest or any other dark place, reality becomes thinner; the balance between the visible and the non-visible realms favours the latter because people can no longer trust their sense of sight. In the jungle of the Morowali reserve, vegetation is sometimes so thick that it is impossible to see more than a few metres around. That which happens in the jungle is almost non-visible; trees cover even the sky, and hearing takes over as the primary sense, particularly for detecting the presence of animals or rivers well before seeing them. While Atkinson states that 'access to extraordinary experience is phrased in terms of sight, not hearing' (Atkinson 1989: 40), I do not totally agree, and I discuss here the role of hearing and music in the relationship with the non-visible spiritual world.

The connections between the non-visible and mythical power are expressed especially strongly during the *momago*. The ritual must take place during the night and end before the sunrise. Moreover, an almost pitch-black darkness is required for the ritual because light pushes away the spirits (just as music attracts them). This darkness helps to set the atmosphere and it is in line with the idea that 'miracles can still happen but only in secret'; great wonders (like the *tau walia*'s powers) can only happen in the dark, where the mystery can be preserved and where non-visible beings dwell. Moreover, the *tau walia* use the *pompolonzu* (ritual cloth) to cover their eyes when they are 'seeing far'. They close their human eyes to activate their spiritual sight: 'there is no elaborated transition between "states." As they sing, shamans close their eyes and see the spirit world' (Atkinson 1989: 92) and 'As he sings he uses "the eyes of his spirit familiars" to see hidden aspects of the world' (Atkinson 1989: 121). Despite Atkinson's suggestion that sight and not hearing is more central to the language of extraordinary experience (Atkinson 1989: 40), the music (the singing) is a constant presence when entering into contact with the non-visible world. Thanks to their liminality, *tau walia* can tap into mythical space-time and use their spiritual power to see the non-visible world. This is a power that is not always active; if it were, *tau walia* would be fully non-visible beings rather than points of contact between humans and spirits. In fact, 'Shamans with such magic insist that they possess such vision only in the context of a shamanic ritual, whereas vampires use such vision at all times' (Atkinson 1989: 96). The shamanic ritual is a context characterized by the presence of music and 'music makes translucent the boundary between human and spirit' (Friedson 1996: 100).

The same powers of the *tau walia* are a connection between the non-visible and the spiritual world. In Chapter 3, I introduced these powers and underlined how most are available to the *tau walia* only during the ritual or while hearing the ritual music. Among these powers, the most pertinent to this discussion is *jampu* (invisibility), a power that allows the *tau walia* to take on the invisibility that is normally enjoyed only by the spirits. Atkinson describes the people who dwell in the forest as '*tau bolag* or *tau wuni* ("non-visible people")'. This group is considered 'another "category" of people like the Wana themselves. Unlike the Wana, however, the Bolag are said to possess *jampu*, the power to become non-visible. Using jampu, they conceal themselves from their Wana neighbours and allow themselves to be seen only when and if they choose' (1992: 37).

Building on these reflections about the opposition between visible and non-visible, other elements of Wana life and rituality can also be categorized following this 'visible-non-visible' dichotomy (Table 3).

There is, however, an important element of Wana life that does not fit into this table: emotions. There is no obvious binary counterpart to emotions in this construction, but the control of emotions in particular ways plays an important role in Wana life, particularly through how people cope with the frustrations of living a 'wretched' life. They are a non-visible force that can bring great danger, and the control of emotions is crucial for the survival of the individual and the community. Despite their power, emotions share the invisibility that I have just discussed as an important shaper of Wana social life.

I would suggest that there is a direct connection between the use of music and communication with the non-visible world. Following the theories of James Frazer (1994) on sympathetic magic, I see important connections between the invisibility of music and other non-visible elements of Wana life (spirits, emotions and so on). I understand music as a bridge and link between the visible and the non-visible world.

Secrecy or invisibility (*jampu*) is the main characteristic of everything that is non-human and, hence, extraordinary. In Chapter 3, I outlined how *jampu* is one of the main powers of *tau walia*, and how this power is strongly related to their spiritual nature. Shamans, in Wana language *tau walia* (literally person spirit), are the living manifestation of liminality between the human and the spirit. As humans they have a body and they live and interact in the same reality as all other Wana people, but as half-spirits they also belong partially to the non-visible world of the spirits. Indeed, spirits are not the only non-visible element of Wana life that is visible to them; illness and emotions are also accessible to them.

Inner illness, by definition, is non-visible to normal people, and only *tau walia* can see and treat it. This kind of illness is caused by problems of the soul

Table 3 Elements of Wana life categorized according to visible–non-visible dichotomy

Visible	Non-visible
Humans	Spirits
Village	Spirit realm (Forest-West)
Body	Souls
Sight	Hearing
Wounds	Inner illness

or wounds caused by *setan*, both of which are also non-visible. It is the role of the *tau walia* to make these illnesses 'visible', by describing them in their *do'a* or in songs, to help the patient in understanding and 'materializing' the illness. In the *momago*, the illness is described as a rock that is thrown away, but also as something that can come in contact with other people and infect them. In the *molawo*, illnesses are fishing hooks that tear the flesh of the patient and that the *tau walia* removes after having obtained permission from *Pue Lamoa*, the vengeful god of lighting that is punishing the patient. For Wana people (along with many other peoples), that which is non-visible is mysterious and often dangerous. It seems likely that the jungle, as the place of spirits, is considered dangerous partly because of the difficulty in seeing more than a few metres around. The *tau walia* acts as a mediator between the visible world of the humans and the non-visible world of the spirits, helping Wana people in understanding what they cannot see and experience by themselves.

Emotions are also non-visible, and Wana people are highly concerned with them. I have already shown how people put in motion a series of cultural rules and behavioural expectations to avoid strong emotion. It is not a coincidence that during the *kayori* sadness can be expressed only when covering the face, and this makes it impossible for the community to see somebody crying. Perhaps this is because crying openly could be contagious, or because catharsis cannot occur if the community is watching. Having in mind Atkinson's statement that miracles can happen only if nobody is watching, being seen by the community prevents emotional catharsis while at the same time making sure that nothing extra-ordinary can happen during the *mandeke*. Another tool, used also to treat inner illness, is music. It cannot reasonably be only a coincidence that music, something non-visible, is used to control emotions and to treat inner illness. In Wana culture, music seems closely linked to these two non-visible elements, emotions and spirits, forming a powerful triad that represents the non-visible and mythical world.

Invisibility is crucial in Wana culture, and Atkinson discusses how this non-visibility is a necessary requirement for wonders to occur. As a result, the best way for people to communicate with the non-visible is through music. Music has power over the emotions, not least because, as I have already shown, it sets up the atmosphere of the room in the *momago*. Everyday instruments such as the *popondo* and the *tutali* have power over people's emotions, and the *balo bombongo*, the war trumpet, has the power to actually unleash war on the world. Similarly, I discussed above that, in the *kayori*, music is a marker for emotions, because it guides people through the dangerous mourning period.

Ultimately, invisibility should be thought of as a special form of existence and, of course, *tau walia* cannot simply interact with it using mundane language.

In this extract from Atkinson, the significance of *reporting* incredible occurrences is clear. In an illiterate culture such as that of the Wana people, this reporting implies experiencing something through sound and hearing. As she also affirms, the important *pangansani* 'applies to the extraordinary and powerful knowledge of an earlier age and to a highly developed understanding of special knowledge obtained from hidden sources in the world today' (Atkinson 1989: 182). This power is expressed thought *do'a*. Wana people take into great consideration the power of words, to the extent that simply the narration of mythological stories has the power to destroy the world. Words have a creative power that derives directly from their connection with the non-visible world. To tell a *katuntu* means to *recreate* a mythical story, to physically bring the space-time of the myth into the realm of humans. This overlapping in a single space of two worlds that nowadays are distinct would destroy both. As I have previously noted, my experience is that Wana people are quite likely to ignore rules. Thus, I never encountered anyone showing concerns about telling a *katuntu*. In fact, Apa Rau and Apa Kode seemed to be very pleased to have somebody, especially a Westerner, interested in it.

Atkinson continues, explaining that 'It is not uncommon for one who is skilled at playing a musical instrument such as flute, tuning fork, or stringed chest resonator to play haunting and plaintive songs to attract hidden beings' (1989: 54). In the previous chapters, I showed that music is present during the entire *momago* and *kayori* rituals and that it takes a very important role. Moreover, non-ritual music also has a great power; the *popondo* and the *tulali* are two instruments with the power to greatly influence people's sexual desires. Atkinson herself even describes the *yori* (tuning fork) as an instrument able to attract the spirits, in a similar way to how the ritual music of the *momago* does so. At the other extreme, instrumental music is forbidden in the *kayori* because the aim of the ritual is not to call the spirits (centripetal force), but actually to keep them away and to send away the soul of the deceased (centrifugal force). Music is thus used as way of calling the spirits, and as a tool for interacting with the non-visible realm that is available not only to the *tau walia* but to everyone. In addition, it is possible to draw a direct connection between the invisibility of emotions and of the spirits, and the invisibility of music. Following Frazer's theories about imitative magic,

If we analyse the principles of thought on which magic is based, they will probably be found to resolve themselves into two: first, that like produces like, or that an effect resembles its cause; and, second, that things which have once been in contact with each other continue to act on each other at a distance after the physical contact has been severed.

(1994: 11)

As noted previously, it is reasonable to conclude that Wana people see a connection between sound and the non-visible world; this is evident considering the Wana belief that sounds produced by non-visible people can be heard. The entire ritual of the *molawo* is based on imitative thinking and magic very much consistent with Frazer's theories. A particularly clear example is that loud noises are forbidden after a *molawo* because they recall the thunder sent by *Pue Lamoa*. Another is the prohibitions that surround illness, such as that someone recently cured of smallpox should not eat red fruit. Sound on its own, however, is not enough to communicate with the non-visible world; normal speech is too mundane for interacting with non-human beings, especially gods. For this reason, Wana people use music to communicate with the spirits and to control emotion. Even in situations where instrumental music is forbidden (the *molawo* and the *kayori*), people do not simply talk to *Pue Lamoa* (*molawo*) or to the deceased (*kayori*), but they sing. A clear distinction must be drawn between the mundane plane and the ritual one, and this difference is perceptible in the soundscape of the ritual. As Rasmussen reports, 'Songs are thoughts, sung out with the breath when people are moved by great forces and ordinary speech no longer suffices' (Rasmussen 1931: 321). Music creates an atmosphere and sets the stage for wonders to happen. During the *momago*, it is the music that marks the beginning and the end of the ritual. Likewise, it is not darkness or not seeing that separates mundane space-time and ritual space-time, but music. Taken in this light, music seems to take on a central role in the relationship between humans and the non-visible people.

So, when Atkinson talks of extraordinary experiences being understood through sight not hearing, she seems to underestimate the role of sound in Wana spirituality. It is music that actually connects mythical space-time and ritual space-time, and that allows *tau walia* to cross the boundary between humans and the non-visible world, and to use the power derived from their non-visible identity.

Conclusions

This chapter has acted as a resume and final exploration of the findings of the two previous chapters. Here I have shown how the *momago* and the *kayori* actively express and address the key values of Wana people. Through understanding these rituals and Wana mythology, it is clear that, like in many other cultures, Wana people categorize the world in terms of centre and periphery. Unlike in many other cultures, however, they see themselves as existing at the powerless centre. The idea of a powerless centre and a powerful periphery is quite unusual in Western culture, but for Wana people it is the perfect exhibition of agency. In this way they express their awareness of being socially and economically subaltern, but they simultaneously express their position of power in respect to other cultures. This is power that originated with them and that one day will come back to them as the people that managed to stay in the physical, social and spiritual centre of the world.

In the same way, this division of power has an impact on the internal power relationships within the community. The individual is constantly placed in a situation of inferiority in respect to the collective, and they are made aware through the rituals that their life has a meaning only inside the group. Moreover, the individuality of a community member is clearly linked to a lack of power, because this is a state displaying low density. In Wana society, the larger the group, the greater is the power.

In Figure 12, we saw how the lowest level of density/power is found with the single member and the highest level comes with the primordial perfect density where everything was one. Between these two extremes, there are smaller kinds of density that mean that each larger collective has more power than the last: from the single member to the family, the village, the community, the *momago* and the *kayori*. Each step offers more *kasintuwu* and support, and an increased level of emotional, physical and spiritual health, not only for the individual but for the entire community.

Even if the community is at the centre of Wana life, this chapter has shown that the division of power in the space has a deep impact on gender relationships inside the group. Keeping the women away from the opportunity to move away from the centre and to have contact with the non-visible world means keeping them away from mythical power. As I have discussed, this relationship between the visible and the non-visible is also pivotal in this culture, and there is a clear separation between these two worlds that is broken only but the *tau walia*, due to their liminal nature between humans and spirits, and by music. It is music, which is in a certain way available to everybody, that acts as a bridge between the two worlds. This bridge is not exclusive to the *tau walia* but open to everybody. Anyone can play an instrument and thus contact the non-visible world, even though they may have less spiritual awareness and control than a *tau walia*. It is possible that in the past Wana religion afforded more space to non-visible experience for individuals than nowadays, when the community is always present when the division between the non-visible and the visible world becomes thin.

Ultimately, Wana people transform their geographical and historical position into the idea of their culture being central. Thus, they show great ability in attaching positive meanings to a reality that it is not always kind to them. Wana manage to defeat death because the last emotion a Wana will feel after a funeral is a positive one. As Morreall wittingly points out, 'the comic vision of life has often been criticized as frivolous and escapist. I would argue the opposite: that given the human condition, it is the most realistic vision we have' (2009: 153).

In the end, the photo I choose as cover perfectly illustrates the Wana playful approach to death. With my students or during conferences I usually ask my interlocutors if they can guess why these people are laughing, and I am asking the same question to you, the reader. Please, take your time to think about what you learned so far. Do you have an answer? (Figure 15).

Figure 15 People laughing and smiling while looking at the recording of a funeral. Source: Giorgio Scalici, photographer.

These people are laughing and smiling while watching the video I made at the funeral of a loved one (wife, daughter in law, daughter, best friend and so on). They asked me to show them. They are laughing not because they didn't suffer, or are suffering in that moment, but because the *kayori* was successful and they managed to transform a terrible event into an opportunity to create positive emotion and memories. These people are laughing because they are watching a friend being silly, somebody doing something goofy or remembering the company of a good friend that was there with and for them.

I truly believe anthropology is not just learning about others but, more than everything else, learning from others, and if there is one thing I have learned from the Wana and I hope this book will leave to the readers is that pain is unavoidable, it is just a part of our lives, but we can work together, as one being, to transform these terrible moment linked to death and illness into opportunities to stay together, to share our time-space with each other and, in the end, to create memories and emotion that will last well beyond the terrible moment we are facing.

Notes

Chapter 1

1 I have decided to use the term 'density' instead of 'unity' to stress the spatial and physical qualities of the event. As explained in detail in the final chapter, this is one of the key terms I employ to understand Wana culture.

2 Some report having been told to their face [by the Wana who became Christian] that they lack the personal worth of a dog or a chicken because they have no religion (Atkinson 1991: 46).

3 Almost never documented. Atkinson briefly, few lines, wrote about it in her essay on gender among the Wana people (1990).

4 Tana Toraja is one of the top ten tourist attractions in Indonesia on many travel websites, including *planetware.com*, *touropia.com*, *theculturetrip.com*, and *thecrazytourist.com*.

5 The source of this quotation is unknown and it has also been attributed to Thomas Morus and Benjamin Franklin. For this reason, I am unable to give a bibliographic reference for it.

6 Tradition is not to preserve the ashes but to pass on the flame. (Translation by the author).

7 What is anthropology if not the study of ourselves through the eyes of the others?

8 The Music department at the University of Palermo was focusing almost exclusively on Sicilian or, in some rarer cases, Mediterranean musical culture.

9 Bahasa means 'language' in Indonesian and Bahasa Indonesia is the local name of the Indonesian language. For this reason, the term *bahasa* will be used to refer to the local languages.

10 *Buleh* is an Indonesian word derived from the Javanese word for 'albino' and used nowadays to refer to white people. Its basic meaning is not negative, but it often expresses a mono-dimensional view of all white people being like rich Australians, carrying US dollars and speaking English.

11 Also known as 'tarantism', it refers to a dancing mania that used to be common in Salento, Puglia. This mania usually affects women and its treatment requires long musical sessions.

12 In UK, anthropology is considered a social science, while ethnomusicology and religious studies are classed among the humanities; in Italy the three fields are seen as more closely connected, and are all part of the humanities denomination.

13 It can help in understanding the situation of the *Meridione* knowing malaria was eradicated in Italy in 1962, less than sixty years ago (Snowden 2005).

14 The Cambridge Torres Strait expedition in 1898 was a turning point in the history of the British anthropology for its interdisciplinarity and for the important role of fieldwork (Hart 2009). The members of this pioneering expedition were William Halse Rivers, Charles Myers and William McDougall (all psychologists), Alfred Haddon (anthropologist), Sidney Ray (linguist), Anthony Wilkin (photographer) and Charles Seligman (medical pathologist) (Haddon 1935: xi–xiii). Sadly, according to anthropologist Keith Hart, the destiny of this expedition was very different from the almost-mythological status that De Martino's expedition acquired among Italian scholars. In the lecture during the conference 'Anthropology and psychology: the legacy of the Torres Strait expedition, 1898–1998', which was held in St. John's College, Cambridge, 10–12 August 1998, Hart stated: 'If Victorian anthropology was largely conducted from the armchair, this event, above all, marked a turn to fieldwork in Britain. But if we ask what impact its participants have made on professional anthropologists and their students today, the answer is likely to be nil or negligible' (2009). He went on: 'The only reason for taking up the cudgels on Rivers's behalf is that his contribution has been all but eliminated from the collective memory of the discipline' (2009).

15 This book has never been translated into English.

16 In this work, to respect Wana culture and to underline the problematic use of the word 'shaman', I will use the term *tau walia*, the Wana term used to indicate a religious figure that could be placed in the very large umbrella-term 'shaman'.

17 As it will be explained in detail later, the concept of West is not geographical but mythological. The West is not the place to the west of the Wana land but the place *outside* of the Wana land, the place where the people of myth went at the end of the mythical era.

18 At least, as a Westerner, I was perceived as a rich person. Dear reader, trust me, I was not and I am not rich.

19 To know more about the problems raised by this mentality during my fieldwork, see *Who Framed Tetebua?* (Scalici 2022).

20 From an interview with Om Suma in 2011.

21 'Lateral thinking' is an indirect approach to a problem. Looking at a problem from different angles instead trying a direct approach. While a direct question involves the use of Western logic, lateral questioning seeks alternative points of view.

22 I am indebted to Helen Limon for a comment on one of my conference presentations that pushed me to rethink my position on gender in my research.

23 Though I do not have any medical training beyond the most basic matters, the Wana trusted my medicines and I knew how to use the medicine I brought with me.

24 Operation Drake (1978–80), named after Sir Francis Drake and supported by the Scientific Exploration Society, was a round-the-world voyage with the participation of an international members. It started in Plymouth in October 1978 the brigantine Eye of the Wind left Plymouth to return to England in December 1980 (Chapman 1982).

25 She briefly wrote about it in *How Gender Makes a Difference in Wana Society* (1990).

Chapter 2

1 https://www.giorgioscalici.eu/kayori/
2 Translated from Italian by the author.
3 Translated from Italian by the author.
4 Translated from Italian by the author.
5 Other trance-like experiences can be possession, Sufi dances, states of Nirvana and so on.
6 The term 'trancer' is also used by Richard B. Lee (1968), among others.
7 I suppose the author intended 'chthonic'.
8 In this situation, 'clearly' is used to indicate a mental clarity.

Chapter 3

1 It surprised me how the Toraja attracted so many scholars over the years (Christu 1999; Hollan 1988; Rappoport 2004; Wellenkamp1988 and Waterson 2018 just to name a few) while the Wana, less than 500 km away from them, did not get the attention deserved; leaving rituals like the *kayori* undocumented until now. This raises few questions on the 'everything has been already studied' myth and the problematic role of trends in academic research. Reflection that has to wait for a more suitable space and time.

2 https://www.giorgioscalici.eu/life-in-the-jungle/

3 *Bahasa* is the Indonesian word for 'language'. Considering that Indonesians call their own language *Bahasa* Indonesia and the Wana also use this term to refer to their own language, I have decided to use the term when referring to Indonesian or Wana language.

4 Dammar, meaning resin in Malay, is a resin obtained from the *shorea* trees. The resin is used in foods, as a clouding or glazing agent, and in the production of incense and varnish (Bulbeck et al. 2016).

5   In 2016, a motorbike was present in the village of Marisa. This motorbike was used to go from the village to the working place of the owner, a lumberjack like many other Wana. The distance between the village and the place is easily covered on foot, especially for the Wana, and there are not many paths available to a motorbike. I believe that this, like the widespread presence of mobile phones or watches, is another evidence of Wana desire for a modern, or we could say Indonesian, life.

6   From a personal conversation with Indo Rahu, June 2011.

7   A reptile belonging to the varanidae family, to which Komodo dragons also belong.

8   This food is known as *papeda* in Maluku, *linut* in Malaysia and *ambuyat* in Brunei. It is made from sago starch, produced by the mixing of the sago flour with water, cooked until it coagulates.

9   Sago is a starch extracted from the marrow of several species of palm belonging to the Metroxylon, Cycas and Phoenix genus. The sago is a staple food for the populations of New Guinea, Molucca and Sulawesi archipelago, where it is commonly called *sagu*. It is traditionally cooked and eaten in various forms, such as in balls, mixed with boiling water to form a paste or as a pancake.

10   Wana inferiority complex reminded me of the word of Aimé Césaire regarding the effects of colonialism: 'I am talking of millions of men who have been skilfully injected with fear, inferiority complexes, trepidation, servility, despair, absement' (Quoted in Fanon 2008: 1).

11   Even the lack of cloths is considered a consequence of the exodus of the *tau baraka*. Atkinson reports that even sewing is considered a skill of the mythical space-time. Leaves, bark cloth and coconuts were 'considered by the Wana to be grievously inferior to cotton cloth' (Atkinson 1979: 65) and another proof of their miserable life.

12   Interview recorded in March 2011.

13   Kruyt describes *Pololoisong* either 'man or god' (1930: 417).

14   The missionaries are part of the Ethnos360, formerly known as New Tribes Mission (NTM), which is an international, theologically evangelical Christian mission organization based in Sanford, Florida, the United States. NTM has approximately 3,300 missionaries in more than twenty nations (Clark 2019).

15   Many people asked me how many helicopters I had at home. It was hard to explain that helicopter ownership does not represent ordinary lifestyles in the West, and that poverty exists in that part of the world too.

16   Interviewed in March 2011.

17   From an interview in March 2011.

18   From a personal conversation with Apa Rahu in June 2011.

19   From a conversation that took place on April 2010.

20 Indonesian Hinduism, called Agama Hindu Dharma Indonesia, has been modified, in order to fit the government definition of a legitimate religion, into a monotheistic religion, with revealed scriptures and moral rules. In the end, Balinese Hinduism is quite different from Hinduism in India (McDaniel 2010).

21 Relationships between Indonesia and Israel have been tense, especially in regard to Palestine, and the two nations do not have formal diplomatic relations. In 2010, while completing the documents for my Darmasiswa scholarship, I was told that the Israeli stamp on my passport could have been a good reason not to let me enter the country. Moreover, the number of publications on Hitler and Nazism that are on sale in any Indonesian bookshop is notable.

22 The newly founded Ministry of Religion was unable to define religion outside its Islamic identity, giving Islamic theology a key role in 'framing and shaping all the debates about religion' (Picard 2011: 13).

23 Abunawas is a *tau baraka*, a human who lived during the mythical space-time and possessed great powers.

24 From an interview with Apa Rahu, June 2011.

25 *Tare pamarentah, tare agama, tare kampung.*

26 'Atheism became a criminal offence, polytheism, too, was outlawed and between 1954 and 1982 the state conducted a rigorous campaign against the followers of tribal spirit religions during which the most stubborn pagans suffered imprisonment or worse' (Harper 1997: 14).

27 Kasintuwu would appear to be similar to the Balinese *ikhlass*: 'a value of sharing that which is dearest, of preparedness to surrender oneself to the collective good' (Wikan 1988: 452).

28 https://www.giorgioscalici.eu/kasi/

29 From one of the stories Apa Rau told me.

30 According to the Bible's book of Genesis, Adam lived 930 years, his son Set lived 912 years, Enos 905 years, Maalaleèl 895 years, Lamech 777 years. Terach, Abraham's father, lived 205 years, and so on.

31 Communism, alongside Marxism-Leninism, was officially banned in Indonesia following the aftermath of the 30 September coup attempt and the subsequent anti-communist killings, by adoption of *TAP MPRS* no. 25/1966 in 1966 and *Undang Undang* no. 27/1999 in 1999, which are still in force. The law does not explicitly declare a ban on symbols of communism, but Indonesian police frequently use the law to arrest people displaying them.

32 Personal conversation in May 2011.

33 Hertz attests a god called Lamoa among the Alfur people of Sulawesi (Hertz 1994: 147). Alfur people is a broad term used to refer to all of the non-Muslim, non-Christian peoples living in the interior areas of Sulawesi and Maluku.

34 The myth continues with the death of *Inkoni* on the shores of the Kolo Sea, which from that day becomes red like blood every time somebody gossips or swears. From that day if somebody says the word *inkoni* or *mankoni*, they will be eaten by the demon. Wana mythology is extremely fascinating, but the sources are few and often contradict one another. This work is not the right place for a study of Wana mythology, but I intend to focus on this topic in future work.

35 Interview with Indo Pino in June 2011.

36 Interview with Apa Rahu in March 2011.

37 The sacred mountain is also known by Wana people under another name: *Taman Sari*, a Javanese word that means 'beautiful garden'.

38 *Poloisong* has a younger brother: Adi Banggai. While *Poloisong*, as a Wana cultural hero, was illiterate, the younger brother was the first Muslim and he knew how to write.

39 *Pue Bunku* could actually be one of the many *tau Baraka* (people of the myth) that inhabited the mythical space-time. It is also possible that he was one of the many divine beings in the Wana ancient pantheon. Sadly, I was not able to obtain more information about it and I can only offer some reflections and speculations.

40 This myth clearly recalls millenarian movements, which are present in Indonesia (Beatty 2012). Some of these movements, as in this case, are responses to colonial oppression and are aimed at overturning the relationship of power between the colonial empire and the indigenous community. They narrate a history in which the wealth of the West derives from the local land and thus one day must return to it (Worsley 1957). Worsley sees cargo cults like this one as a rational response to colonial oppression (Worsley 1957), and this is clearly pertinent in the Wana case. Moreover, ignorance of the real sources of Westerners' power is something that the indigenous community needs to face and overcome (Burridge 1969: 71), and the result is the local community creating stories and explanations for the condition of both them and the outsiders.

41 The *salia*, called *padunku* in the area in which I conducted my study, continues to the present day, although not annually because of change to the climate and the impact of the cultivation of rice. Nowadays, the ritual lasts just one night, during which a *momago* (the main shamanic ritual) is celebrated. It is possible that in the past, when the harvest was more abundant, the Wana people were able to celebrate for more days.

42 Porath reports that among the Riau of Indonesia 'One of the classic examples in the performance of healing is the extraction of a material object from the patient's body' (2015: 369).

43 https://www.giorgioscalici.eu/molawo/

44 In 1878, the German scholar Richard Andree already theorized sympathetic magic in his work *Ethnographische Parallelen und Vergleiche*.

45 This part dedicated to Wana music is based on *The Musical Instruments of Wana Tradition (Indonesia)* (Scalici 2023).

46 https://www.giorgioscalici.eu/traditional-music/

47 When looking for somebody to make me instruments, I had trouble finding a volunteer, even if the work was paid. All of the instruments that I brought back from the field were all made especially for me, and I paid for them all. Knowing the Wana approach towards replacing objects, I never took an instrument from a Wana owner.

48 By classification, I mean 'a scheme that organizes knowledge about selected entities from a chosen domain, grouping them in one or more steps (stages of subdivision) into sets of classes' (Kartomi 1990: 16).

49 For a wider discussion about this part of Wana culture and its effects on my fieldwork, I suggest looking at Scalici (2019b).

50 https://www.giorgioscalici.eu/yori/

51 I theorize the gongs arrived with the help of the transmigration programme, thus during the twentieth century. The transmigration programme, *transmigrasi* in Indonesian, was an initiative of the Dutch colonial government, and currently of the Indonesian government, to move people from densely populated areas, mainly Java and Bali, to less populous areas of the archipelago (Elmhirst 1999).

52 Gong chimes are extremely common in the musical world of the Southeast Asia, and can be found in different forms in Indonesia, Cambodia, Thailand, Burma and Vietnam (Heins 2001).

53 I met Dr Groumblies in 2011 during our first fieldwork among the Wana.

54 Reptile belonging to the family of monitor lizards which also includes Komodo dragons.

55 Mammal of the marsupial family of the order diprotodont. They are commonly called possums.

56 Particles of the whole natural kingdom: reed or bamboo, shell of some fruits, metal, hard wood, stone (sonorous), animal skins, carapace, bones, horns hollows, silk, woven raffia, horsehair, guts; the instruments constitute a synthesis of the cosmos (Translation by the author).

57 https://www.giorgioscalici.eu/popondo/

58 Considering the lack, in Wana language, of names used to indicate the different notes, due to the major attention given to the timbre of a note, I have decided to use the Western terminology to indicate the tuning of the Wana instruments. Obviously, the reader must keep in mind that indications are not absolutes, and they are warmly invited to listen to the tuning of each musical instruments on the website: giorgioscalici.eu/music/

59 https://www.giorgioscalici.eu/tetebua/

60 https://www.giorgioscalici.eu/geso/

61 https://www.giorgioscalici.eu/tulali/
62 https://www.giorgioscalici.eu/linga-linga/
63 During my fieldwork, I've met a woman who was a rare kind of shaman, called a *walia muansang*, who breathe from their armpits while dancing the *motaro*, because 'they are like fish that breathe from their gills'. If fish-shamans exist, it is highly possible that the common shamans were chicken-shamans and henceforth the resemblance between their dance and the chickens. Sadly, this theory hasn't been yet supported or negated by the Wana.
64 Moreover, according to Wana mythology, one of the people of mythical space-time saw a tree fall and not get up again. In that moment, he understood that humans could die, and he started to cry. From then on, people that lay down dead did not get up again.

Chapter 4

1   'In many cultures, gong ensemble music in ritual is seen as the actual medium through which the human and spiritual worlds merge' (Pugh-Kitingan 2012: 149).
2   It is important to underline that few Wana people use pills with caution. This habit, beyond the danger of an allergic attack, can be quite dangerous as it can lead to the inopportune, or overuse, of antibiotics and medicines.
3   In the past, there were different kinds of demons like the liver-eater *measa* or *pongko*, the soul trader *tau tolo*, the *salibi*, which punished those who spoke badly, the *tabar*, which crossed the rainbow to hurt Wana people, and so on (Atkinson 1992: 48).
4   The occipital bone is the main bone of the back and lower part of the skull.
5   From an interview with Indo Pino, May 2011.
6   Translation from Italian by the author.
7   From an interview with Ajeran Donda in April 2011.
8   Interview with Apa Oki, March 2011.
9   Interview with Apa Doti, April 2011.
10 'Mastery over fire, insensibility to heat, and, hence, the "mystical heat" that renders both extreme cold and the temperature of burning coals supportable, is a magico-mystical virtue that, accompanied by no less marvelous qualities (ascent, magical flight, etc.) translates into sensible terms the fact that the shaman has passed beyond the human condition and already shares in the condition of "spirits"' (Eliade 1972: 335).
11 One of the many names used by Wana people to refer to their cultural hero and trickster.

12   No, it isn't a mistake. I wrote 'funeral' and 'enjoying' in the same sentence. As
      the reader will soon learn, Wana funerals are more a matter of playfulness than
      dreadfulness.

13   https://www.giorgioscalici.eu/momago/

14   An example is the '18 happenings in 6 Parts' by Allan Kaprow in the Reuben
      Gallery of New York in 1959.

15   Wana people have a truly lax attitude regarding rules. Even if there are many things
      that should never be done (playing the war trumpet, playing ritual music outside
      the ritual, using red *pompolonzu* and so on), people do these things anyway.

16   During my research, I was not able to discover why a tube of toothpaste was among
      the offerings to the spirits. It could be that as something introduced into this
      society quite recently from outside, perhaps by missionaries or the government, it is
      considered extraordinary and therefore valuable, despite its daily use. It may also be
      important that it is a substance related to the mouth; almost all the other offerings
      are food, beverages or things to be chewed.

17   Translated from Italian by the author.

18   A programme in which the Dutch government and the Indonesian government
      moved landless people from densely populated areas of Indonesia (Java and Bali)
      to less populous areas (Papua, Kalimantan, Sumatra and Sulawesi). The aim of the
      programme was to reduce poverty and overpopulation but it raised many issues of
      the so-called 'Javanization' and 'Islamization' of these destination territories.

19   The reader can know more about this in Scalici (2022).

20   https://www.giorgioscalici.eu/momago/

21   https://www.giorgioscalici.eu/momago/

22   In interlocking music of this type, one musician's positive action of striking a note
      always coincides with a negative action, or 'non-strike', of his fellow musician, who
      at that moment lifts his beater. The effect is such that both series of equally spaced
      notes seem to interlock like the teeth of a cogwheel. Each of the two musicians,
      however, feels his own series of notes as 'on beat'. (https://www.britannica.com/art/
      African-music/Musical-structure#ref519774).

23   From an interview with Apa Ede, April 2016.

24   Translation from Italian by the author.

25   For an in-depth and complete analysis of Wana shamanic lyrics, please refer to the
      remarkable work of Atkinson in *The Art and Politics of Wana Shamanship* (1989); a
      great part of this work is dedicated to the study and translation of shamanic chants.

26   As Atkinson notes, 'Shamanic vocabulary borrows eclectically from other
      languages as well as from archaic and arcane ritual forms. Familiar Wana words
      are transformed by substitutions, contractions, and reduplications of sounds. [...]
      Shamans' songs are fully comprehensible to Wana audience' (Atkinson 1992: 16).

27   Translation from Italian by Scalici.

28 This prop is often fashioned from a t-shirt. The shaman Apa Ede told me that 'the *pompolonzu* helps the shaman to see far'. Usually, it is used to cover the shaman's face, to remove the illness from the sick patient, or to be a connection between a shaman and the other shamans, the spirits, or music instruments.

29 Interview with Apa Ede, May 2011.

Chapter 5

1   For the discussion about Wana souls, see the previous chapter.

2   In previous chapters, we already saw how Wana people tend to use humour, instead of violence or aggression, to control the behaviour of their members.

3   'Stories also say that in the past death was a temporary state from which people returned in three days' (Atkinson 1992: 46).

4   Rappoport reports a similar myth among the Lamaholot: 'He then let for the sea and cut a branch and tied the two inseparable [bamboo], hung his dance costume, and his bells to a post and leant back against it, then he climbed down into the hole, onto the coffin. He was playing the flute. [...] When the sound of the flute stopped, he was dead' (2014: 234).

5   The ritual power of the double eight is also present among the Taman of Borneo (Bernstein 1991, 1997).

6   Interview with Apa Rau, March 2011.

7   There are various versions of the origin of human beings. One of these is clearly influenced by the Old Testament and tells us of the cremation of the first woman from the ribs of the first man.

8   From a conversation with Apa N'Te.

9   A *sarong* is a large tube or length of fabric often wrapped around the waist. It is a garment worn in South Asia, Southeast Asia, the Arabian Peninsula, East Africa and on many Pacific islands.

10 The shells of this animal are put inside a piece of bamboo and cooked for hours, reducing them to powder.

11 It was described in this way to me by Om Manggi during a conversation on 18 May 2016.

12 Also, in Korean shamanism 'the deceased's final entry into paradise and permanent separation from the world of the living is enacted through another deeply symbolic psychodrama' (Mills 2014: 150).

13 The presence of gambling behaviour during funerals is also reported by Praet (2014: 118).

14 Rappoport reports a similar ritual behaviour in Flores: 'the beginning of each planting season, the final seat is depicted as a stone and a stake, at the top of which

is a coconut (representing the washing of hair with coconut milk before death)'
(2017: 471).

15 Indeed, one of the songs she describes is the story of 'The Lovers' Flute', in which 'a
violent death keeps the two lovers apart forever' (Rappaport 2014: 235). There are
links here with the myth of the origin of death and the presence of the *tulali*, the
flute that is connected to love in Wana culture.

16 During my fieldwork I saw three-year-old children smoking. According to the
Wana, if somebody can sit with a cigarette in their hand, they can smoke.

17 I would like to have the opportunity to do more studies on the relationship between
death and hair, but it is interesting to note that in *The Libation Bearers* (Χοηφόροι,
Choēphóroi), Orestes offers a lock of hair as a sign of mourning (Aeschylus 1984).

18 While *pongas* is Wana rice wine, *chaptikus* is a common Indonesian palm wine,
often made illegally.

19 Conversation with Apa Ede, March 2011.

20 https://www.giorgioscalici.eu/kayori/

21 These lyrics were told to me by Apa Dheri in 2011.

22 Translated from Italian by the author.

23 Translated from Italian by the author.

24 From a conversation with Apa Rau, May 2011.

25 Translated from Italian by the author.

26 Wana people often refer to people of the recent past as even poorer than
themselves, since they only had coconuts and leaves as clothing.

Chapter 6

1 Wana hospitality was illustrated very clearly to me when I told Om Manggi that
my homeland Italy also had poor people. Previously imagining only riches in this
distant land, he told me that all of the Italian poor would be welcome in Morowali
and would have land to work.

2 Indonesia was a Dutch colony from 1602 until 1949. For many years, Dutch people
were the only non-Asians that Wana people ever met. Still now many footpaths
inside the Morowali reserve are called '*jalan Belanda*' (literally Dutch streets)
because they were made by the Dutch.

3 Wana people have terms for male and female, and they are aware of homosexuality.
I never encountered any homosexual couples, although it is possible this was a
matter of homosexually not being expressed openly. Outside the forest, I met gay
men, a lesbian couple living together and a transgender person. These people
are accepted and not considered negatively at all, but I never witnessed open
homosexuality among Wana people. Atkinson writes about women who transition

to becoming men but not of men becoming women, and these passages were complete, considering that one of the examples had a wooden penis and a wife (Atkinson 1990).

4   Grumblies spells the word *tau* differently from Atkinson and myself.

5   https://www.giorgioscalici.eu/kayori/

6   All these sound samples can be found at the bottom of this webpage: www. giorgioscalici.eu/kayori/

7   In my experience of death studies conferences, I had the impression that showing or listening to people crying was almost a taboo. I am aware of the emotional discomfort in hearing somebody crying but I think that this is also an important part of our work as death scholars.

8   Atkinson also uses the term 'unseen', writing that *tau walia* 'treat not overt symptoms, but unseen causes' (1989: 75).

9   The term non-visible is also preferred by Robert J. Barrett in his essay 'Performance, Effectiveness and the iban manang' (1993), in an edited volume titled *The Seen and the Unseen: Shamanism, Mediumship and Possession in Borneo.*

Bibliography

Abasi, Augustine Kututera. 1995. '"Lua-Lia", the "Fresh Funeral": Founding a House for the Deceased among the Kasena of North-East Ghana'. *Africa: Journal of the International African Institute*, Vol. 65, No. 3: 448–75.

Aberle, David. 1970. 'A Note on Relative Deprivation Theory as Applied to Millenarian and Other Cult Movements'. In *Millenial Dreams in Action*, edited by Sylvia Thrupp, 209–14. New York: Schocken Books.

Adams, Kathleen M. 1997. 'Ethnic Tourism and the Renegotiation of Tradition in Tana Toraja (Sulawesi, Indonesia)'. *Ethnology*, Vol. 36, No. 4: 309–20.

Aggarwal, Ravina. 2001. 'At the Margins of Death: Ritual Space and the Politics of Location in an Indo-Himalayan Border Village'. *American Ethnologist*, Vol. 28, No. 3: 549–73.

Alea, Nicola and Bluck, Susan. 2003. 'Why Are You Telling Me That? A Conceptual Model of the Social Function of Autobiographical Memory'. *Memory*, Vol. 11: 165–78.

Alford, Finnegan and Alford, Richard. 1981. 'A Holo-Cultural Study of Humor'. *Ethos*, Vol. 9, No. 2: 149–64.

Alighieri, Dante. 2005. *La Divina Commedia*. Milano: Mondadori.

Alvard, Michael. 2000. 'The Potential for Sustainable Harvests by Traditional Wana Hunters in Morowali Nature Reserve, Central Sulawesi, Indonesia'. *Organization*, Vol. 59, No. 4: 428–40.

Andree, Richard. 1878. *Ethnographische Parallelen und Vergleiche*. Stuttgart: Verlag von Julius Maier.

Aragon, Lorraine V. 1996. 'Suppressed and Revised Performances: Raego' Songs of Central Sulawesi'. *Ethnomusicology*, Vol. 40, No. 3, Special Issue: Music and Religion: 413–39.

Asad, Talal. 2003. *Formations of the Secular: Christianity, Islam, Modernity*. Stanford, CA: Stanford University Press.

Atkinson, Jane Monnig. 1983. 'Religions in Dialogue: The Construction of an Indonesian Minority Religion'. *Ethnologist*, Vol. 10, No. 4: 684–96.

Atkinson, Jane Monnig. 1987. 'The Effectiveness of Shamans in an Indonesian Ritual'. *American Anthropologist*, New Series, Vol. 89, No. 2: 342–55.

Atkinson, Jane Monnig. 1988. 'Religion and the Wana of Sulawesi'. In *The Real and Imagined Role of Culture in Development: Case Studies from Indonesia*, edited by Michael Dove, 41–61. Honolulu: University of Hawaii Press.

Atkinson, Jane Monnig. 1989. *The Art and Politics of Wana Shamaniship*. Berkeley: University of California Press.

Atkinson, Jane Monnig. 1990. 'How Gender Makes a Difference in Wana Society'. In *Power and Difference: Gender in Island Southeast Asia*, edited by Jane Monnig Atkinson and Shelly Errington, 59–93. Stanford: Stanford University Press.

Atkinson, Jane Monnig. 1992. 'Shamanisms Today'. *Annual Review of Anthropology*, Vol. 21, No. 3: 307–30.

Atkinson, Jane Monnig. 2003. 'Who Appears in the Family Album? Writing the History of Indonesia's Revolutionary Struggle'. In *Cultural Citizenship in Island Southeast Asia: Nation and Belonging in the Hinterlands*, edited by Renato Rosaldo, 134–61. Berkeley: University of California Press.

Baily, John. 2001. 'Learning to Perform as a Research Technique in Ethnomusicology'. *British Journal of Ethnomusicology*, Vol. 10, No. 2: 85–98.

Balzer, Marjorie Mandelstam. 1997. *Shamanic Worlds: Rituals and Lore of Siberia and Central Asia*. London: North Castle Books.

Barker, Joshua. 2012. 'The Ethnographic Interview in an Age of Globalization'. In *The SAGE Handbook of Social Anthropology*, edited by Richard Fardon, 54–69. London: SAGE.

Barnes, Robert. 1974. *Kédang*. Oxford: Clarendon.

Barrett, Frederick S.; Grimm, Kevin J.; Robins, Richard W.; Wildschut, Tim; Sedikides, Constantine and Janata, Petr. 2010. 'Music-Evoked Nostalgia: Affect, Memory, and Personality'. *Emotion*, Vol. 10, No. 3: 390–403.

Bascom, William. 1984. 'The Forms of Folklore: The Prose Narrative'. In *Sacred Narrative: Readings in the Theory of Myth*, edited by Alan Dundes, 5–29. London: University of California Press.

Bastide, Roger. 1972. *Le rêve, La Trance et la Folie*. Paris: Flammarion.

Beatty, Andrew. 2005. 'Emotions in the Field: What Are We Talking About?' *Journal of the Royal Anthropological Institute*, Vol. 11: 17–37.

Beatty, Andrew. 2010. 'How Did It Feel for You? Emotion, Narrative, and the Limits of Ethnography'. *American Anthropologist*, Vol. 112, No. 3: 430–43.

Beatty, Andrew. 2012. 'The Tell-Tale Heart: Conversion and Emotion in Nias'. *Ethnos*, Vol. 77, No. 3: 295–320.

Beatty, Andrew. 2014. 'Anthropology and Emotion'. *Journal of the Royal Anthropological Institute*, Vol. 20: 545–63.

Beatty, Andrew. 2019. *Emotional Worlds: Beyond an Anthropology of Emotion*. Cambridge: Cambridge University Press.

Becker, Judith. 1994. 'Music and Trance'. *Leonardo Music Journal*, Vol. 4: 41–51.

Becker, Judith. 2000. '*Listening Selves and Spirit Possession*'. *World Music*, Vol. 42, No. 2: 25–55.

Becker, Judith. 2003. '*Musica e Trance*'. In *Enciclopedia Della Musica Einaudi*, edited by Jean-Jacques Nattiez, Vol. II: 409–36. Turin: Einaudi.

Becker, Judith. 2004. *Deep Listeners: Music, Emotion, and Trancing*. Indianapolis and Bloomington: Indiana University Press.

Belo, Jane. 1960. *Trance in Bali*. New York: Columbia University Press.

Benedict, Ruth. 1934. 'Anthropology and the Abnormal'. *Journal of General Psychology*, Vol. 10: 77.

Bernstein, Jay H. 1991. *Taman Ethnomedicine: The Social Organization of Sickness and Medical Knowledge in the Upper Kapua*, PhD Dissertation. Berkeley: University of California.

Bernstein, Jay H. 1997. *Spirits Captured in Stone: Shamanism and Traditional Medicine among the Taman of Borneo*. Boulder: Lynne Rienner Publishers.

Biehl, João, Good, Byron and Kleinman, Arthur. 2007. *Subjectivity: Ethnographic Investigations*. Berkeley: University of California Press.

Bloch, Maurice. 1971. *Placing the Dead: Tombs, Ancestral Villages and Kinship Organization in Madagascar*. London and New York: Seminar Press.

Bloch, Maurice and Parry, Jonathan (Eds.). 1982. *Death and the Regeneration of Life*. Cambridge: Cambridge University Press.

Blood, Anne J.; Zatorre, Robert J.; Bermudez, Patrick and Evans, Alan C. 1999. 'Emotional Responses to Pleasant and Unpleasant Music Correlate with Activity in Paralimbic Brain Regions'. *Nature Neuroscience*, Vol. 2: 382–7.

Bollig, Michael and Finke, Peter. 2014. 'Explanatory Models in Anthropology: Methodological Refinements, Cross-Cultural Comparison and Theoretical Developments'. *Zeitschrift für Ethnologie*, Vol. 139, No. 1: 39–54.

Bonanno, George. 2004. 'Loss, Trauma, and Human Resilience: Have We Underestimated the Human Capacity to Thrive after Extremely Aversive Events'. *American Psychologist*, Vol. 59, No. 1: 20–8.

Bonini Baraldi, Filippo. 2013. *Tsiganes, Musique et Empathie*. Paris: MSH Paris.

Bourguignon, Erika. 1976. *Possession*. Novato State, CA: Chandler and Sharp Publishers.

Bourguignon, Erika. 1979. *Trance Dance*. In *The Highest State of Consciousness*, edited by John White, 331–43. Garden City: Doubleday.

Briggs, Jean. 1970. *Never in Anger: Portrait of an Eskimo Family*. Cambridge: Harvard University Press.

Brosius, Christiane. 2007. 'The Unwanted Offering. Ubiquity and Success of Failure in a Ritual of the Hindu Right'. In *When Rituals Go Wrong: Mistakes, Failure, and the Dynamics of Ritual*, edited by Ute Hüsken, 291–324. Leiden and Boston: Brill.

Bruner, Edward. 1994. 'Abraham Lincoln as Authentic Reproduction: A Critique of Postmodernism'. *American Anthropologist*, Vol. 96, No. 2: 397–415.

Bulbeck, David; Aziz, Fadhila Arifin; O'connor, Sue; Calo, Ambra; Fenner, Jack N.; Marwick, Ben; Feathers, Jim; Wood, Rachel and Prastiningtyas, Dyah. 2016. 'Mortuary Caves and the Dammar Trade in the Towuti–Routa Region, Sulawesi, in an Island Southeast Asian Context'. *Asian Perspectives*, Vol. 55, No. 2: 148–83.

Bultmann, Rudolf. 1985. *New Testament and Mythology: And Other Basic Writings*. London: SCM Press.

Cady, Elizabeth; Harris, Richard and Knappenberger, Bret. 2008. 'Using Music to Cue Autobiographical Memories of Different Lifetime Periods'. *Psychology of Music*, Vol. 36, No. 2: 157–77.

Canave-Dioquino, Corazon; Santos, Ramón P. and Maceda, Josè. 2008. 'The Philippines'. In *The Garland Handbook of Southeast Asian Music*, edited by Terry E. Miller and Sean Williams, 415–45. New York: Routledge.

Cardeña, Etzel. 1989. 'The Varieties of Possession Experience'. *Association for the Anthropological Study of Consciousness Quarterly*, Vol. 5: 1–17.

Cavalli-Sforza, Luigi and Feldman, Marcus. 1981. *Cultural Transmission and Evolution: A Quantitative Approach*. Princeton, NJ: Princeton University Press.

Chapman, Roger. 1982. *In the 'Eye of the Wind': Story of Operation Drake*. London: Hamilton.

Chappie, Eliot and Coon, Carleton S. 1942. *Principles of Anthropology*. New York: Henry Holt Company.

Christian, Willima. 2004. 'Provoked Religious Weeping in Early Modern Spain'. In *Religion and Emotion. Approaches and interpretation*, edited by John Corrigan, 33–50. Oxford: Oxford University Press.

Christou, Maria. 1997. *An Ethnographic Study of the Loom and Weaving of the Sa'dan Toraja of To'Barana*. MA Dissertation, Ann Arbor: University of Alberta.

Churchill, Nancy. 2006. 'Dignifying Carnival: The Politics of Heritage Recognition in Puebla, Mexico'. *International Journal of Cultural Property*, Vol. 13: 1–24.

Clark, Scott. 1994. *Japan: A View from the Bath*. Honolulu: University of Hawai'i.

Cohen, Anthony. 1985. *Symbolic Construction of Community*. London: Routledge.

Coleman, Elizabeth. 2018. 'Cross-Cultural Aesthetics and Etiquette'. In *Social Aesthetics and Moral Judgment*, edited by Jennifer McMahon, 44–61. New York: Routledge Taylor and Francis Group.

Combarieu, Jules. 1982. *La musique et la magie: etude sur les origines populaires de l'art musical, son influence et sa fonction dans les societes*. Paris: Alphonse Picard et fils.

Conway, Martin A. 1993. 'Emotion and Memory'. *Science*, Vol. 261: 369–70.

Conway, Martin A.; Turk, David J.; Miller, Shannon L.; Logan, Jessica; Nebes, Robert D.; Meltzer, Carolyn C. and Becker, James T. 1999. 'A Positron Emission Tomography (PET) Study of Autobiographical Memory Retrieval'. *Memory*, Vol. 7: 679–702.

Cook, Nicholas. 2021. *Music: A Very Short Introduction*. Oxford: Oxford University Press.

Coté, Joost. 1996. 'Colonising Central Sulawesi. The 'Ethical Policy' and Imperialist Expansion 1890–1910'. *Itinerario*, Vol. 20, No. 3: 87–107.

Cowlishaw, Gillian. 1997. 'Race at Work: Reflecting on Fieldwork in the Northern Territory'. *The Journal of the Royal Anthropological Institute*, Vol. 3, No. 1: 95–113.

Cowlishaw, Gillian. 2001. '"Contempt and New Solicitude": Race Relations and Australian Ethnography'. *Oceania*, Vol. 71, No. 3: 169–87.

Cowlishaw, Gillian. 2010. 'Mythologising Culture Part 1: Desiring Aboriginality in the Suburbs'. *The Australian Journal of Anthropology*, Vol. 21: 208–27.

Cowlishaw, Gillian. 2017. 'Tunnel Vision: Part One – Resisting Postcolonialism in Australian Anthropology'. *The Australian Journal of Anthropology*, Vol. 28: 324–41.

Cowlishaw, Gillian. 2018. 'Tunnel Vision: Part Two – Explaining Australian Anthropology's Conservatism'. *The Australian Journal of Anthropology*, Vol. 29: 35–52.

Cox, Rupert and Christopher Wright. 2012. 'Blurred Visions: Reflecting Visual Anthropology'. In *The SAGE Handbook of Social Anthropology*, edited by Richard Fardon; Oliva Harris; Trevor H. J. Marshand; Mark Nuttall; Cris Shore; Veronica Strang and Richard A. Wilson, 84–101. London: Sage Publications.

Crapanzano, Vincent. 1973. *The Hamadsha: A Study in Moroccan Ethnopsychiatry.* Berkeley: University of California Press.

Crapanzano, Vincent. 1980. *Tuhami: Portrait of a Moroccan*. Chicago: University of Chicago Press.

Cresswell, Tim. 2010. 'Towards a Politics of Mobility'. *Environment and Planning: Society and Space*, Vol. 28, No. 1: 17–31.

Crowe, Barbara. 2004. *Music and Soul Making toward a New Theory of Music Therapy.* Lanham: Scarecrow Press.

Darwin, Charles. 1872. *The Expression of the Emotions in Man and Animals.* London: John Murray.

Davies, Douglas. J. 2002. *Anthropology and Theology*. Oxford: Berg.

Davies, Douglas J. 2015. *Mors Britannica: Lifestyle and Death-Style in Britain Today.* Oxford: Oxford University Press.

Davies, Douglas J. 2017. *Death, Ritual and Belief. The Rhetoric of Funerary Rites.* London: Bloomsbury.

De Jong, Ferdinand. 2007. 'A Masterpiece of Masquerading: Contradictions of Conservation in Intangible Heritage'. In *Reclaiming Heritage: Alternative Imaginaries of Memory in West Africa*, edited by Ferdinand De Jong and Michael Rowlands, 161–84. Walnut Creek, CA: Left Coast Press.

De Martino, Ernesto. 1958. *Morte e pianto rituale nel mondo antico. Dal lamento funebre antico al pianto di Maria*. Turin: Edizioni scientifiche Einaudi.

De Martino, Ernesto. 1961. *La terra del rimorso: Contributo a una storia religiosa del Sud*. Milan: il Saggiatore.

De Martino, Ernesto. 1967. *Il mondo magico. Prolegomeni a una storia del magismo.* Turin: Bollati Boringhieri.

Demetrio, Francisco R. 1978. 'The Shaman as Psychologist'. *Asian Folklore Studies*, Vol. 37, No. 1: 57–75.

Dennis, Rutledge M. 2007. 'Marginality'. In *Blackwell Encyclopedia of Sociology*, edited by George Ritzer, 2763–5. Oxford: Blackwell Publishing.

Denvens, Carol. 1992. 'If We Get the Girls, We Get the Race': Missionary Education of Native American Girls. *Journal of World History*, Vol. 3, No. 2: 219–37.

Desjarlais, Robert R. 1989. 'Healing through Images: The Magical Flight and Healing Geography of Nepali Shamans'. *Ethos*, Vol. 17, No. 3: 289–307.

Desjarlais, Robert R. 1992. *Body and Emotion: The Aesthetics of Illness and Healing in the Nepal Himalayas*. Philadelphia: University of Pennsylvania Press.

Desjarlais, Robert R. and Throop, Jason. 2011. 'Phenomenological Approaches in Anthropology'. *Annual Review of Anthropology*, Vol. 40: 87–102.

Douglas, Mary. 1999. *Implicit Meanings: Selected Essays in Anthropology*. New York: Routledge Taylor and Francis Group.

Drucker-Brown, Susan. 1982. 'Joking at Death: The Mamprusi Grandparent-Grandchild Joking Relationship'. *Man*, Vol. 17, No. 4: 714–27.

Dundes, Alan (Ed.). 1984. *Sacred Narrative: Readings in the Theory of Myth*. London: University of California Press.

Durkheim, Emile. 1915. *The Elementary Forms of Religious Life*. London: George Allen & Unwin Lt.

Durkheim, Emile. 1997. *The Division of Labour in Society*. New York: Free Press.

Dziegielewski, Sophia; Jacinto, George; Laudadio, Angela and Legg-Rodriguez, Loloma. 2003. 'Humor: An Essential Communication Tool in Therapy'. *International Journal of Mental Health*, Vol. 32, No. 3: 74–90.

Ebersole, Gary L. 2004. 'The Function of Ritual Weeping Revisited'. In *Religion and Emotion. Approaches and Interpretation*, edited by John Corrigan, 185–222. Oxford: Oxford University press.

Eddington, Arthur Stanley. 1948. *The Nature of the Physical World*. New York: The Macmillan Company.

Ekman, Paul. 1980. 'Biological and Cultural Contributions to Body and Facial Movement in the Expression of Emotions'. In *Explaining Emotions*, edited by Amélie Oksenberg Rorty, 73–101. Berkeley: University of California Press.

el-Aswad, el-Sayed. 1987. 'Death Rituals in Rural Egyptian Society: A Symbolic Study'. *Urban Anthropology and Studies of Cultural Systems and World Economic Development*, Vol. 16, No. 2: 205–41.

El Haj, Mohamad. 2012. 'The Involuntary Nature of Music-Evoked Autobiographical Memories in Alzheimer's Disease'. *Consciousness and Cognition*, Vol. 21, No. 1: 238–46.

El Haj, Mohamad; Fasotti, Luciano and Allain, Philippe. 2001. 'The Effect of Auditory Stimulation on Autobiographical Recall in Dementia'. *Experimental Aging Research*, Vol. 27, No. 3: 215–28.

Eliade, Mircea. 1968. *Myths, Dreams and Mysteries: The Encounter between Contemporary Faiths and Archaic Reality*. London: Fontana.

Eliade, Mircea. 1971. *The Myth of the Eternal Return: Or, Cosmos and History*. Princeton: Princeton University Press.

Eliade, Mircea. 1972. *Shamanism: Archaic Techniques of Ecstasy*. Princeton: Princeton University Press.

Eliade, Mircea. 1987. *The Sacred and the Profane: The Nature of Religion*. San Diego: Harcourt Brace Janovich.

Emmerich, Christoph. 2007. '"All the King's Horses And All the King's Men": The 2004 Red Matsyendranatha Incident in Lalitpur'. In *When Rituals Go Wrong: Mistakes, Failure, and the Dynamics of Ritual*, edited by Ute Hüsken, 133–64. Leiden: Bill.

Evans-Pritchard, Edward Evan. 1937. *Witchcraft, Oracles and Magic among the Azande.* Oxford: Clarendon Press.

Evans-Pritchard, Edward Evan. 1956. *Nuer Religion.* Oxford: Clarendon Press.

Fabietti, Ugo. 1991. *Storia dell'Antropologia.* Bologna: Zanichelli.

Fanon, Franz. 1961. *Les Damnés de la terre.* Paris: Éditions Maspero.

Favara, Alberto. 1921. *Canti della terra e del mare di Sicilia.* Milan: Ricordi.

Feld, Steven. 1982. *Sound and Sentiment: Birds, Weeping, Poetics and Song in Kaluli Expression.* Philadelphia: University of Pennsylvania Press.

Fischer, Agneta H. and Manstead, Antony S. R. 2000. 'The Relation between Gender and Emotions in Different Cultures'. In *Gender and Emotion: Social Psychological Perspectives*, edited by Agneta H. Fischer, 71–94. Cambridge: Cambridge University Press.

Frazer, James George. 1994. *The Golden Bough: A Study in Magic and Religion.* Oxford and New York: Oxford University Press.

Friedberg, Claudine. 2011. 'O imaginário e as praticas nas relações com os outros seres; Algumas pistas de reflexão com base em dados timorenses'. In *Ita maun alin ... O livro do irmão mais novo; Afinidades Anthropologicas em torno de Timor-Leste*, edited by Kelly Silva and Lucio Sousa, 46–61. Lisbon: Edições Colibri.

Friedson, Steven M. 1996. *Dancing Prophets: Musical Experience in Tumbuka Healing.* Chicago and London: University of Chicago Press.

Fuller-Torrey, Edwin. 1972. *The Mind Game.* New York: Emerson Hall Publishers.

Geertz, Clifford. 1973. *The Interpretation of Cultures.* New York: Basic Books.

Gell, Alfred. 1992. *The Anthropology of Time: Cultural Constructions of Temporal Maps and Images.* Oxford: Berg.

Gennep, Arnold Van. 1960. *The Rites of Passage.* London: Routledge & Kegan Paul.

Gilsenan, Michael. 1973. *Saint and Sufi in Modern Egypt.* Oxford: Clarendon Press.

Goody, Jack. 1961. 'Religion and Ritual: The Definitional'. *The British Journal of Sociology*, Vol. 12, No. 2: 142–64.

Grambo, Ronald. 1971. 'Ritual Crying in Folk Tradition'. *Anthropos*, Vol. 66, No. 5/6: 938–45.

Gramsci, Antonio. 1948–51. *I quaderni dal carcere.* Turin: Einaudi.

Gregory, Christopher A. 1980. 'Gifts to Men and Gifts to God: Gift Exchange and Capital Accumulation in Contemporary Papua'. *Man*, Vol. 15: 626–52.

Grimes, Ronald L. 1985. *Research in Ritual Studies.* Washington, DC: University Press of America.

Grumblies, Anna-Teresa. 2013. 'Being Wana, Becoming an "Indigenous People". Experimenting with Indigeneity in Central Sulawesi'. In *Adat and Indigeneity in Indonesia: Culture and Entitlements between Heteronomy and Self-ascription*, edited by Brigitta Hauser-Schäublin, 81–98. Göttingen: Universitätsverlag Göttingen.

Grumblies, Anna-Teresa. 2016. *The Construction of Marginality among Upland Groups in Indonesia: The Case of the Wana of Central Sulawesi.* PhD Doctoral Thesis, Cologne: University of Cologne.

Guggino, Elsa. 2004. *I canti e la magia. Percorsi di una ricerca.* Palermo: Sellerio.

Gupta, Akhil and Ferguson, James. 1992. 'Beyond "Culture": Space, Identity, and the Politics of Difference'. *Cultural Anthropology*, Vol. 7, No. 1: 6–23.

Gurvich, Georges. 1961. *The Spectrum of Social Time.* Dordrecht: Reidel.

Haddon, Alfred. 1901–1935. *Reports of the Cambridge Anthropological Expedition to Torres Straits.* Cambridge: Cambridge University Press.

Hallpike, Christopher R. 1969. 'Social Hair'. *New Series*, Vol. 4, No. 2: 256–64.

Hamayon, Roberte N. 1993. 'Are "Trance," "Ecstasy," and Similar Concepts Appropriate in the Study of Shamanism?' *Shaman*, Vol. 1, No. 2: 1–15.

Hammond, Peter. 1964. 'Mossi Joking'. *Ethnology*, Vol. 3, No. 3: 259–67.

Harlow, Ilana. 2003. 'Practical Jokes and the Revival of the Dead in Irish Tradition'. In *Of Corpse: Death and Humor in Folklore and Popular Culture*, edited by Peter Narvaez, 83–112. Louisville: University Press of Colorado.

Harms, Erik; Hussain, Shafqat; Newell, Sasha; Piot, Charles; Schein, Louisa; Shneiderman, Sara; Turner, Terence S. and Zhang, Juan. 2014. 'Remote and Edgy: New Takes on Old Anthropological Themes'. *HAU: Journal of Ethnographic Theory*, Vol. 4: 361–81.

Harper, Martin. 1997. 'Shamanism and Traditional Healers in Modern Day Indonesia'. *Shaman*, Vol. 5, No. 1: 13–34.

Harré, Rom. 1991. *Physical Being: A Theory for a Corporeal Psychology.* Oxford: Basil Blackwel.

Harris, Jack. 1940. 'The White Knife Shoshone of Nevada'. In *Acculturation in Seven American Indian Tribes*, edited by Ralph Linton, 39–166. New York: Appleton-Century.

Hashimoto, Hiroyuki. 2003. 'Between Preservation and Tourism: Folk Performing Arts in Contemporary Japan'. *Asian Folklore Studies*, Vol. 62, No. 2: 225–36.

Hauser-Schäublin, Brigitta. 2013. 'Introduction: The Power of Indigeneity. Reparation, Readjustments and Repositioning'. In *Adat and Indigeneity in Indonesia: Culture and Entitlements between Heteronomy and Self-ascription*, edited by Brigitta Hauser-Schäublin, Göttingen Studies in Cultural Property 7, 5–15. Göttingen: Universitätsverlag Göttingen.

Hertz, Robert. 2004. *Death and the Right Hand.* London: Routledge.

Hiatt, Lester Richard. 1965. *Kinship and Conflict.* Canberra: Australian National University.

Hochschild, Arlie Russel. 1983. *The Managed Heart: The Commercialization of Human Feeling.* Berkeley: University of California Press.

Hollan, Douglas. 1988. 'Staying "Cool" in Toraja: Informal Strategies for the Management of Anger and Hostility in a Nonviolent Society'. *Ethos*, Vol. 16: 52–72.

Hollan, Douglas. 2001. 'Developments in Person-Centered Ethnography'. In *The Psychology of Cultural Experience*, edited by Carmella Moore and Holly Mathews, 48–67. Cambridge: Cambridge University Press.

Hollan, Douglas and Wellenkamp, Jane. 1994. *Contentment and Suffering. Culture and Experience in Toraja*. New York: Columbia University Press.

hooks, bell. 1990. 'Marginality as a Site of Resistance'. In *Out There: Marginalization and Contemporary Cultures*, edited by Russell Ferguson, 341–3. Cambridge: MIT Press.

Huang, Julia. 2003. 'Weeping in a Taiwanese Buddhist Charismatic Movement'. *Ethnology*, Vol. 42, No. 1: 73–86.

James, Diana. 2015. 'Tjukurpa Time'. In *Long History, Deep Time: Deepening Histories of Place*, edited by Ann McGrath and Mary Anne Jebb, 33–45. Canberra: ANU Press.

Janata, Petr; Tomic, Stefan T. and Rakowski, Sonja K. 2007. 'Characterization of Music Evoked Autobiographical Memories'. *Memory*, Vol. 15: 845–60.

Jäncke, Lutz. 2008. 'Music, Memory and Emotion'. *Journal of Biology*, Vol. 7, No. 6: 21–45.

Jones, Rex L. 1968. 'Shamanism in South Asia: A Preliminary Survey'. *History of Religions*, Vol. 7, No. 4: 330–47.

Juslin, Patrick; Harmat, László and Eerola, Toumas. 2014. 'What Makes Music Emotionally Significant? Exploring the Underlying Mechanisms'. *Psychology of Music*, Vol. 42, No. 4: 599–623.

Kapferer, Bruce. 1979. 'Emotions and Feeling in Sinhalese Healing Rites'. *Social Analysis*, Vol. 1: 153–76.

Kartomi, Margaret J. 1973a. 'Music and Trance in Central Java'. *Ethnomusicology*, Vol. 17, No. 2: 163–208.

Kartomi, Margaret J. 1973b. 'Jaran Kepang and Kuda Lumping: Trance Dancing in Java'. *Hemisphere*, Vol. 17: 20–7.

Kartomi, Margaret J. 1998. 'The Music-Culture of South-Coast West Sumatra: Backwater of the Minangkabau "Heartland" or Home of the Sacred Mermaid and the Earth Goddess?' *Asian Music*, Vol. 30, No. 1: 133–81.

Kartomi, Margaret J. 2008. 'Indonesia'. In *The Garland Handbook of Southeast Asian Music*, edited by Terry E. Miller and Sean Williams, 334–405. New York: Routledge.

Kendall, Laurel. 2011. 'The Contraction and Expansion of Shamanic Landscapes in Contemporary South Korea'. *CrossCurrents*, Vol. 61, No. 3: 328–44.

Kho, Nishimura. 1987. 'Shamanism and Medical Cures'. *Current Anthropology*, Vol. 28, No. 4: S59–S64.

Kiev, Ari. 1961. 'Spirit Possession in Haiti'. *American Journal of Psychiatry*, Vol. 118: 133–8.

Kim, Hyunchul. 2012. 'The Purification Process of Death: Mortuary Rites in a Japanese Rural Town'. *Asian Ethnology*, Vol. 71, No. 2: 225–57.

Kleinman, Arthur. 1980. *Patients and Healers in the Context of Culture: An Exploration of the Borderland between Anthropology, Medicine, and Psychiatry*. Berkeley: University of California Press.

Kluckhohn, Clyde. 1944. *Navaho Witchcraft*. Boston: Beacon Press.

Koelsch, Stefan. 2014. 'Brain Correlates of Music-Evoked Emotions'. *Nature Neuroscience*, Vol. 15: 170–80.

Kondi, Bledar. 2012. *Death and Ritual Crying: An Anthropological Approach to Albanian Funeral Customs*. Berlin: Logos Verlag Berlin.

Krumhansl, Carol and Zupnick, Justin. 2013. 'Cascading Reminiscence Bumps in Popular Music'. *Psychological Science*, Vol. 24, No. 10: 2057–68.

Kruyt, Albert. 1930. 'De To Wana op Oost-Celebese'. *Tijdschrift voor indische taal-, land-, en volkenkunde,* Vol. 70: 110–20.

Kuipers, Joel C. 2011. 'The Society and Its Environment'. In *Indonesia: A Country Study*, edited by William Frederick and Robert Worden, 45–78. Washington, DC: Library of Congress.

Lahadji, Jabar. 1999. 'Morowali Nature Reserve and the Wana People, in Indigenous Peoples and Protected Areas'. In *South and Southeast Asia: From Principles to Practice*, edited by Marcus Colchester and Christian Erni, 228–49. Amsterdam: Aksant Academic Publisher.

Lahadji, Jabar. 2008. 'People, Park and Partnership. Problems and Possible Solutions in the Morowali Nature Reserve'. *IIAS* Newsletter, Vol. 46: 2–23.

Lambek, Michael. 1989. 'From Disease to Discourse: Remarks on the Conceptualisation of Trance and Spirit Possession'. In *Altered States of Consciousness and Mental Health: A Cross Cultural Perspective*, edited by Colleen Ward, 36–61. Newbury Park: Sage Publications.

Lambert South, Andrea; Elton, Jessica and Lietzenmayer, Alison. 2020. 'Communicating Death with Humor: Humor Types and Functions in Death over Dinner Conversations'. *Death Studies*, Vol. 46, No. 4: 851–60.

Lansdown, Richard. 2014. 'Crucible or Centrifuge? Bronislaw Malinowski's A Diary in the Strict Sense of the Term'. *Configurations*, Vol. 22, No. 1: 29–55.

Laughlin, Charles and John Langdon, Esther Jean. 2013. 'New Perspectives of Shamanism in Brazil: Shamanisms and Neo-Shamanisms as Dialogical Categories'. *Civilisations*, Vol. 61, No. 2: 19–35.

Leach, Edmund A. 1958. 'Magical Hair'. *Journal of the Royal Anthropological Institute*, Vol. 88: 147–54.

Leach, Edmund A. 1961. *Rethinking Anthropology*. London: Athlone Press.

Leavitt, John. 1996. 'Meaning and Feeling in the Anthropology of Emotions'. *American Ethnologist*, Vol. 23, No. 3: 514–39.

LeCompte, Margaret. 1987. 'Bias in the Biography: Bias and Subjectivity in Ethnographic Research'. *Anthropology & Education Quarterly*, Vol. 18, No. 1: 43–52.

Leeming, David. 1990. *The World of Mythology*. Oxford: Oxford University Press.

Lévi-Bruhl, Lucien. 1985. *How Natives Think*. Princeton: Princeton University Press.

Lévi-Strauss. 1955. 'The Structural Study of Myth'. *The Journal of American Folklore*, Vol. 68, No. 270: 428–44.

Lévi-Strauss. 1958. *Structural Anthropology*. New York: Basic Books.

Lévy, Robert and Rosaldo, Michelle. 1983. 'Issue Devoted to Self and Emotion'. *Ethos*, Vol. 11, No. 3.

Lewis, Ioan Myrddin. 1972. *Ecstatic Religion. An Anthropological Study of Spirit Possession and Shamanism*. Hammondsworth: Penguin.

Li, Tania M. 1999. 'Marginality, Power and Production: Analysing Upland Transformations'. In *Transforming the Indonesian Uplands: Marginality, Power and Production*, edited by Tania M. Li, 1–45. Amsterdam: Harwood.

Ludwing, Arnold M. 1968. 'Altered States of Consciousness'. In *Trance and Possession States*, edited by Raymond Prince. Montreal: R. M. Bucke Memorial Society.

Luhrmann, Tanya Marie. 2006. 'Subjectivity'. *Anthropological Theory*, Vol. 6: 345–61.

Lutz, Catherine. 1985. 'Depression and the Translation of Emotional Worlds'. In *Culture and Depression: Studies in the Anthropology and Cross-Cultural Psychiatry of Affect and Disorder*, edited by Arthur Kleinman and Byron Good, 63–100. Berkeley: University of California Press.

Lutz, Catherine and Geoffrey White. 1986. 'The Anthropology of Emotions'. *Annual Review of Anthropology*, Vol. 15: 405–36.

Lynch, Owen. 1990. 'The Social Construction of Emotion in India'. In *Divine Passions: The Social Construction of Emotion in India*, edited by Owen Lynch, 3–34. Berkeley: University of California Press.

MacIver, Robert. 1917. *Community: A Sociological Study. Being an Attempt to Set Out the Nature and Fundamental Laws of Social Life*. London: Routledge.

Magowan, Fiona. 2001. 'Shadows of Song: Exploring Research and Performance Strategies in Yolngu Women's Crying-Songs'. *Oceania*, Vol. 72, No. 2: 89–104.

Magowan, Fiona. 2007. *Melodies of Mourning: Music and Emotion in Northern Australia*. Santa Fe: School for Advanced Research.

Malinowski, Bronislaw. 1989. *A Diary in the Strict Sense of the Term*. Stanford: Stanford University Press.

Manning, Frank E. 1976. 'The Rediscovery of Religious Play: A Pentecostal Case'. In *The Anthropological Study of Play: Problems and Prospects, Proceedings of the First Annual Meeting of the Association of the Anthropological Study of Play*, edited by David F. Lancy and Allan B. Tindall, 140–4. Cornwall: Leisure Press.

Marris, Peter. 1974. *Loss and Change*. London: Routledge.

Martin, Rod and Lefcourt, Herbert. 1983. 'Sense of Humor as a Moderator of the Relation between Stressors and Moods'. *Journal of Personality and Social Psychology*, Vol. 45, No. 6: 1313–24.

Martineau, Harriet. 1972. 'A Model of the Social Functions of Humor'. In *The Psychology of Humor*, edited by Jeffrey Goldstein and Paul McGhee, 101–25. New York: Academic Press.

Matarrita-Cascante, David and Brennan, Mark A. 2012. 'Conceptualizing Community Development in the Twenty-first Century'. *Community Development*, Vol. 43, No. 32: 93–305.

Matusky, Patricia and Chopyak, James. 2008. 'Peninsular Malaysia'. In *The Garland Handbook of Southeast Asian Music*, edited by Terry E. Miller and Sean Williams, 222–46. New York: Routledge.

McDaniel, June. 2010. 'Agama Hindu Dharma Indonesia as a New Religious Movement: Hinduism Recreated in the Image of Islam'. *Nova Religio: The Journal of Alternative and Emergent Religions*, Vol. 14, No. 1: 93–111.

McVey, Ruth T. 1999. *Redesigning the Cosmos: Belief Systems and State Power in Indonesia*. Copenhagen: Nordic Institute of Asian Studies.

Mead, Margaret and Bateson, George. 1942. *Balinese Character, a Photographic Analysis*. New York: New York Academy of Sciences.

Metcalf, Peter. 1982. *A Borneo Journey into Death. Berawan Eschatology from Its Rituals*. Philadelphia: University of Pennsylvania Press.

Metcalf, Peter and Richard Huntington. 1991. *Celebrations of Death. The Anthropology of Mortuary Ritual*. New York: Cambridge University Press.

Meyer, Leonard. 1956. *Emotion and Meaning in Music*. Chicago: University of Chicago Press.

Miller, Frank. 1967. *Humor in a Chippewa Tribal Council*. Pittsburgh: University of Pittsburgh Press.

Mills, Simon. 2012. 'Sounds to Soothe the Soul: Music and Bereavement in a Traditional South Korean Death Ritual'. *Mortality*, Vol. 17, No.2: 145–57.

Mischel, Walter and Mischel, Frances. 1958. 'Psychological Aspect of Spirit Possession'. *American Anthropologist*, Vol. 60: 149–260.

Mitchell, Andrew W. 1981. *Operation Drake: Voyage of Discovery*. London: Severn House Publisher Limited.

Miyazaki, Koji. 2000. 'Javanese-Malay: Between Adaptation and Alienation'. *Sojourn: Journal of Social Issues in Southeast Asia*, Vol. 15, No. 1: 76–99.

Morreall, John. 2009. *Comic Relief: A Comprehensive Philosophy of Humor*. Oxford: Blackwell Publishing.

Mosko, Mark. 1985. *Quadripartite Structures Categories, Relations and Homologies in Bush Mekeo Culture*. Cambridge: Cambridge University Press.

Mosquera, Alexander. 2018. 'The Anthroposemiotics of Jokes in Funeral Rituals: Humor as a Mask for Humans in the Face of Death'. *Chinese Semiotic Studies*, Vol. 14, No. 2: 171–92.

Müller, Klaus E. 2001. *Sciamanismo. Guaritore, Spiriti, Rituali*. Turin: Bollati Boringhieri.

Myers, Fred. 1986. *Pintupi Country, Pintupi Self*. Canberra and Washington, DC: AIAS with Smithsonian Institution Press.

Nguyễn, Phong T. 2008. 'Minority Musics of Vietnam'. In *The Garland Handbook of Southeast Asian Music*, edited by Terry E. Miller and Sean Williams, 297–302. New York: Routledge.

Noorduyn, Jacobus. 1991. *A Critical Survey of Studies on the Languages of Sulawesi*. Leiden: KITLV Press.

Norbeck, Edward. 1976. 'Johan Huizinga and Modern Anthropology'. In *The Anthropological Study of Play: Problems and Prospects, Proceedings of the First Annual Meeting of the Association of the Anthropological Study of Play*, edited by David F. Lancy and Allan B. Tindall, 13–22. Cornwall: Leisure Press.

Oesterreich, Traugott K. 1966. 'Possession, Demoniacal and Other, among Primitive Races'. In *Antiquity, the Middle Ages, and Modern Times*. New Hyde Park,

NY: University Books. First English-language edition, 1930: Original German publication, 1921.

Ohnuki-Tiernery, Emiko. 1981. *Illness and Healing among the Sakhalin Ainu. A Symbolic Interpretation.* Cambridge: Cambridge University Press.

Ortner, Sherry B. 1974. 'Is Female to Male as Nature Is to Culture?' In *Women, Culture, and Society*, edited by Michelle Z. Rosaldo and Louise Lamphere, 61–95. Stanford: Stanford University.

Osterweis, Mariam; Frederic, Solomon and Green, Morris (Eds.). 1984. *Reactions, Consequences and Care.* Washington, DC: National Academy Press.

Otto, Walter Friedrich. 1996. *Theophania. Lo Spirito Della Religion Greca Antica.* Geneva: Il Melangolo.

Palmer, Jerry. 1993. *Taking Humour Seriously.* New York: Routledge Taylor and Francis Group.

Panksepp, Jaak and Trevarthen, Colwyn. 2009. 'The Neuroscience of Emotion in Music'. In *Communicative Musicality: Exploring the Basis of Human Companionship*, edited by Stephen Malloch and Colwyn Trevarthen, 105–46. New York: Oxford University Press.

Parkinson, Brian. 1995. *Ideas and Realities of Emotions.* London: Routledge.

Parry, Jonathan. 1994. *Death in Banaras.* Cambridge: Cambridge University Press.

Perlman, Janice E. 1976. *The Myth of Marginality: Urban Poverty and Politics in Rio de Janeiro.* Berkeley: University of California Press.

Permanent Committee on Geographical Names. 2003. *Indonesia. Population and Administrative Divisions.* London: Crown.

Peters, Larry G. 1978. 'Psychotherapy in Tamang Shamanism'. *Ethos*, Vol. 6, No. 2: 63–91.

Peters, Larry G. 1981. *Ecstasy and Healing in Nepal: An Ethnopsychiatric Study of Tamang Shamanism.* Malibu: Undena Publications.

Peters, Larry G. 1982. 'Trance, Initiation, and Psychotherapy in Tamang Shamanism'. *American Ethnologist*, Vol. 9, No. 1: 21–46.

Peters, Larry G. 1989. 'Shamanism: Phenomenology of a Spiritual Discipline'. *Journal of Transpersonal Psychology*, Vol. 21, No. 2: 115–37.

Picard, Michel. 2011 'Introduction: "Agama," "Adat," and Pancasila'. In *The politics of Religion in Indonesia: Syncretism, Orthodoxy, and Religious Contention in Java and Bali*, edited by Michel Picard and Rémy Madinier, 1–20. Oxon: Routledge.

Plato. 2004. *The Laws*, edited by Trevor Saunders. London, New York: Penguin.

Platz, Friedrich.; Kopiez, Reinhard.; Hasselhorn, Johannes and Wolf, Anna. 2015. 'The Impact of Song-specific Age and Affective Qualities of Popular Songs on Music-Evoked Autobiographical Memories (MEAMs)'. *Musicae Scientiae*, Vol. 19, No. 4: 327–49.

Pollard, Amy. 2009. 'Field of Screams: Difficulty and Ethnographic Fieldwork'. *Anthropology Matters Journal*, Vol. 11, No. 2: 1–24.

Porath, Nathan. 2008. 'Seeing Sound: Consciousness and Therapeutic Acoustics in the Inter-sensory Shamanic Epistemology of the Orang Sakai of Riau (Sumatra)'. *The Journal of the Royal Anthropological Institute*, Vol. 14, No. 3: 647–63.

Porath, Nathan. 2010. '"They Have Not Progressed Enough": Development's Negated Identities among Two Indigenous Peoples (Orang Asli) in Indonesia and Thailand'. *Journal of Southeast Asian Studies*, Vol. 41, No. 2: 267–89.

Porath, Nathan. 2013a. 'Freud among the Orang Sakai the Father Archetype, the Talking Cure, and the Transference in a Sumatran Shamanic Healing Complex'. *Anthropos*, Vol. 108, No. 1: 1–17.

Porath, Nathan. 2013b. '"Not to Be Aware Anymore": Indigenous Sumatran Ideas and Shamanic Experiences of Changed States of Awareness/Consciousness'. *Anthropology of Consciousness*, Vol. 24, No. 1: 7–31.

Porath, Nathan. 2015. 'Physicalising the Spirit-Dimension by Song, Dance and "fakery" in Indigenous Mainland Riau, Indonesia'. *Journal of Southeast Asian Studies*, Vol. 46, No. 3: 368–90.

Porterfield, Amanda. 1987. 'Shamanism: A Psychosocial Definition'. *Journal of the American Academy of Religion*, Vol. 55, No. 4: 721–39.

Pottier, Eugène. 1871. *L'Internationale*. Paris: Dentu.

Praet, Istvan. 2014. *Animism and the Question of Life*. New York, London: Routledge.

Pressel, Esther. 1974. 'Umbanda Trance and Possession in Sao Paulo, Brazil'. In *Trance, Healing and Hallucination*, edited by Felicitas Goodman, Jeannette H. Henney and Esther Pressel, 113–225. London: Wiley.

Prewiranegara, Shafruddin. 1984. 'Pancasila as the Sole Foundation'. *Indonesia*, No. 38: 74–83.

Prosser, Jon and Andrew Loxley. 2008. *Introducing Visual Methods*. Paris: National Centre for Research Methods, NCRM Review Papers, NCRM/010.

Pugh-Kitingan, Jacqueline. 2012. 'Gong Ensemble Music of the Dusun Tinagas of Sabah through the Gaze of movement'. *Yearbook for Traditional Music*, Vol. 44: 149–65.

Quinn, Naomi and Dorothy Holland. 1987. *Cultural Models in Language and Thought*. Cambridge: Cambridge University Press.

Radcliffe-Brown, Alfred. 1965. *Structure and Function in Primitive Society: Essays and Addresses*. New York: Free Press.

Rappoport, Dana. 2004. 'Ritual Music and Christianization in the Toraja Highlands, Sulawesi'. *Ethnomusicology*, Vol. 48, No. 3: 378–404.

Rappoport, Dana. 2011. 'To Sing the Rice in Tanjung Bunga (Eastern Flores, Indonesia)'. In *Austronesian Soundscapes: Performing Arts in Oceania and Southeast Asia*, edited by Birgit Abels, 103–31. Amsterdam: Amsterdam University Press.

Rappoport, Dana. 2014. 'Songs and Sorrow in Tanjung Bunga: Music and the Myth of the Origin of Rice (Lamaholot, Flores, Indonesia)'. *Bijdragen tot de Taal-, Land- en Volkenkunde/Journal of the Humanities and Social Sciences of Southeast Asia*, Vol. 170, No. 2–3: 215–49.

Rappoport, Dana. 2016. 'Why Do They (Still) Sing Stories? Singing Narratives in Tanjung Bunga (Eastern Flores, Lamaholot, Indonesia)'. *Wacana, Journal of the Humanities of Indonesia*, Vol. 17, No. 2: 163–90.

Rappoport, Dana. 2017. 'Singing in Dangerous Places (Flores, Lamaholot, Indonesia)'. *The Asia Pacific Journal of Anthropology*, Vol. 18, No. 5: 462–82.

Rappaport, Roy A. 1974. 'Obvious Aspects of Ritual'. *Cambridge Journal of Anthropology*, Vol. 2, No. 1: 3–69.

Rappaport, Roy A. 1979. *Ecology, Meaning, and Religions*. Berkeley: North Atlantic Books.

Rasmussen, Knud. 1931. *The Netsilik Eskimos*. Copenhagen: Thule Report, Vol. 8.

Riccardi, Cynthia. 1999. *Indigenous Swidden Agriculture of the Wana within the Morowali Nature Reserve of Central Sulawesi, Indonesia*. MA Dissertation, Athens: Ohio University.

Roe, Keith. 1985. 'Swedish Youth and Music: Listening Patterns and Motivations'. *Communication Research*, Vol. 12: 353–62.

Rosaldo, Renato. 1989. 'Grief and a Headhunter's Rage: On the Culture Force of Emotions'. In *Culture and Truth*, edited by Renato Rosaldo, 1–21. Boston: Beacon Press.

Roseman, Marina. 1984. 'The Social Structuring of Sound: The Temiar of Peninsular Malaysia'. *Ethnomusicology*, Vol. 28, No. 3: 411–45.

Roseman, Marina. 1990. 'Head, Heart, Odor, and Shadow: The Structure of the Self, the Emotional World, and Ritual Performance among Senoi Temiar'. *Ethos*, Vol. 18, No. 3: 227–50.

Roseman, Marina. 1993. *Healing Sounds from the Malaysian Rainforest*. Berkeley: University of California Press.

Roseman, Marina. 1998. 'Singers of the Landscape: Song, History, and Property Rights in the Malaysian Rain Forest'. *American Anthropologist*, New Series, Vol. 100, No. 1: 106–21.

Roseman, Marina. 2008. 'The Indigenous Peoples (Orang Asli) of the Malay Peninsula'. In *The Garland Handbook of Southeast Asian Music*, edited by Terry E. Miller, and Sean Williams, 317–25. New York: Routledge.

Rosenblatt, Paul; Walsh, Patricia and Jackson, Douglas. 1976. *Grief and Mourning in Cross-Cultural Perspective*. New Haven: Human Relations Area Files.

Rottenberg, Jonatha; Bylsma, Lauren M. and Vingerhoets, Ad J. J. M. 2008. 'Is Crying Beneficial?' *Current Directions in Psychological Science*, Vol. 17, No. 6: 400–4.

Rouget, Gilbert. 1985. *Music and Trance: A Theory of the Relations between Music and Possession*. Chicago: University of Chicago Press.

Rubin, David C. 1995. *Memory in Oral Traditions: The Cognitive Psychology of Epic, Ballads, and Counting-out Rhymes*. New York: Oxford University Press.

Rubin, David C.; Wetzler, Scott; and Nebes, Robert. 1986. 'Autobiographical Memory across the Adult Lifespan'. In *Autobiographical Memory*, edited by David C. Rubin, 202–21. Cambridge: Cambridge University Press.

Sachs, Curt. 1962. *Wellsprings of Music*. The Hague: Nijhoff.

Said, Edward W. 1978. *Orientalism*. New York: Pantheon Books.

Salamone, Frank A. 2009. *The Hausa of Nigeria*. Lanham: University Press of America.

Sanga, Imani. 2009. 'Teaching-Learning Processes in "Muziki Wa Injili" in Dar Es Salaam'. *African Music*, Vol. 8, No. 3: 132–43.

Sangaji, Arianto. 2007. 'The Masyarakat Adat Movement in Indonesia: A Critical Insider's View'. In *The Revival of Tradition in Indonesian Politics: The Deployment of Adat from Colonialism to Indigenism*, edited by Jamie S. Davidson and David Henley 319–36. London: Routledge.

Sangay, Thupten and Kilty, Gavin. 2011. 'Tibetan Ritual for the Dead'. *The Tibet Journal*, Vol. 36, No. 3: 49–59.

Sanjek, Roger. 1990. 'The Secret Life of Fieldnotes'. In *Fieldnotes: The Makings of Anthropology*, edited by Roger Sanjek, 187–270. Ithaca: Cornell University Press.

Scalici, Giorgio. 2019. *Healing the Individual, Healing the Community Shamanic Rituals and Funerals of the Wana People of Morowali*. PhD Thesis. Durham: Durham University.

Scalici, Giorgio. 2022. 'Who Framed Tetebua?' In *Patterns of Change in the Traditional Music of Southeast Asia*, edited by Giovanni Giuriati, 160–85. Udine: Nota.

Scalici, Giorgio. 2023. 'The Musical Instruments of Wana Tradition (Indonesia)'. *Etnografie sonore/Sound Ethnographies*, Vol. 5, No. 1: 82–104.

Scarduelli, Pietro. 1992. *Lo Specchio del Cosmo. Il Simbolismo Spaziale Nelle Culture dell'Indonesia*. Turin: Il Seganalibro.

Scarduelli, Pietro. 2007a. *Sciamani, Stregoni, Sacerdoti: Uno Studio Antropologico dei Rituali*. Palermo: Sellerio.

Scarduelli, Pietro (Ed.). 2007b. *Antropologia del rito. Interpretazioni e Spiegazioni*. Turin: Bollati Boringhieri.

Scarduelli, Pietro. 2009. *Culture dell'Indonesia*. Palermo: Sellerio.

Schaeffner, André. 1978. *Origine Degli Strumenti Musicali*. Palermo: Sellerio.

Schieffelin, Edward L. 1996. 'On Failure and Performance. Throwing the Medium out of the Séance'. In *The Performance of Healing*, edited by Carol Laderman and Marina Roseman, 59–89. New York and London: Routledge.

Schiller, Anne. 1996. 'An "Old" Religion in "New Order" Indonesia: Notes on Ethnicity and Religious Affiliation'. *Sociology of Religion*, Vol. 57, No. 4: 409–17.

Schneider, David Murray. 1984. *A Critique of the Study of Kinship*. Ann Arbor: University of Michigan.

Schulkind, Matthew D.; Hennis, Laura K. and Rubin, David C. 1999. 'Music, Emotion, and Autobiographical Memory: They're Playing Your Song'. *Memory & Cognition*, Vol. 27: 948–55.

Schutz, Alfred and Luckmann, Thomas. 1973. *The Structures of the Life-World*, Vol. I. Evanston: Northwestern University Press.

Sciannameo, Gianluca. 2006. *Nelle Indie di quaggiù: Ernesto De Martino e il Cinema Etnografico*. Bari: Palomar.

Shepard, Glenn H. 2002. 'Three Days for Weeping: Dreams, Emotions, and Death in the Peruvian Amazon'. *Medical Anthropology Quarterly*, Vol. 16, No. 2: 200–29.

Sherzer, Joel. 1983. *Kuna Ways of Speaking. An Ethnographic Perspective.* Austin: University of Texas Press.

Shields, Rob. 1991. *Places on the Margin: Alternative Geographies of Modernity.* London: Routledge.

Shils, Edward. 1982. *The Constitution of Society. The Heritage of Sociology.* Chicago: University of Chicago Press.

Shirokogoroff, Sergei Mikhailovich. 1935. *Psychomental Complex of the Tungus.* London: Kegan Paul.

Shor, Ronald E. 1959. 'Hypnosis and the Concept of the Generalized Reality Orientation'. *Journal of Psychotherapy*, Vol. 13: 582–602.

Shweder, Richard A. and Levine, Robert A. 1984. *Culture Theory: Essays on Mind, Self and Emotion.* Cambridge: Cambridge University Press.

Simpson, George E. 1970. *Religious Cult of the Caribbean.* Puerto Rico: Institute of Caribbean Studies.

Smart, Ninian. 1981. *Beyond Ideology.* London: Collins.

Smith, Jonathan. 1980. 'The Bare Facts of Ritual'. *History of Religions*, Vol. 20, No. ½: 112–27.

Smith, Jonathan. 1992. *To Take Place.* Chicago and London: University of Chicago Press.

Smith, William Robertson. 1889. *Lectures on the Religion of the Semites.* London: Adam & Charles Black.

Snowden, Frank. 2005. *The Conquest of Malaria: Italy, 1900–1962.* New Haven: Yale University Press.

Solomon, Jennifer. 1996. 'Humor and Aging Well: A Laughing Matter or a Matter of Laughing?' *American Behavioral Scientist*, Vol. 39, No. 3: 249–71.

Spiro, Melford. 1986. 'Cultural Relativism and the Future of Anthropology'. *Cultural Anthropology*, Vol. 1, No. 3: 259–86.

Stebbins, Robert. 1979. 'Comic Relief in Everyday Life: Dramaturgic Observations on A Function of Humor'. *Symbolic Interaction*, Vol. 2, No. 1: 95–104.

Stephenson, Richard. 1951. 'Conflict and Control Functions of Humor'. *American Journal of Sociology*, Vol. 56, No. 6: 569–74.

Steward, Julian H. 1941. 'Culture Element Distribution, XIII: Nevada Shoshoni'. *University of California Anthropological Records*, Vol. 4: 209–360.

Stoller, Paul. 1989. *Fusion of the Worlds: An Ethnography of Possession among the Songhay of Niger.* Chicago: University of Chicago Press.

Stuart, Kevin and Narsu. 1994. 'Funerals in Alxa Right Banner, Inner Mongolia'. *Mongolian Studies*, Vol. 17: 99–103.

Sturm, Brian W. 2000. 'The "Storylistening" Trance Experience'. *The Journal of American Folklore*, Vol. 113, No. 449: 287–304.

Svašek, Maruška. 2005. 'The Politics of Chosen Trauma. Expellee Memories, Emotions and Identities'. In *Mixed Emotions. Anthropological Studies of Feeling*, edited by Kay Milton and Maruška Svašek, 195–214. Oxford: Berg.

Svašek, Maruška and Skrbiš, Zlatko. 2007. 'Passions and Powers: Emotions and Globalisation'. *Identities: Global Studies in Culture and Power*, Vol. 14, No. 4: 367–83.

Sweetman, Paul. 2009. 'Revealing Habitus, Illuminating Practice: Bourdieu, Photography and Visual Methods'. *The Sociological Review*, Vol. 57, No. 3: 491–511.

Symmons-Symonolewicz, Konstantin. 1982. 'The Ethnographer and His Savages: An Intellectual History of Malinowski's Diary'. *Polish Review*, Vol. 27, No. 1–2: 92–8.

Tart, Charles. 1975. *State of Consciousness*. New York: Dutton.

Telle, Kari G. 2000. 'Feeding the Dead: Reformulating Sasak Mortuary Practices'. *Bijdragen tot de Taal-, Land- en Volkenkunde*, Vol. 156, No. 4: 771–805.

Terwiel, Barend Jan. 1979. 'Tai Funeral Customs: Towards a Reconstruction of Archaic-Tai Ceremonies'. *Anthropos*, Vol. 74, No. 3/4: 393–432.

Thomas, Louis-Vincent. 1976. *Antropologia Della Morte*. Milan: Garzanti.

Tolbert, Elizabeth. 1990. 'Women Cry with Words: Symbolization of Affect in the Karelian Lament'. *Yearbook for Traditional Music*, Vol. 22: 80–105.

Traube, Elizabeth G. 1989. 'Obligations to the Source: Complementarity and Hierarchy in an Eastern Indonesian Society'. In *The Attraction of Opposites: Thought and Society in a Dualistic Mode*, edited by David Maybury-Lewis and Uri Almagor, 321–44. Ann Arbor: University of Michigan Press.

Tsing, Anna L. 1993. *In the Realm of the Diamond Queen: Marginality in an out-of-the-way Place*. Princeton: Princeton University Press.

Turner, Edith. 2011. *Communitas: The Anthropology of Collective Joy*. New York: Palgrave Macmillan.

Turner, Victor. 1986. *The Anthropology of Performance*. New York: PAJ Publications.

Tylor, Edward Burnett. 2010. *Primitive Culture: Researches into the Development of Mythology, Philosophy, Religion, Art, and Custom*. Cambridge: Cambridge University Press.

Urban, Greg. 1988. 'Ritual Wailing in Amerindian Brazil'. *American Anthropologist*, Vol. 90: 385–400.

Vaitl, Dieter; Birbaumer, Niels; Gruzelier, John; Jamieson, Graham; Kotchoubey, Boris; Kübler, Andrea; Lehmann, Dietrich; Miltner, Wolfang; Püts, Peter; Ott, Ulrich; Sammer, Gebhard; Strauch, Inge; Strehl, Ute and Wackermann, Jiri. 2005. 'Psychobiology of Altered States of Consciousness'. *Psychological Bulletin*, Vol. 131, No. 1: 98–127.

Van Groenendael, Victoria M. Clara. 2008. *Jaranan. The Horse Dance ad Trance in East Java*. Leiden: KITLV Press.

Vander, Judith. 1997. *Shoshone Ghost Dance Religion. Poetry Songs and Great Basin Context*. Urbana and Chicago: University of Illinois Press.

Wagner, Frits A. 1961. *Indonesia*. Milan: il Saggiatore.

Wallace, Anthony F. C. 1966. *Religion, an Anthropological View*. New York: Random House.

Walsh, Roger. 1980. 'The Consciousness Disciplines and the Behavioral Sciences'. *American Journal of Psychiatry*, Vol. 137: 663–74.

Waterson, Roxana. 1993. 'Taking the Place of Sorrow: The Dynamics of Mortuary Rites among the Sa'dan Toraja'. *Southeast Asian Journal of Social Science*, Vol. 21, No. 2, Special Issue: Social Constructions of Death in Southeast Asia: 73–96.

Waterson, Roxana. 2018. 'Learning to Share Emotions through Ritual Participation among the Toraja of Sulawesi'. In *Expressions of Austronesian Thought and Emotions*, edited by James Fox, 81–127. Canberra: ANU Press.

Wellenkamp, Jane. 1988. 'Notions of Grief and Catharsis among the Toraja'. *American Ethnologist*, Vol. 15, No. 3: 486–500.

Whiting, Beatrice. 1950. *Paiute Sorcery*. New York: Viking Fund Publications in Anthropology, No. 15.

Wier, Dennis R. 1996. *Trance: From Magic to Technology*, translated by Media. Ann Arbor, Michigan: Trans Media Inc.

Wierzbicka, Anna. 2009. 'Language and Metalanguage: Key Issues in Emotion Research'. *Emotion Review*, Vol. 1: 3–14.

Wikan, Unni. 1988. 'Bereavement and Loss in two Muslim Communities: Egypt and Bali Compared'. *Social Science & Medicine*, Vol. 27, No. 5: 451–60.

Wikan, Unni. 1989a. '*Managing the Heart to Brighten Face and Soul: Emotions in Balinese Morality and Health Care*'. *American Ethnologist*, Vol. 16: 294–312.

Wikan, Unni. 1989b. 'Illness from Fright or Soul Loss: A North Balinese Culture-Bound Syndrome?' *Culture, Medicine and Psychiatry*, Vol. 13: 25–50.

Wikan, Unni. 1990. *Managing Turbulent Hearts: A Balinese Formula for Living*. Chicago: University of Chicago Press.

Wilder, William D. (Ed.). 2003. *Journey of the Soul: Anthropological Studies of Death, Burial, and Reburial Practices in Borneo*. Phillips: Borneo Research Council.

Wildschut, Tim; Sedikides, Constantine; Arndt, Jamie and Routledge, Clay Carver. 2006. 'Nostalgia: Content, Triggers, Functions'. *Journal of Personality and Social Psychology*, Vol.91, No. 5: 975–93.

Winkelman, Michael James. 1990. 'Shamans and other "Magico-Religious" Healers: A Cross-Cultural Study of Their Origins, Nature, and Social Transformations'. *Ethos*, Vol. 18, No. 3: 308–52.

Winkelman, Michael James. 2010. *Shamanism. A Biopsychosocial Paradigm of Consciousness and Healing*. Santa Barbara, Denver and Oxford: Praeger.

Winzeler, Robert. 1990. 'Amok: Historical, Psychological, and Cultural Perspectives'. In *Emotions of Culture: A Malay Perspective*, edited by Wazir Jahan Karim, 96–122. Singapore: Oxford University Press.

Wolf, Richard. 2001. 'Emotional Dimensions of Ritual Music among the Kotas, a South Indian Tribe'. *Ethnomusicology*, Vol. 45, No. 3: 379–422.

Wolf, Richard. 2006. *The Black Cow's Footprint. Time, Space, and Music in the Lives of the Kotas of South India*. Urbana and Chicago: University of Illinois Press.

Yoder, Lonnie. 1986. 'The Funeral Meal: A Significant Funerary'. *Journal of Religion and Health*, Vol. 25, No. 2: 149–60.

Zinker, Joseph. 2003. 'Beauty and Creativity in Human Relationships'. In *Creative License*, edited by Margherita Lobb and Nancy Amendt-Lyon, 141–51. Vienna: Springer.

Sitography

BPSP Sulteng. 2013. *Statistik Kependudukan Sulteng 2013* (Badan Pusat Statistik Provinsi Sulawesi Tengah), available at: http://sulteng.bps.go.id/endback/ pdf_publikasi/Statistik-Kependudukan-Sulawesi-Tengah-2013.pdf [Accessed 27 February 2018].

Clark, Bob. 2019. *Ethnos 350, about,* available at: https://blogs.ethnos360.org/bob-clark/ about/ [Accessed 23 June 2019].

Embassy of the Republic of Indonesia in Romania. n.d. Available at: http://www.indonezia. ro/republic.htm [Accessed 27 February 2018].

Encyclopedia Brittanica. n.d. 'African Music', available at: https://www.britannica.com/ art/African-music/Musical-structure#ref519774 [Accessed 23 September 2018].

Hart, Keith. 2006. 'The Cambridge Torres Strait Expedition and British Social Anthropology', *Memory Bank,* 6 November, available at http://thememorybank. co.uk/2009/11/06/the-cambridge-torres-strait-expedition-and-british-social-anthropology/ [Accessed 23 September 2018].

Hasani, Ismail. 2016. *Not Allowed to not Believe? The Troubled Place of Atheism in Indonesia,* https://indonesiaatmelbourne.unimelb.edu.au/not-believing-not-allowed-the-troubled-place-of-atheism-in-indonesia/ [Accessed 29 July 2022].

Hynes, Casey. 2022. *15 Top-Rated Tourist Attractions in Indonesia,* available at: https://www.planetware.com/tourist-attractions/indonesia-ina.htm [Accessed 23 October 2022].

No Author. n.d. *15 Best Places to Visit in Indonesia,* available at: https://www. thecrazytourist.com/15-best-places-visit-indonesia/ [Accessed 23 September 2018].

No Author. 2015. 'Indonesia Second Biggest Marine Pollutant, after China', *Jakarta Post,* 6 November, available at: http://www.thejakartapost.com/news/2015/11/06/ indonesia-second-biggest-marine-pollutant-after-china.html [Accessed 27 February 2018].

No Author. n.d. *10 Top Tourist Attractions in Indonesia,* available at: https://www. touropia.com/tourist-attractions-in-indonesia/ [Accessed 23 September 2018].

Osman, Salim. 2012. 'Is Atheism Illegal in Indonesia?' *Jakarta Globe,* available at: http:// jakartaglobe.id/archive/is-atheism-illegal-in-indonesia/ [Accessed 27 February 2018].

Putri, Edira. 2017. *The 15 Most Beautiful Places to Visit in Indonesia,* available at: https:// theculturetrip.com/asia/indonesia/articles/the-10-most-beautiful-places-to-visit-in-indonesia/ [Accessed 23 September 2018].

Vidal, John. 2014. 'Rate of Deforestation in Indonesia Overtakes Brazil', *Guardian,* 29 June, available at: https://www.theguardian.com/environment/2014/jun/29/rate-of-deforestation-in-indonesia-overtakes-brazil-says-study [Accessed 27 February 2018].

Videography

Journet, Martine and Nougarol, Gérard. 2005. *Gods and Satans*. Le miroir, Paris, 87min.

Journet, Martine and Nougarol, Gérard. 2007. *The Shadow*. Institut für Visuelle Ethnographie (IVE), Göttingen, 69min.

Journet, Martine and Nougarol, Gérard. 2011. *Indo Pino*. Marseille: IRD audiovisuel, 85min.

Index

www.ingramcontent.com/pod-product-compliance
Lightning Source LLC
Chambersburg PA
CBHW071853270326
41929CB00013B/2214